To Jo[...]

No obligation to read!

Love,
lol

Sir Thomas Roe and the Mughal Empire

Sir Thomas Roe and the Mughal Empire

Colin Paul Mitchell

ASCE
AREA STUDY
CENTRE FOR
EUROPE

© Colin Mitchell, 2000

All rights reserved. 2000. No part of this publication may be reproduced, stored in a retrieval system, or transmitted, in any form or by any means electronic, mechanical, photocopying, recording or otherwise without the prior permission of the publisher.

The views expressed in this book are those of the authors and do not purport to reflect the position of the Centre.

ISBN 969 8551 01 8

Cover designed by Ishrat Rizvi

Printed at
Mehran Printers, Karachi.
Published by
The Area Study Centre for Europe,
University of Karachi.

This book is dedicated to the memory of my mother, Linda.

CONTENTS

	page
Note on Transliteration	ix
Acknowledgments	xi
Introduction	xiii
1. Sir Thomas Roe and the Mughal Context	1
2. Sir Thomas Roe As *Litterateur*	48
3. Sir Thomas Roe As Courtier	90
4. Sir Thomas Roe As Ambassador	132
5. Sir Thomas Roe As Politician and Historian	173
6. Tracing the Historiography of *The Embassy of Sir Thomas Roe*	205
Conclusion: Sir Thomas Roe As Orientalist	230
Bibliography	236
Index	251

NOTE ON TRANSLITERATION

It should be noted that there are several transliteration systems available for rendering the Persian and Arabic languages into Roman script, such as those offered by the *Encyclopedia of Islam*, the Library of Congress and the professional Middle East Studies Association. The system used here is a simple one, with only the alif (ا), the wauw (و), and the yaa(ي) being represented by â, û, and î respectively. The letters saa (ث), haa (ح), dhaa (ذ), saud (ص), daud(ض), taa (ط), and zaa (ظ) are not distinguished. I take responsibility for any spelling or typographical errors.

ACKNOWLEDGMENTS

This book originally appeared as my M.A. McGill thesis The Embassy of Sir Thomas Roe *and its Primacy in Seventeenth Century Mughal Historiography: A Re-Evaluation.* I would like to thank my advisor, Sajida Alvi, who originally helped see it through to its completion. The revisions of the thesis into book length have been made possible thanks to financial assistance from the University of Toronto's School of Graduate Studies, and the Social Science and Humanities Research Council of Canada. I would like to express my appreciation for the editorial suggestions by my family, especially Jeanne Shami, Ken Mitchell, and Rod Manchee. Above all, the support of my family and friends, especially Liane, Mark, Luke, and Emma, was deeply valued.

INTRODUCTION

When one enters the Victoria Memorial Hall in Calcutta, you cannot help but be impressed by the British Raj's need to celebrate their administrative and cultural accomplishments. The Memorial indeed is an aesthetically-pleasing testimony to roughly two hundred years of rule; a well-ordered museum, lavish displays, and an impressive collection of Persian documents all combine to dictate a message: the British experience in India had been 'glorious.' Probably the most striking feature, however, was the interior of the massive domed hall. A series of somewhat ostentatious panels record the British Raj experience: portraits of Clive and Hastings, the visit by Queen Victoria, etc. One panel, however, caught my attention. It depicted a seventeenth-century Englishman, in full Jacobean regalia, exiting a resplendent carriage surrounded on all sides by a sizeable entourage of Mughal officers and nobles. I hurriedly looked around for a caption to confirm my suspicions, but to my mind it could be no other than Britain's first ambassador to India, Sir Thomas Roe. It seemed that, from the Memorial architect's perception, Roe's four-year mission to the court of the Mughals ranked as one of the pivotal moments in the history of British India.

Earlier, in 1995, I had completed my M.A. at McGill's Institute of Islamic Studies by submitting my thesis entitled The Embassy of Sir Thomas Roe *and Its Primacy in Seventeenth Century Mughal Historiography: A Re-evaluation.* While reading and analyzing this account, I would like to think that, in some strange fashion, I became very close to its author. Two years later, I learned that I had been awarded a research fellowship and, not unlike that early seventeenth century Englishman, I was suddenly introduced to a puzzling and exotic culture. My transition into this society had been made smooth thanks to the widespread nature of the English language and the recent trends in cultural and commercial globalization. Thomas Roe, however, had no such luxuries. Although limited European excursions had been made in the preceding century, the subcontinent very much remained *terra incognita* for early seventeenth century Westerners. If I, a twentieth-century scholar trained in the history, culture, and languages of the Indo-Islamic world, was overwhelmed with the ineffability of the subcontinent, one can only imagine the difficulties encountered by Roe.

"No where else is to be found so full and so trustworthy an account of events in the time of the Moghul court," concludes W. Foster in his introduction of *The Embassy of Sir Thomas Roe*. This statement, written in 1899, was consistent with colonial scholarship's reliance on European primary sources in early modern Mughal studies. A nascent stage of scholarship was still struggling to translate and make available the massive number of Indo-Islamic memoirs (*nâmahâ*) and histories (*tavârîkh*). In addition to just beginning to understand the complexities of deciphering the palaeographic niceties of various Persian scripts, British historians were also labouring to compile vocabularies and grammars to facilitate their translation projects. Eventually interpreting native historical sources as self-aggrandizing and unreliable, European travel accounts and ambassador reports were deemed 'objective' and heavily relied upon. Later decades have since witnessed a generation of historians dedicated to translating and discussing Mughal diplomatic sources, such as imperial letters, royal decrees, bureaucratic manuals, administrative missives, and legal documents. Nonetheless, *The Embassy of Sir Thomas Roe*, a compilation of the English ambassador's journal entries, notes, and correspondence from 1615 to 1619, is still considered a valuable first hand account of the court of the Mughal Emperor Jahângîr (r. 1605-1627). Despite the detail of Roe's observations of the court machinations between Khurram (the later emperor "Shâh Jahân"), Âsaf Khân (empress Nûr Jahân's brother and father of Mumtâz Mahal), and Nûr Jahân, or of Jahângîr's propensity for vice, their use necessitates extreme caution.

The Mughal empire, established by the Tîmûrid exile Bâbur in the early sixteenth century and systematized by his descendent Akbar later in the century, was a relatively new phenomenon for expansionary Europe. Its adoption of both Perso-Islamic principles of kingship, combined with certain Tîmûrid characteristics, guaranteed the Mughal dynasty a unique complexity among early modern Islamic empires. Moreover, while other Islamic systems of rule, like that of the Ottomans or the Safavids, were able to rationalize themselves with promulgations of either *sunnî* or *shî`î* religious orthodoxy, the Mughals were uncharacteristic in their status as minority Muslim rulers. Is it possible for the complexity of such a system to be accurately represented by a seventeenth-century European with absolutely no experience in an Islamic environment? Nonetheless, scholars to date have accredited Roe's account as rigorous and meticulous with little appreciation for the cultural and linguistic discrepancies existing between the worlds of seventeenth-century Europe and Mughal India.

Moreover, the perceptions recorded in *The Embassy of Sir Thomas Roe* serve as a good introduction to the larger issues addressed in the discipline of 'encounter studies.' A composite of history, literature, and anthropology, the study of how Europe interacted with both the Old and New Worlds in the early modern setting has grown significantly in the last two decades. The underlying theses of many scholars exploring this area (Stuart Schwartz, Peter Hulme, Seymour Phillips, Anthony Reid), is that the 'discovery' of non-European cultures delivered a dramatic and unsettling blow to European world conceptions. As Spain, Portugal, England, and Holland began establishing their transoceanic empires, European theologians and humanists were faced with an unprecedented level of cultural heterogeneity. Their rationalization of non-European cultures was rooted in ethnographies developed during the mediaeval period; Biblical tradition dictated how, after the Great Flood, Noah allotted the three existing continents (Africa, Asia, and Europe) among his three sons, Japeth, Shem, and Ham.[1] With the growth of humanism in the fourteenth and fifteenth centuries, it was commonly understood that the cultures of Africa and Asia were essentially polluted remnants of ancient Christian societies. Descriptions by men like Marco Polo and the Franciscan missionaries Carpine and William of Rubruck struggled with the cultural diversity of the Middle East and Asia and its apparent incompatibility with its supposed European ancestry. With Vasco da Gama's circumnavigation of Africa in 1498, a new era of European participation in the Indian Ocean area was ushered in. Portuguese chroniclers like Barbosa, Pires, and Castanheda began providing detailed accounts of the political, cultural, and religious features of Vijayanagar, Malabar, and the Coromandel Coast. Our understanding of pre-modern India, and more importantly how Europeans initially perceived it, has been helped considerably by the Vatican's collection of *relaciones*, or written reports, sent by Jesuit missionaries stationed in various cities across the subcontinent.[2]

European awareness of the Old World expanded significantly with the arrival of the English East India Company and the Dutch *Vereenigde Oost-Indische Compagnie* in the early seventeenth century. Written accounts of these north Atlantic trading agents and factors to their superiors in London and Amsterdam were strictly confined to commercial transactions and market speculations. While there were previous descriptions by Englishmen who had individually travelled through Persia and India (Anthony

Jenkinson (1561), Arthur Edwards (1568), Ralph Fitch (1583), James Lancaster (1591), and Richard Steele (1614)), these men were either agents of the English Muscovy Company or independent merchants, and their accounts were essentially commercially based. Thomas Roe, as is discussed later on, was no "mean, middling" merchant when he arrived in Sûrat in 1615; he was a man of many qualities whose presentation of the Mughal empire went beyond economic or trade agendas. His extensive education and training in the Humanist arts, including history, biblical studies, and philosophy, distinguished him from his East India Company colleagues. His account, as I contend, was representative of this aforementioned problem of explaining or rationalizing non-European cultures; moreover, his description of Jahângîr and the Mughal empire catered specifically to early seventeenth-century English analogies and terminology. The purpose here is not to expose examples of spuriousness in Roe's account, thereby providing a 'true' or 'real' assessment of Jahângîr's court. Rather, this investigation purports to a) understand and highlight the various features of Jacobean English society of which Roe was a product; b) recognize and reveal existing subjective elements hidden among his account's perceptions and conclusions regarding Mughal India; and, c) examine some of the underlying causes explaining *The Embassy of Sir Thomas Roe's* historiographical domination.

One would be perfectly within their rights to ask why *The Embassy of Sir Thomas Roe* deserves a book-length investigation. It is, after all, only one seventeenth-century travel account among many. This particular examination, however, is not just about what a Jacobean Englishman had to say about the Mughal Indian environment. Sir Thomas Roe stood as a bridge or gateway between seventeenth-century England and the strange, exotic reality of Mughal India; this book, in many ways, reflects this original nexus of relations. Not only is it a study of what Roe perceived and wrote about Jahângîr's court, it is also a study of both Jacobean and Mughal society and culture. To fully appreciate the way Roe chose to represent certain features of what he was observing, we also have to be very aware of the environment from which he came. At the same time, we cannot understand how Roe chose to describe something without understanding what exactly he was attempting to relate. While, indeed, the bulk of this book revolves around *The Embassy of Sir Thomas Roe*, there is an underlying structure dedicated to mapping out this tripartite relationship between Sir Thomas Roe, the Mughal empire, and Jacobean England.

This book is divided according to themes. There is an initial chapter designed to introduce the reader to the Mughal empire and the developments explaining how Roe found himself appointed as England's first ambassador to India. The next four chapters are divided according to what I believe are the major themes of Roe's writing and areas in which he had substantial training or professional experience. For instance, we find a strong literary element in Roe's journal which I think justifies a chapter ("Sir Thomas Roe as *Litterateur*)". Likewise, someone reading *The Embassy of Sir Thomas Roe* will be struck with the constant references to diplomacy and the status of ambassadors; this, in turn has resulted in a chapter entitled "Sir Thomas Roe as Ambassador." In each of these chapters, a simple methodology is followed. Firstly, I trace Roe's education and training regarding the area in question, be it literature, courtier skills, diplomacy, politics, or history. Subsequently, I examine the larger Jacobean definitions and approaches to the area and how these might have influenced how Roe recorded his perceptions in the Mughal context. Basing myself on indigenous Mughal sources, I then look at the topic from an Indo-Islamic perspective. For example, the chapter "Sir Thomas Roe as Courtier" begins with a narrative of how Roe worked as a professional courtier for both Elizabeth I and James I. The chapter then continues with an examination of how Jacobean England defined the royal court and how courtier relationships should be conducted. The discussion then moves to *The Embassy of Sir Thomas Roe* and whether or not we can find any overtly Jacobean metaphors or similes in Roe's depiction of the Mughal Indian court. To reinforce the 'Anglified' rendition of Jahângîr's court, we then present how the Mughals perceived and practiced court politics. Perhaps the last chapter, "Tracing the Historiography of *The Embassy of Sir Thomas Roe*," partially explains the previous question of why Sir Thomas Roe deserves such a lengthy study. It is here that we prove how this seventeenth-century source has come to occupy a central position in the current Mughal historiography and how Roe's unique perceptions have unduly influenced how historians interpret the Mughal empire today. The conclusion, "Sir Thomas Roe as Orientalist," looks at this source and how it has been used with respect to larger, ongoing arguments in the South Asian scholarly community.

There is a tendency in this field to chart out 'development' in the Mughal empire, with Akbar representing the 'pinnacle' of Mughal accomplishments and a ruler like Bahâdur Shâh signaling a decline into depravity and corruption. There is no mistaking where Jahângîr Shâh was supposed to stand *vis-à-vis* these issues of enlightened rule or tyrannical despotism. *The Embassy* is important as an historical source because of the breadth and detail of its commentary on Mughal politics and court events, but it has also had an important historiographical dimension. Its characterization of Jahângîr is of an ineffective ruler whose proclivity for sport and drink facilitated the growth of disruptive elements in the immediate family and court. While working on his translation of *Tûzuk-i Jahângîrî*, Henry Beveridge wrote an article in 1907 for the *Indian Magazine* in which he stated that Jahângîr's "account of himself also has its charm, for it reveals the real man, and so he lives for us in his Memoirs just as James VI—to whom he bears a strange and even ludicrous resemblance—

lives in the 'Fortunes of Nigel' or Claudius in "Suetonius and Tacitus."³ Beveridge's close comparison of Jahângîr with his English contemporary is not surprising. While the 'Whig' trend of nineteenth-century scholarship depicted a slovenly and inept, yet strangely contemplative, James I, the colonial era of Mughal historiography presented his Indo-Muslim counterpart as "fond of sport, art and good living and by the lack of the finer intellectual qualities [unable] to attain the ranks of great administrators."⁴ Later scholars have discreetly ignored the significance of Jahângîr's hedonist qualities, but E.B. Findly has recently revived their importance in an effort to prove "he had neither the desire nor the temperament to tinker with regional boundaries or with the machinery of government"⁵ and that "he was not willing to dirty his hands in the building and maintenance of a political state."⁶ For someone like Findly, "what most satisfied Jahângîr was what gave him pleasure, and what gave him most pleasure were things he could see."⁷.

Generally speaking, scholars relying on European accounts, specifically *The Embassy*, have failed to appreciate the underlying sophistication of the Mughal empire's structure and, possibly motivated by a sense of drama and intrigue, have focused on the proceedings of a few, well-placed court personalities.⁸ Many historians, however, have succeeded in illustrating the intricacy and individuality of the Mughal administration and its incorporation of the nobility.⁹ This study is neither an apology for Jahângîr nor a study detailing the Mughal administration. Rather, it hopes to call into question how and why Jahângîr's reign became widely accepted as the beginning of the end for the Mughal empire.

NOTES

1. John B. Friedman, "Cultural Conflicts in Medieval World Maps," in *Implicit Understandings: Observing, Reporting, and Reflecting on the Encounters Between Europeans and Other Peoples in the Early Modern Era*, ed. S. Schwartz (Cambridge: 1994), p. 67.
2. For a good study of the various letters sent by Jesuit agents to the Vatican, see John Correia-Alfonso, *Jesuit Letters and Indian History, 1542-1773* (Bombay: 1969).
3. Henry Beveridge, "Preface," in *Tûzuk-i Jahângîrî*, p. ix.
4. Lt. Col. Sir Wolseley Haig and Sir Richard Burns, *The Cambridge History of India*, Vol. IV (Delhi: 1937), p. 182. For another James I-Jahângîr comparison, see Stanley Lane-Poole's *Mediæval India Under Mohammedan Rule* (New York: 1906), pp. 298-99.
5. E.B. Findly, *Nur Jahan: Empress of Mughal India* (Oxford: 1993), p. 63.
6. Findly, *Nur Jahan*, p. 65.
7. Findly, *Nur Jahan*, p. 65.
8. Probably the most absurd example of this brand of scholarship is Waldemar Hansen's *The Peacock Throne*, New York: 1972; however, Findly's 1993 work on Nûr Jahân perpetuates this trend on a subdued scale.
9. While many works exist on this subject, noteworthy texts include M. Athar Ali, *The Mughal Nobility Under Aurengzeb* (Bombay: 1965), and I.H. Qureshi, *Administration of the Mughal Empire* (Karachi: 1966).

1
SIR THOMAS ROE AND THE MUGHAL CONTEXT

Sir Thomas Roe's arrival in 1615 came at an auspicious time. Muhammad Sultân Salîm, crowned as Nûr al-Dîn Muhammad Jahângîr Pâdshâh Ghâzî in 1605, had inherited a well-organized and territorially impressive empire from his father, Jalâl al-Dîn Muhammad Akbar. The transition to what many scholars consider the zenith of Muslim rule in India was, nonethless, a slow and painful one. Prior to the reign of Akbar, Islamic governance of northern India had been largely understood as a powerful and ethnically-distinct minority exerting its will, through taxation and coercion, over a non-Muslim majority. Alternating between Turkish and Afghân periods of domination, the early medieval period (1000-1500 ACE) witnessed the continued conquest and subjugation of indigenous kingdoms in Râjpûtânâ, Râthor, Bihâr, Bengâl, and Gujarât. Moreover, Islamic theories of kingship became seriously diluted as Turkish slaves, initially serving as shock troops and military commanders, began assuming control.[1] Indo-Islamic administration underwent various systemizations during the reigns of 'Alâ al-Dîn Khaljî (r. 1296-1329), Muhammad ibn Tughluq (r. 1329-1351) and Fîrûz Tughluq (r. 1351-1388); nonetheless, the Turkish dynasty was essentially an orthodox *sunnî* institution and ruled according to the *sharî'ah* (Islamic law) and traditional Muslim methods of taxation.[2]

Indo-Turkic rule, centered in Delhî, was seriously disrupted by Tîmûr's invasion of India in 1398, thus allowing a proliferation of independent territories during the fifteenth century in Malwâ, Gujarât, Bengâl, Khândesh, and the Deccan.[3] The ethos of 'foreign rule' in northern India continued under the governance of the Afghân Lodîs (1414-1526) as indigenous Hindu and Muslim converts found themselves displaced from the feudal aristocracy by the resulting influx of Central Asian *amîrs* and *khâns*. While the Hindu majority became alienated under the orthodox rule of Sultân Iskandar (r. 1488-1517), discontent spread among the Afghân ruling elite when Iskandar's successor, Ibrâhîm, attempted to introduce a strict policy of centralization.[4] Ibrâhîm's response was anything but conciliatory as he systematically eliminated the leaders of any opposition; when one of the premier Afghân Lodîs, Daulat Khân, realized he and his family were under imperial scrutiny, he sought assistance from the north.

Zahîr al-Dîn Muhammad Bâbur, Chaghtâ'î ruler of Farghânah and descendent of Tîmûr, had spent much of his youth defending his hereditary claims to Transoxania and Khurâsân against the powerful Uzbekî chief, Shîbânî Muhammad Khân.[5] After his defeat at Archian in 1503 and the loss of the traditional Tîmûrid capital Samarqand, Bâbur and his royal camp became mobile as they roamed Central Asia in search of powerful military allies.[6] Central Asian dynamics, however, were radically changed in 1510 when the Safavî shâh, Isma'îl, marched east from Tabrîz and routed Shîbânî's troops at Marv. Realizing the military potential of this new Iranian power, Bâbur continued his policy of convenient diplomacy by concluding a treaty with Isma'îl which stipulated, among other things, that the *khutbah* be read in the shâh's name and the recently-titled Central Asian *pâdshâh* embrace *shî'ism*.[7] The *sunnî* Uzbekî chiefs, using Bâbur's adoption of such *bid'a* (innovation) as a rallying point, were able to reconsolidate after the debacle of Marv and defeated the joined forces of Isma'îl and Bâbur at Ghijdavân in 1512. Isolated to a fiefdom around the area of Kâbul, Bâbur decided to reorient his policy towards the south and, for the next decade, organized raids into Sindh and Multân. When the emissary of the disgruntled Afghân noble Daulat Khân arrived in Kâbul in 1524, Bâbur seized the opportunity to orchestrate a massive invasion of the Indian subcontinent.[8] "Having placed [his] foot in the stirrup of resolution and [his] hand on the reins of confidence in God," Bâbur reenacted his ancestor's infamous 1398 *tour de force* by routing all Afghân resistance mustered by Ibrâhîm Lodî at Panîpât in April 1526.[9] After several battles (Khânwâh, Chandirî, Gogra) in which he managed to subdue most Lodî and Râjpût opposition, the Chaghtâ'î Turk assumed control of Hindûstân.

Chingîzîd and Turkic tradition stipulates that, upon the death of an overlord, all territory be divided among the inheriting royal family; with the absence of any law of *primogeniture*, periods of succession in Central Asian history have been marked by fratricide and familial civil wars.[10] Nasîr al-Dîn Muhammad Humâyûn was no exception to this eventuality and, soon after ascending the throne at Âgrâ on 29 December 1530, he parceled out portions of his father's dominions to his four brothers.[11] Stability only lasted a year when Kâmrân marched south from Kâbul and conquered Panjâb. After a period of limited territorial expansion in Gujarât at the expense of the local ruler Bahâdur Shâh, Humâyûn's most serious crisis came when disgruntled Afghân nobles rallied around a prominent *jâgîrdâr* in Bengâl named Sher Khân Sûr.[12] Following two decisive defeats at Chausâ and Qanauj, Humâyûn was forced to flee in 1542 and, after a short time in Sindh and Râjasthân, sought asylum at the Persian court of the Shâh Tahmâsp.

This interlude in Mughal rule in India was by no means a dark one since Sher Shâh is credited with a number of administrative and judicial reforms; moreover, he ignored the advice of his orthodox *sunnî 'ulamâ* and introduced a policy of limited toleration for Hindus.[13] Meanwhile, Humâyûn was involved in a bitter dispute with his brothers for the control of Afghânistân. With the help of 14,000 Persian troops, he managed to dislodge Kâmrân and 'Askarî from Kâbul and Qandahâr in 1545. These victories in the northwest, coinciding with the death of Sher Shâh during his siege of the Râjpût fort at Kâlinjar, seemed promising for a restoration of Mughal power in India. Humâyûn was content to let his enemies do his work for him. Sher Shâh's successor, Islâm Shâh Sûr, faced several rebellions and acts of sedition and, by the time of his death in 1554, Afghân rule in northern India was rife with factionalism and civil war.[14] Humâyûn's return to the throne was virtually unopposed after his defeat of the Afghâns at Lahore in February 1555, but his accidental death one year later came at a critical period since Mughal rule had yet to be fully restored.

When Jalâl al-Dîn Muhammad Akbar assumed the throne on 14 February 1556 at the age of thirteen, the prospects of a single Muslim political entity in northern India seemed remote. Akbar's step-brother, Mîrzâ Muhammad Hakîm, was essentially an autonomous ruler in Kâbul; several independent states had sprung up during the period of decentralization following Sher Shâh's death, and a debilitating famine was spreading through Delhî and Âgrâ. Bengâl was now under the direct suzerainty of the Afghân Sûr dynasty and, to the west, Râjpût princes had reestablished formidable centers of power in Mewâr, Jaisalmîr, Bundî, and Jodhpûr. Hoping to monopolize on the precarious Mughal hold on central India, Muhammad 'Âdil of the Sûr Afghâns marched west towards Âgrâ. The Mughal forces, led by Akbar's *vakîl-i saltanat* (vice regent) Bairâm Khân, were initially driven from both Delhî and Âgrâ but, after a spirited stand at Panîpât, succeeded in defeating the invading forces.[15] It was largely due to the efforts of Akbar's vice regent that the Mughal empire was not consumed by internal civil strife and factional politics early on. Moreover, it was under Bairâm Khân that the young king was able to secure a number of agriculturally-rich territories desperately needed to ensure Mughal stability—Lahore, Multân, Ajmîr, and Jaunpûr. Internal dissension grew further in 1560 when Akbar's foster-mother, Mahâl Angâh, engineered the down fall of Bairâm Khân who was now bearing the title *khân-i khânân* ("greatest of the khâns").[16] Likewise, one year later, Akbar ordered the execution of Mahâl Angâh's son, Adham Khân, for the murder of the emperor's proposed *vakîl-i saltanat*, Shams al-Dîn Muhammad Atga Khân. By 1564, Akbar had suppressed such divisive elements and by replacing the office of *vakîl* with four ministerial positions (military, financial, bureaucratic, and religious), he effectively eliminated chances of one member of the Mughal nobility exercising undue power over others.

Akbar's first serious test as an independent ruler came when a majority of the Uzbekî nobility revolted in the mid-1560s. These Uzbek elites traced their lineage back to Shîbânî Muhammad Khân but, seeking fortune and booty under Bâbur, had pledged allegiance to the House of Tîmûr; in fact, when Humâyûn fled, a majority of these Central Asian *amîrs* had accompanied their overlord to Persia. However when Akbar started initiating his policy of absolutist, centralized rule, their political sensibilities, more oriented towards consensus and shared power, were offended. The revolt of 'Abd Allâh Khân, governor of Malwâ, in 1564 was soon supplemented by a series of Uzbekî uprisings in Bihâr and Bengâl.[17] The emperor's legitimacy was seriously challenged when the insurgents proclaimed Akbar's half-brother, Mîrzâ Muhammad Hakîm, the true Mughal ruler. To further complicate this issue of legitimacy, some of Tîmûr's distant descendants, the family of Muhammad Sultân Mîrzâ, also revolted and tried to capture Delhî.[18] Through suppression and negotiation, Akbar was ultimately able to disperse these threats but it was becoming evident that his ancestry was a double-edged tool: while it provided the legitimacy needed to rule, Tîmûrid rules of succession would continue to permit legal claims to the throne by royal family members.

Akbar's policy of political assimilation in Râjpûtânâ in the late 1560s proved beneficial in two ways. First, by enticing key Râjpûts like the family of Bihârî Mal headed by the Kachwâha Râjah of Amber into imperial service, Akbar lessened his reliance on the politically turbulent *amîrs* of Central Asia. Second, securing such allies provided key access to military *entrepôts* and supply routes.[19] Between 1567 and 1569, the Mughal emperor mounted a series of invasions into Râjasthân. After the subjugation of Chitor, Ranthanbhûr, and Kâlinjar, many Râjpût nobles submitted but, unlike previous Muslim rulers, Akbar appeased his defeated enemies by allowing them to retain their territories as fiefdoms under Mughal suzerainty. Ironically, when one of the more serious Râjasthânî rebellions began in 1576 under Rânâ Partâb Singh, Akbar dispatched a Râjpût, Râjah Mân Singh, to quell it. Despite an initial defeat at Haidighat in 1576, Rânâ Partâb would continue to dominate remote parts of Râjasthân through guerrilla tactics until his death in 1597. The inability of Akbar to eliminate this clandestine Mewarî military activity was due, in no small part, to his intermittent strategic commitments to Bengâl[20], Kâbul[21], Gujarât[22], Kashmîr[23], Sindh[24], and Qandahâr.[25] After finally subduing the Râjpûts in the late 1590s, and with much of northern India now consolidated under Mughal rule, Akbar turned to the *shî'î* states of the Deccan as a new area of expansion and wrestled Ahmadnagar away from the Nizâmshâhs in 1601.

With the arrival of Alvarez de Cabral off the coast of Diu in 1501, sixteenth-century subcontinent dynamics would be introduced to a new player in the *Estado da India*, the crown corporation of the Spanish-Portuguese empire. The Iberian approach to overseas trade was essentially imperial in design: the use of small, well-fortified ports from which Indian Ocean traffic could be controlled and regulated. The relative sophistication of ship-board ordinance, combined with the daunting size of caravels and galleons, allowed the Portuguese to reorient the flow of trade, specifically pepper, through their principal ports of Goa and Diu.[26] Moreover, Iberian expansion into the Indian Ocean coincided with the height of the Catholic Reformation in the mid-sixteenth century; one of the strategies adopted by the Catholic Church was to initiate a programme of aggressive proselytism under the auspices of recently created monastic orders, most notably Ignatius Loyala's Military Order of the Jesuits. Missionaries like the Jesuits were instructed by both their own Order General and the Vatican to travel and interact with indigenous Indian rulers, both Muslim and non-Muslim, in an attempt to win over potential political and military allies. Akbar's annexation of Gujarât in the early 1570s made the Portuguese realize not only the proximity but also the importance of this powerful Muslim empire to the northeast. When Akbar was forced to return to Gujarât and suppress a rebellion led by Ibrâhîm Husain Mîrzâ in January 1573, a Portuguese entourage arrived at the Mughal's siege camp near Sûrat. Initially they hoped to act as mediators in this dispute but when they "saw...the largeness of the army, and of the extent of the siege-train, they represented themselves as ambassadors and performed the *kornish*."[27]

In 1579, the first Jesuit mission, led by Father Anthony Monserrate, arrived from Goa at Akbar's capital in Fâtehpûr Sikrî.[28] The missionaries spent the next two years at the Mughal court, indulging in theological debates and discussing points of similarity (and dissimilarity) between Christian and Muslim doctrine. Initial European perception of Islam in the Indian context, however, was consistent with the discourse cultivated earlier during the Crusades of the Middle Ages and the recent Habsburg-Ottoman wars in south-central Europe; Europeans categorized Indian Muslims as 'moors' (very much a North African designation) and 'Turks'. When Akbar dispatched a letter to the Goan Jesuit Society in 1590 inviting another delegation, the ecclesiastical authorities believed the Mughal emperor was contemplating conversion to Christianity. Father Edward Leiton and Christopher de Voga arrived in Lahore in 1591 but after several days of rhetoric and discussion, the Europeans realized that Akbar was simply interested in the theoretical implications of the Christian doctrine and had no serious interest in converting. Nonetheless, these two missions, plus a third in 1594, allowed for the Portuguese to establish limited diplomatic contact with the Mughal emperor which, in turn, resulted in certain trade concessions being allotted to the *Estado da India*.

Mentioned earlier, much of the history of northern India after 1000 ACE is characterized by foreign invasions and the establishment of intermittent Muslim minority regimes. Looking to the Mughals as the first 'indigenous' Islamic rulers would be ambitious considering the dynasty's early history. Bâbur, a self-professed Chaghtâ'î, never entirely assimilated himself into the Indian environment and, to his mind, Hindûstân was a land of people with "no genius, no comprehension of mind, no politeness of manner, skill or knowledge in design or architecture." True to his Tîmûrid *ghâzî* ancestry, he considered northern India's most positive features to be its large mineral deposits of gold and silver.[29] Humâyûn's temporary exile to Persia, a result of his inability to control the centrifugal Afghân elements, only reinforces the superficiality of early Mughal rule. Moreover, the tendency of both Bâbur and Humâyûn to parcel out *jâgîrdâr* appointments to kin and clan members did little to reconcile the displaced elite of both Muslim and non-Muslim circles. In this sense, the early Mughal dynasty was nothing more than a continuation of previous ruling strategies practiced by Turkish and Afghân *khândâns*.

Appreciating the events of the last three centuries, Akbar correctly understood that Mughal rule could not hope to avoid the rude fate of its predecessors without a radical departure from contemporary Indo-Islamic political theory. The *dâr al-Islâm* was no longer characterized by a plethora of minor parochial dynasties making nominal recognition of the caliphate. With the Ottomans expanding into Europe, the Levant, Mesopotamia, and the Maghrib, along with the Safavid empire securing large swathes of territory in the Caucasus, `Irâq-i `Arab, and Khurâsân, the age of "gunpowder empires" was in full swing.[30] Maintaining such expansive territories required sophisticated administrations, organized and well disciplined armies, regulated religious institutions, and the consistent sponsorship of craftsmen, architects, painters, and artisans. Emperors and ministers alike realized the incompatibility of tribal, specifically Turkic, culture with the sedentary, urban-based societies that were now developing in the premodern period. In the case of the Indo-Pak subcontinent, this tension was exacerbated by the growing resentment of an alienated indigenous population.

Early on, we can detect Akbar's struggle to distance himself from Central Asian steppe culture by accessing a hitherto untapped reservoir of sedentarized nobility. When the emperor ascended to the throne in 1556, Chaghtâ'î and Uzbekî nobles comprised half of the ruling elite but within twenty-five years Akbar had reduced this fraction to one-quarter. Downsizing of the Central Asian contingent went hand in hand with a general increase in the overall number of Mughal nobility.[31] In addition to those who had joined Humâyûn during his stay in Iran, some of the new inductees were Persian *emigrés* fleeing Qizilbâsh persecution or Uzbekî invasions; notable examples include Bairâm Khân, Mîrzâ Muzaffar Husain, Mîrzâ Rustam, Pîr Muhammad Khân Shîrvânî, Zain Khân Koka of Herât, Mîrzâ Yûsuf Khân, Muzaffar Khân Turbatî, and Muhammad Qâsim Khân.[32] Akbar also looked to indigenous Muslim converts, like the Sayyids of Bârha (Sâdât-i Bârha) and Bilgrâm, who would later prove to be some of the empire's most worthy and loyal military commanders.³³ Above all, the Mughal ruler's most innovative, construed by some as heretical, measure was the recruitment of Râjpût and non-Râjpût Hindu nobility. While satisfying certain strategic objectives, the recruitment of men like the Kachwâha Râjah of Amber was central to Akbar's program of 'de-Turkicification.' As both Richards and Ziegler have pointed out, Râjpûts maintained their social systems of brotherhoods *(bhai-bambh)* and patrilineal kin groups but, through the use of diplomatic marriages, could now access the Mughal royal house for military and political advancement. Akbar intensely cultivated the deeply embedded Râjpût codes of loyalty and warfare, and by concentrating on this relationship between master and warrior, he de-emphasized his technical status as a Muslim overlord and simply became "the greatest of the Râjpût masters."³⁴ Râjah Bhagwân Dâs, son of Râjah Bihârî Mal, was governor of Panjâb (1585-87) while his son, Râjah Mân Singh, has been considered one of Akbar's greatest generals.³⁵ Non-Râjpût Hindus were now also part of the Mughal infrastructure; Râjah Todar Mal, a Khatrî, was appointed *vakîl* in 1583 and many of his financial reforms, including rent and currency regulation, were included in the Â'în-i-Akbarî.³⁶

Such developments, i.e. the displacement of Turkic elements and corresponding substitution of non-Muslims or Muslim converts, are not unique to the Indo-Islamic context. In the latter years of Tahmâsp's reign, the Safavid shâh enlisted thousands of Christian Caucasian slaves *(ghulâmân)* into the military corps; this process was accelerated by 'Abbâs I and many of these *ghulâmân* rose to elevated positions in the Safavid state.³⁷ Likewise, we see a similar phenomenon in the Ottoman empire with the *sultâns* of Istânbûl relying increasingly on the European, Muslim-converted slaves being trained in the *devshirme* institution as a pool of future bureaucrats, ministers, and military commanders.³⁸ Thus, we have parallel developments in the three major Islamic political states of the premodern period: the sponsorship and encouragement of non-tribal, occasionally non-Muslim, elements in the ruling infrastructure. The reasons for this are complicated and many-fold. Traditional Islamic conceptions of government, as espoused by political theorists like al-Ghazâlî, Nizâm al-Mulk, and Nasîr al-Dîn Tûsî, agree that the maintenance of justice, through *sharî'ah*, is the penultimate goal of any Muslim state.[40] However, guaranteeing justice necessitates a strong military which is in turn funded through responsible taxation of the peasantry (*ra'âyâ*) by an efficient bureaucracy. The axial feature of this system is the appeasement of the military elite *(umarâ')* through land and tax grants. As the early Ottomans built their empire with the tribal power of the Anatolian *beylerbegs*, the initial success of Shâh Isma'îl in creating the Safavid state was predicated on the military support of the Türkmen Qizilbâsh; in both cases, this relationship between tribal *umarâ'* and the ruler eventually became strained.[40] The rulers removed the power of this turbulent elite by substituting a professional corps of non-tribal, and initially non-Muslim, bureaucrats and military commanders. It is from this context that we have to understand Akbar's policy of incorporating indigenous Indian, Muslim and non-Muslim, elements into the governmental structure. As long as the Indo-Islamic state was reliant on the Afghân and Turkic military, dynastic stability and responsible governance would continue to be problematic.

This is not to say that Akbar's reign was free of dissension. Besides the earlier mentioned political rebellions, one of the most discussed developments was the hostile reaction of the orthodox *sunnî 'ulamâ* to the emperor's infallibility decree in 1579. Akbar's assumption of the role of supreme interpretative guide (*mujtahid*) significantly alarmed the religious establishment. This decree, in conjunction with the emperor's keen interest in other religious traditions (Sufism, Bakhtism, Hinduism,

Buddhism, Christianity), signaled to many a dangerous departure from the traditional *sunnah*. We should, however, be cautious in asserting that the *dîn-i illâhî* and the *mazhar* promulgation were interdependent developments. The holistic religious doctrine promulgated by Akbar was essentially a court phenomenon. By M. Athar Ali's account, it was a "select group of disciples"—probably 18-19 adherents—including the emperor's principal *vakîl* and propagandist, Abû al-Fazl.[41] The *mazhar*, however, is much more profound and should be seen not in terms of religious heterodoxy but in the light of *realpolitik*. By positioning himself as the supreme head and arbiter of doctrinal issues, Akbar was expanding the imperial presence to include both the temporal and spiritual world; as Abû al-Fazl observed: "God be praised for that at this day the Lord of Lords of inspired wisdom is represented by the Holy Personality of the Shâhinshâh [Akbar]."[42] Once again, we have a certain parallelism in Ottoman Turkey and Safavid Iran. When Sultân Salîm I captured the holy cities of Mekkah and Madînah in his invasion of the Arabian Peninsula in 1517, one of his first steps was to appropriate the office of *khalîfah*. With such a title, the *sultân* was now the nominal head of the Muslim community (*ummah*) in both worldly and spiritual affairs. Likewise, when Isma'îl Safavî proclaimed himself shâh in Tabrîz in 1501, it was commonly understood that he was the spiritual master (*murshid-i kâmil*); this dual understanding of the *shâh* as both a temporal and spiritual leader was continued well into the seventeenth century.[43]

By the turn of the sixteenth century, the Mughal empire was no longer characterized by overt tribalism and ethnic-dominated dynasticism. Rather, not unlike their contemporaries in Anatolia and Iran, the Mughals adopted a style of rule modeled on syncretism and increased bureaucratic and religious centralization. We should not believe, however, that there was a complete rejection of Turkic-Mongol traditions; the continued adherence to certain ceremonial procedures, honorifics and titles, and symbols of imperial legitimacy, suggests that Akbar and later Mughal emperors never entirely dismissed their ancestral heritage.

Prince Salîm (later crowned as Jahângîr) and his decision to expedite his accession to the throne through rebellion was indeed indicative of such Chingîzîd traditions. While campaigning in Mewâr during 1599, the young prince became unduly influenced by his immediate circle of advisors including the later leading courtier and military commander, Mahâbat Khân. After a failed bid to seize Âgrâ, Salîm commissioned a number of ships and sailed for Allâhabâd.[44] There, the prince proclaimed independence and appointed his principal supporters, Qutb al-Dîn Khân, Lâl Beg, and Yatîm Bahâdur to the respective *jâgîrs* of Bihâr, Jaunpûr, and Kâlpî.[45] For the next two years, Salîm continued to control the territory of western Bihâr but made the serious strategic error of involving himself in a conspiracy leading to the assassination of Akbar's chief administrator and dear friend, Abû al-Fazl.[46] The prince was ultimately reconciled to his father in 1603 and allowed to continue ruling his court in Allâhabâd which, by 1604, had taken on some rather Byzantine features. Râjah Mân Singh and Mîrzâ 'Azîz Koka, making note of such debauch behavior as well as the emperor's failing health, looked to an alternate candidate for the throne: Khusrau.[47] In 1605, as Akbar lay on his deathbed, the two nobles began making preparations for Salîm's arrest and confinement. However, the Sayyids of Bârha learned of the plot and insisted that a general council of *khâns* and *amîrs* be held. The majority of the grandees agreed with Sayyid Khân Bârha and announced unanimous support for Salîm.[49] On 24 October 1605, one week after the death of Akbar, the *khutbah* was read with the name of the new emperor, Nûr al-Dîn Muhammad Jahângîr Pâdshâh Ghâzî. Heralds were dispatched to the various provinces, royal decrees *(farâmîn)* and land appointments *(tuyûl)* were affixed with Jahângîr's *tughrâ* and seal, and imperial mints were directed to prepare a new line of currency.

Whether or not the young emperor felt overshadowed by the recent military accomplishments of his father is unclear but, nonetheless, he decided to inaugurate his reign with a show of force. Rânâ Partâb Singh had passed away in 1597 but his son, Amar Singh, had continued to harry Mughal troops from the Mewârî mountain passes. Dispatching a cavalry force of 20,000 under the joint command of his son Parvaiz and Âsaf Khân Ja'far Beg, Jahângîr hoped to settle the Râjpût question once and for all.[49] Amar Singh rallied his nobles and continued his father's strategy of avoiding pitched battle. Pressing developments in other parts of the empire (see below) forced the Mughals to withdraw and sign a truce with Amar Singh at Mândalgarh. Jahângîr's decision to commit his forces to such a project was not wise. If anything, past Mughal experiences have shown the futility of depending on the traditional mode of Tîmûrid warfare, large organized divisions of armored cavalry, in the mountainous Mewârî terrain. Any such endeavors would only prove to be costly and demoralizing. Moreover, the young emperor should have realized the vulnerability of his position in this first year of rule since conflicting claims to the throne and foreign aggression were inevitable during such periods of succession.

It was made quickly clear that Jahângîr could not equal his father's territorial ambitions nor his gift for military strategy. While he prided himself on his daily involvement in administration and judicial arbitration, the new emperor clearly lacked Akbar's tenacity and commitment. On the other hand, Jahângîr's extensive education as a youth left him with a deep passion for natural sciences, painting, philosophy, mysticism, and the Persian literary tradition. His consistent patronage of artists like Abû al-Hasan, Âqâ Rizâ, Ustâd Mansûr, and Bishân Dâs contributed significantly to the evolution of Mughal miniature painting.⁵⁰ Jahângîr's penchant for court culture also had an important literary dimension. Akbar's sponsorship of court poets was continued by Jahângîr when he nominated Tâlib Âmulî as the poet laureate *(malik shu'arâ')*. Âmulî, Nizâmî, 'Abd al-Nabî Fakhr al-Zamânî Qazvînî, Ahsan, Bahjâtî, and other poets furthered the development of *sabk-i hindî*, a style of poetry known for its philosophical twist of the traditionally love-oriented *ghazal*. In the genre of prose writing, scribes *(munshîs)* and scholars such as Nûr al-Dîn Muhammad 'Abd Allâh, Bâqir Khân Najm-i Sânî, and Harkarn Dâs produced a substantial number of *inshâ'* works. One the most well known Persian dictionaries, the *Farhang-i Jahângîrî*, was compiled and dedicated to Jahângîr by Jamâl al-Dîn Husain Injû. It was also during this reign that the 'mirrors-for-princes' genre blossomed with Bâqir Khân Najm-i Sânî's writing of the famous *Mau'izah-i Jahângîrî*.⁵¹ Histories written during this period include the celebrated *Ma'âthir-i Jahângîrî* by Kâmgâr Husainî and *Iqbâl nâmah-i Jahângîrî* by Mu'tamad Khân, as well as 'Abd Allâh's *Târîkh-i Dâ'ûdî*, Gaibî's *Bahâristân-i Ghaibî*, Kanbô's *Ma'din-i akhbâr-i Ahmadî*, and Shîrâzî's *Ahsan al-tavârîkh*. In fact, one of our most valued historical sources for this period was penned by Jahângîr himself: the *Tûzuk-i Jahângîrî*. Fruitful *sûfî* biographies *(tadhkiras)*, such as Dehlavî's *Akhbâr al-akhyâr* and Shattarî's *Gulzâr-i abrâr*, as well as religious treatises like Mahjûr's *Sahîfat al-kirâmî*, were written between 1605 and 1627.

Although Khusrau was reconciled to his father after the accession, it took only six months before the young prince "unfurled the banner of sedition" by escaping to Panjâb with 350 retainers on horse. Intercepting and winning over a number of nobles on their way to pay homage to Jahângîr, Khusrau soon amassed an army of 12,000. When he attempted to enter Lahore, he encountered resistance from the governor, Dilâvar Khân. After nine days of siege, Khusrau learned that a relief force, led by his father, was imminent and fled. Jahângîr eventually caught up with

Khusrau and soundly defeated the rebels at Sultânpûr.[52] While Khusrau was spared, other nobles involved with the insurrection were summarily executed; likewise, the emperor ordered the arrest and execution of the fifth Sikh Guru, Arjun, who had aided Khusrau during his stay in the Panjâb.

The problems of the inevitable instability following a succession was not just an internal problem; like ambitious family members and disgruntled *khâns*, rulers of neighboring political states looked upon such transition periods as opportunities for territorial expansion. When Shâh ʿAbbâs I (r. 1588-1629) learned of Akbar's death, he instructed his Khurâsânî governors to consolidate their levies and co-ordinate an attack on the city of Qandahâr. Qandahâr, located between the Arghandâd and Shurâb rivers and representing a component in the Kâbul-Qandahâr-Herât triangle, was one of the principal *entrepôts* of Central Asia. Textiles, spices, slaves, gold, and silver were transported by Indian merchants via Qandahâr to Persia; likewise, Persian and Armenian traders used the city as a conduit to the subcontinent for their commodities of silk, porcelain, wine, and European-manufactured goods.[53] More importantly, Qandahâr was key to the overall defense of northern India. Since its proximity to Lahore and the Indo-Gangetic plain made it an ideal launching point for invasions, Akbar and previous Indo-Islamic rulers had made the defense and maintenance of the fort a priority issue. Luckily, the governor of Qandahâr, Shâh Beg Khân, was able to withstand the initial assault of the Persian army and gave Jahângîr the time he needed to organize a successful relief expedition.[54] ʿAbbâs I sent the ambassador Husain Beg to convey his shock and dismay that the Khurâsânî *khâns* had engaged such hostilities with no prior royal approval.[55] The Mughal emperor apparently thought it prudent not to press the matter and accepted the *shâh's* explanation but not without posting a further 15,000 cavalry at the fort. Jahângîr went on to enjoy the summer of 1607 with a number of hunting expeditions in the province of Kâbul but this was spoiled when two nobles, Khvâjah Vais and Pîr Khân Lodî, arrived at the royal camp and announced their discovery of a conspiracy to kill the emperor. Khusrau, only recently released from house arrest in Kâbul, had already enlisted several hundred nobles to his cause and was organizing a plan to strike down his father on a hunting trip. Four of the ring leaders, Nûr al-Dîn, I'tibâr Khân, Sharîf ibn Ghiyâs al-Dîn, and Badâgh Khân, were arrested and executed; apropos of Tîmûrid tradition, Khusrau was partially blinded to prevent any such future inclinations.[56]

With the distractions of Khusrau's rebellion and 'Abbâs I's probing attack at Qandahâr now settled, the emperor was relatively free to continue his planned subjugation of Mewâr. Unfortunately, both Jahângîr and his military commander, Mahâbat Khân, continued to believe in the merits of a cavalry-oriented military strategy. With 12,000 horse, 2,000 musketeers, and eighty pieces of artillery, Mahâbat Khân's successes were confined to low-lying terrains and cities. Hilly forts and mountain ranges continued to elude the large and overly encumbered Mughal armies. Mahâbat Khân's successor, 'Abd Allâh Khân, was slightly more successful with significant victories at Mihrpûr and Ranpûr, but any serious followthrough was prevented by the Mughal general's sudden transfer to the Deccanî theater in 1611.[57] One year earlier, Jahângîr had become alarmed by the resurging Nizâmshâh dynasty and ordered Prince Parvaiz, along with his *vazîr-i-dîvân* Âsaf Khân, Râjah Mân Singh, and Sharîf Khân, to proceed to the provinces of Khândesh and Birar. Parvaiz assumed the governorship at the provincial capital Bûrhânpûr but the original governor, Mîrzâ 'Abd al-Rahîm (*Khân-i Khânân*), continued to make the actual decisions. Together, 'Abd al-Rahîm and Parvaiz attempted to curtail and reverse the recent success of the Nizâmshâhî kingdom of Ahmadnagar, ruled now for all intents and purposes by a military slave officer and minister, Malik 'Ambar. Uninspiring leadership and mismanagement took its toll on the Mughal forces and before long Jahângîr entrusted the Deccanî campaign to one of his most powerful amîrs, Pîr Khân Lodî, whom he had recently bestowed with the title of *Khân-i Jahân* ("Khân of the World").[58] By the time Khân-i Jahân arrived in Bûrhânpûr, Malik 'Ambar had routed a Mughal army and was able to re-conquer Ahmadnagar. To worsen matters, there were allegations that 'Abd al-Rahîm had allowed his enemy's victory after receiving a sizeable cash gift. The Khân-i Khânân was arrested and replaced by the Khân-i Jahân who was now promising a complete restoration of Mughal dominion in two years.[59] With close to 12,000 reinforcements and a treasury of 30 *lakhs* (3 million rupees), Khân-i Jahân redoubled the Mughal drive into the Deccan; not unlike the Mewârî campaign, Jahângîr's cumbersome military machine found itself outpaced by the guerrilla tactics of Malik 'Ambar's Maratha troops. Once again, Jahângîr purged the upper military echelons and appointed 'Abd Allâh Khân, experienced and hardened by several months of campaigning in Mewâr, as the new Deccanî campaign commander. His plan to co-ordinate a pincher offensive from the north and the east failed miserably and, like his predecessors, 'Abd Allâh Khân found himself reappointed elsewhere.[60]

With his armies pinned down in a war of attrition with the Râjpûts and the Deccanî frontier consuming men and revenue at an alarming rate, Jahângîr spread his resources even thinner by planning an invasion in the east. The Afghânî landholders (*zamîndârs*) of Bengâl had been resisting Mughal centralization ever since their subjugation by Akbar in the 1570s, and in 1608, 'Usmân Khân threw off Tîmûrid suzerainty and proclaimed independence. It was not until 1612 that an expeditionary force, under the command of Shujâ'at Khân and the governor of Bengâl, Islâm Khân, was organized. Shujâ'at Khân met 'Usmân at the river of Nek Ujyal on 12 March 1612 and, to Jahângîr's delight, routed the enemy. This success, combined with the efficient suppression of the heretical Raushânîyya sect in the province of Kâbul and the militant tribal peoples of Ahom, ensured at least some level of stability in the north and east. By 1614 the Mughal emperor was confident enough to attempt another series of operations in Mewâr; moreover, Prince Khurram, now twenty-two years of age, was proving himself an apt and efficient military commander. The prince adopted a scorched earth strategy by burning crops, dismantling irrigation networks, and destroying granaries. Realizing the futility of assaulting the mountainous Râjpût fortresses, he established a series of forts and guard posts along every major thoroughfare to prevent the movement of foodstuffs and supplies. Faced with dwindling supplies and imminent starvation, the Râjpûts emerged from their retreats and faced the Mughal armies in their preferred mileu: the open plains. The prince used his overwhelming cavalry and artillery to exact a number of victories over the Râjpûts until Amar Singh capitulated and concluded a peace treaty within a few months.[61] Khurram's heeling of the Râjpût nobility was not insignificant. For the last four decades, Rânâs Partâb and Amar Singh had successfully resisted Tîmûrid sovereignty; fiercely supported by their nobility and the local population, these indigenous rulers were a constant threat, not to mention a distinct affront, to the Mughal household and its claim to northern India. Khurram's campaign was so devastatingly effective that it would be nearly fifty years before another independence movement appeared in Mewâr. Consistent with his father's policy of conciliating Râjpûts, Jahângîr gave Rânâ Amar Singh *zât* and *savâr* since his "lofty mind was always desirous, as possible, not to destroy the old families."[62]

The early 1610s, in addition to being a period of successful territorial expansion, were also characterized by an increase of Persian notables in the upper echelons of the Mughal administration. While this of course was a trend put in motion by Akbar, it was a policy his son continued wholeheartedly. Mîrzâ Ghiyâs al-Dîn Muhammad, whose father had been *vazîr* of Yazd, emigrated to India from Iran in 1577 and secured admittance into Akbar's court. Initially serving as the *vazîr-i-dîvân* for Kâbul, he was soon transferred to the royal court as *dîvân-i buyûtât*.[63] With Jahângîr's accession, he was appointed to the central *dîvân* and entitled *I'timâd al-daulat* ("pillar of the state"); when his daughter, Mihr al-Nisâ (later known as Nûr Jahân), was married to Jahângîr in 1611, I'timâd al-daulat was elevated to *vazîr*.[64] Nûr Jahân's extended family, descended from the great Persian houses of Sharîf Tihrânî and Âqâ Mullâh Davated, formed the "core of the Khurâsânî element" in the Mughal nobility after 1611.[65] Nûr Jahân's brother, Abû al-Hasan Âsaf Khân, enjoying the titles *Khân-i Sâmân* and *I'tiqâd Khân*, shared the post of *vakîl* with his father. Other Persian notables included Khvâjah Abû al-Hasan Turbatî, *mîr bakshî* from 1613 to 1620, Bâqir Khân Najm-i Sânî, governor of Multân, Ja'far Beg Âsaf Khân, *vazîr-i-dîvân-i kull* between 1605 and 1607, and Qâsim Khân Juvainî, the governor of Bengâl from 1613 to 1617.[66]

It was also during the early seventeenth century that Mughal India began to emerge as a central hub in the developing world economies of proto-capitalist powers like England and Holland. While Portugal had attempted to manipulate pre-existing trade patterns by diverting the flow of trade, specifically pepper, towards Europe, the North Atlantic trade companies shied away from such ambitions and simply entrenched themselves as one of the many indigenous trading groups operating in the Indian Ocean environment.[67] However, as Stephen Dale reminds us, it would be a mistake to believe that European maritime expansion overwhelmed the local economies; Indian merchants continued to traffic large amounts of trade stuffs into Iran, Central Asia, and Russia well into the eighteenth century.[68] Mughal India's relatively large population, combined with its extensive agricultural wealth, allowed for a prominent economic position in the Eurasian commercial theater. Principal exports to surrounding territories were calicoes, muslins, sugar, indigo, and tobacco; this, in turn, allowed for the importing of specialized commodities rare to India such as silk, horses, and precious metals.[69] The exchange of such goods was facilitated by the establishment and growth of a healthy 'diaspora' of Indian mercantile communities in Qandahâr, Balkh, Isfahân, Shîrâz, and Astrakhân. With the Portuguese *cartaze* system heavily regulating oceanic trade for much of the sixteenth century, Indian merchants reoriented their goods through Lahore to access the Bolan, Sanghar, and Gomal mountain passes into Iran and Central Asia. However, the arrival of the European joint-stock companies substantially altered trade dynamics in the Indian Ocean. After using their superior naval firepower to overwhelm the Portuguese at Swally Road in 1612 and 1615, the English made it clear that the days of Iberian hegemony in western India were coming to a close. With respect to indigenous trade, Indian merchants were now free to import and export goods via Sûrat; in fact, East India Company ship registers suggest a number of Indian traders used the cargo holds of European ships to ferry goods between Sûrat and Bandar `Abbâs.[70]

Once again, we have to be cautious in overestimating the role of players like the East India Company and the *Vereenigde Oost-Indische Compagnie*. When Sir Thomas Roe arrived in 1615, his employers only had fifteen years experience in the east. Likewise, the VOC had only received its monopoly from the Estates General in 1602. Initially, Dutch and English ships were directed towards the Indonesian archipelago and the Spice Islands, areas of the east where the Portuguese were thought to be the weakest. After eleven naval trade expeditions, English merchants realized the advantage of establishing a permanent Indian trading station and storehouse, or factory, and did so in 1613 at Sûrat.[71] When Roe arrived two years later, this was the only official EIC station in Mughal India while individual English merchants were operating in Ahmadâbâd, Âgrâ, and Ajmîr. Likewise, the Dutch were successful in establishing factories in Java and Sumatra and had secured trading concessions from the Qutbshâh of Golkundâ but they would not open their first factory in the Mughal empire (at Sûrat) until 1616. These moves, of course, were bitterly resisted by the *Estado da India,* but Portuguese difficulties with mismanagement, financial insolvency, and lack of local support had taken their toll. It appears that the Dutch and English soon realized that "the commercial realities of trade in the Indian Ocean were inseparable from its Indian framework."[72] Moreover, the ability of the North Atlantic joint-stock companies to gather information and "visualize" their prospective markets gave them a tangible advantage over their Iberian rivals.[73] This directive to EIC agents by their Board of Directors to file meticulous reports of their observations and findings has also provided historians with a body of helpful, albeit occasionally inaccurate, historical literature.[74] EIC prospects in India improved considerably in 1613 when *Estado da India* authorities boarded and seized a royal Mughal vessel. Muqarrab Khân, the governor of Sûrat at the time, was ordered to besiege the Portuguese-held port of Damân and the Jesuit church at Âgrâ was closed down. Jahângîr's frustration with the Portuguese now gave the EIC the opportunity to secure further access to the rich textile industry of the Mughal empire interior. Late in 1614, the Board of Directors petitioned King James I to appoint an official English ambassador to the Mughal court in the hope of negotiating further economic concessions and trade agreements.

The Arrival of Sir Thomas Roe

As this book later details, Thomas Roe was certainly a capable candidate. Already distinguished by a decade of service to the royal family as a gentleman-in-waiting and a short tenure as a Minister in Parliament, Roe was nominated and selected as England's first ambassador to the court of the Mughal emperor. Roe's status as gentry certainly contributed to his selection by the East India Company; previous expedition leaders and ship captains, like Nicholas Downton and Thomas Best, had reported to their superiors that the Mughal emperor was reticent to deal with "mean" merchants and insisted on a "comeley personage." With the appropriate entourage in tow, Roe set sail aboard the *Lion*, one of four ships in the expedition commanded by Captain William Keeling, on 2 February 1615. After an eight-month voyage around the Cape of Good Hope and through the Arabian and Indian Oceans, the fleet arrived off the coast of Sûrat. Problems seemed to have immediately beset the newly arrived ambassador. Roe refused to debark from the ship until he was accorded the proper respect from the resident governor of Sûrat who predictably had converse feelings on the matter. This diplomatic snag was compounded by the governor's insistence that all incoming baggage, including Roe's, was to be searched. For one week, messages were ferried back and forth between the *Lion* and the port authorities until the governor finally agreed to permit the unloading of English goods free of molestation. Diplomatic hassles continued to plague negotiations until the governor solemnly agreed to welcome the visiting dignitary and ratify existing trade agreements with the English.

Roe spent the next five weeks in Sûrat meeting with the authorities, attending to Company grievances, and dispatching letters to factors in Ahmadâbâd and Ajmîr. Roe, however, also encountered difficulties with resident English trading factors who resented his interference and defied his claim as chief Company official in India. The situation peaked when one of the chief factors, stationed in Ajmîr, Edwardes, allegedly declared himself the true English ambassador to the Mughal court, and Roe was forced to order his immediate arrest and confinement. With his appointment in apparent jeopardy and local negotiations proving futile, Roe redoubled his efforts to alert the king of his situation and attain permission to leave Sûrat. On 30 October, permission was finally granted and Roe's ambassadorial train began its slow journey to the royal court.

After two weeks of travel, Roe arrived at the city of Burhânpûr, at that time controlled by Jahângîr's son Parvaiz and Parvaiz's advisor, the *Khân-i Khânân*. True to his mandate, Roe secured a *farmân* from the prince allowing the establishment of an English factory in Burhânpûr. The ambassador's program of reaching Ajmîr as soon as possible was postponed by a vicious bout of fever. Weakened significantly and confined to a litter, Roe must have been seriously disappointed by his inability to effect a regal entry at the Mughal court two weeks later. After a month of recovery, Roe's health had improved sufficiently and he was able to make the requisite ceremonial presentation of James I's letter and gifts to the Mughal emperor on 10 January 1616. Roe immediately set to the task of negotiating a formal treaty between the EIC and the Mughal empire; his principal points of contact on this matter were Prince Khurram and Âsaf Khân. Roe met with these *amîrs* on several occasions, feeling increasingly frustrated with their unwillingness to commit to any of the Englishman's proposals. This reticence is not surprising given the scope of Roe's demands—unrestricted EIC access to Mughal ports, exemption from custom duties and port fees, local and judicial autonomy for English expatriates, and a restriction against all future Portuguese mercantile activity. On 12 March, Roe was able to temporarily bypass these intermediaries and organized a personal meeting with the emperor during the Naurûz celebrations. In addition to reintroducing the proposed comprehensive treaty, Roe also took this opportunity to discuss the governor of Sûrat's harassment, specifically financial extortion, of English agents. In a short time, *farmâns* were issued to Zû al-Faqâr Khân which allowed free passage for English goods through Sûrat and called for reparation to the English traders. With the treaty negotiations obviously going nowhere, Roe concentrated on ensuring a redress of these English financial grievances; Zû al-Faqâr Khân did eventually offer 17,000 *mahmûdis*, but Roe deemed it insufficient and rejected the offer.[75]

Roe had no way of knowing it but his best chance for establishing his proposed treaty came and went during these nine months in Ajmîr. In November 1616, the emperor decided to settle the Deccanî problem once and for all and, not surprisingly, appointed Khurram as the supreme military commander. Keen to have quick and reliable news of his son's military operations, Jahângîr ordered the royal court to break camp in Ajmîr and proceed for Mandû. For the next year, Roe's ambassadorial mission was overshadowed by the military campaign. Moreover, the novelty of the English embassy had obviously worn away. In October 1617, the royal camp shifted again to Ahmadâbâd and then back to Mandû five months later, further disrupting any chance for Roe to meet consistently with the emperor. In May 1618, Roe witnessed a devastating plague epidemic which claimed the lives of seven of his fellow Englishmen. By the winter of 1619, Roe had decided that his presence in the Mughal court was pointless and he terminated his appointment as ambassador to the Mughal empire and boarded the London-bound *Anne* on 17 February 1619.

While ultimately failing to procure the coveted bilateral trading agreement, the EIC could not have been entirely dissatisfied with his performance during his four and a half years in India. He did succeed in soliciting *farâmîn* for trading stations in Burhânpur, Ahmadâbâd, and other Mughal trading *entrepôts*; furthermore, the arrival of his embassy, replete with gifts for Jahângîr, contributed to the decline of Portuguese influence in the Mughal court. From the perspective of an historian, Roe's greatest achievement during this time was the writing of his two-volume journal, *The Embassy of Sir Thomas Roe*. Few travellers, before and after Roe, had the inclination or the commitment to meticulously record court compositions, current events, and ongoing trends in the Mughal political landscape. The combination of Roe's consistent presence in Jahângîr's court and his resolve to present a future reference work has shaped *The Embassy of Sir Thomas Roe* as one of the preeminent non-Persian, historical sources for early seventeenth-century Mughal India. What interests us here, however, is the manner in which Roe expressed his observations during these four years. *The Embassy*, comprising roughly 600 pages, is replete with descriptions, analyses, comparisons, and anecdotes and has been described as a "picture of the India of the early seventeenth century which is of exceptional value and interest" and, moreover, "[Roe's] position afforded him excellent opportunities for observation, while a natural gift for literary expression imparted a vividness to his descriptions which is often lacking in the writings of other travellers of the period."[77]

While such laudatory statements from the nineteenth century have since been qualified, it is difficult to contest the importance of Roe's station. He was an "undoubted Attorney, Procurator, Legate and Ambassador" royally commissioned to represent both the king of England and the Honourable English East India Company.[77] His familiarity with international protocol and court politics was augmented by a comprehensive Humanist education and training in the *belles artes*. Earlier accounts, offered by Company expedition leaders James Best and Henry Middleton, could not match Roe's literary skill and political acumen. However, acknowledging Roe as the best English, or possibly European, source of Jahângîr's reign does not necessarily entail blindly accepting *The Embassy* as gospel. Incorporating such a European account into Mughal historiography without appreciating the critical issue of perspective is dangerous; its accredited 'objectivity' needs to be reinterpreted. The hypothesis of this work is predicated on the need to understand more about the context in which Roe was writing his observations. While the immediate surrounding environment was a Mughal Indian one, Roe's tools and means of description were forged in early seventeenth-century England. His rendition of pre-modern India, of which elements continue to linger in current scholarship, can be better understood and reinterpreted by learning more about Roe and the early Jacobean English society that moulded his phenomenological outlook and perception.

Seventeenth-century English and European studies are well-trammeled areas historiographically. The English civil war (1642-49) coinciding with other major European revolutionary developments in France, Holland, and Spain has convinced certain historians that the early seventeenth-century Europe was in the grip of a political and economic crisis.[78] There can be little doubt that England, like the rest of Europe, was undergoing a massive demographic upsurge and, as a result, more and more people were emigrating to large towns and cities. As cities expanded, market demands were created both in industry and agriculture; traditional lines of social stratification became blurred as gentry shifted away from traditional agricultural practice and began hiring dispossessed agricultural communities to staff their seedling industries in textiles and mining. Mercantilism, already well established in the Italian city-states of Venice, Genoa, and Florence, expanded significantly in the late sixteenth century, especially in the metropolises of London, Antwerp, and Amsterdam. New trading organizations, or 'companies' were being created and given monopolies for exclusive trade with potential commercial areas like the Americas, the Mediterranean, Muscovy, and the Levant. Alongside these socioeconomic changes, the northern Renaissance was in full swing by the end of the sixteenth century. The scientific endeavours of men like Francis Bacon were now challenging the biblically-sponsored Aristotelian views of the world and universe. Literary giants such as Donne, Shakespeare, Jonson, and Milton, were modifying or renovating traditional, mediaeval literary styles. Social and religious frustration with trends in crypto-Catholic absolutism ushered in new debates regarding the issue of constitutional monarchy and the rights of the English peoples; this coincided with the popular fear that Jesuits and other Catholic fifth-columnists were roaming the English countryside plotting the destruction of Protestant England. Moreover, anxiety with corruption and favouritism in court politics resulted in vigorous petition and pamphleteer drives; satirical plays and essays protesting certain unpopular governmental practices abounded and it is in these dynamic, if not turbulent, times that we find Thomas Roe.

While being educated at Oxford, he shared friendships with blossoming literary figures such as John Donne and Ben Jonson. When he moved to London after matriculation, Roe continued these relationships and was esteemed a capable poet and author in his own right. Shortly afterwards, Roe turned to courtly ambitions and served as the Esquire of the Body to the Queen Elizabeth, a position introducing him to Renaissance court culture and its underlying system of sponsorship and patronage. After Elizabeth's death in 1603 and the succession of James I, Roe expanded his repertoire by attaining an appointment as an ambassadorial envoy to continental Europe. Having built a number of connections in his eight years in the court, Roe briefly associated himself in 1612 with a gentry-sponsored trading expedition to the New World. And finally in 1614, one year before his departure to India, Roe was nominated and elected as a member of parliament. This man's education and early career was certainly consistent with other early modern English contemporaries. Men like

Roe shifted freely between literary *tête à têtes* and national political committees; careers were equally heterogeneous with landed gentry dabbling in overseas commerce and mercantile elites occupying state offices. When Roe sailed from Tilbury Hope on 18 September 1615, he was only beginning a new stage in an already eclectic career. Instructed to "vse all the Meanes you can to advance the Trade of the East India Company," the King of England had entrusted Roe with an important commercial and political station.[79]

While James I was probably too preoccupied with continental foreign policy to consider political relations with the Mughal empire an important matter, the EIC certainly felt differently. The Board of Directors realized that the Mughal empire was a sovereign state and expected to be treated as such; without a formal ambassador and embassy, it was unlikely Jahângîr would be amenable to English overtures. Destined to act in the capacity of a leading trade official and England's first official diplomatic representative to India, Roe must have also felt a certain scholarly excitement. The sixteenth century had been, among many things, the 'age of exploration' in which European navigators and pilots were 'discovering' lands and cultures hitherto confined to the domain of fantasy and imagination. Explorers, adventurers, and Jesuits were recording their observations of these new encountered cultures in the New and Old World and, not surprisingly, found an eager and curious audience among the literate elite of Europe. Whether it was Anthony Jenkinson's *Voyage...made from the citie of Mosco in Russia, to the citie of Boghar in Bactria* (1568) or the Huguenot missionary Lefèvre's famous *Rélation d'une voyage à Brésil* (1555), Europeans were becoming increasingly interested in this exotic genre of 'encounter' literature. When Roe initially submitted his draft of *The Embassy of Sir Thomas Roe* to Samuel Purchas, that great compiler of sixteenth and early seventeenth-century travelogues, he was the first to offer systematic descriptions of the empire of the 'Great Mogor' and the literati of London must have eagerly awaited its publication.

Some Theoretical Considerations

A number of questions regarding the nature of historical sources, particularly the dynamic nature of history and historiography in the early modern era, need addressing here. Following the eighteenth-century fascination with reason and rationality, the interdependence of disciplines like philosophy, history, and rhetoric began to dissolve. By the nineteenth century, centers of learning had extensively categorized different areas of knowledge, with each subject comprising its own discipline. This trend of categorization was accompanied by the introduction and application of scientific principles to the humanities and social sciences. Men like Weber introduced the concept of mathematical statistics to the study of societies, while Hegel attempted to literally 'chart' the surrounding universe. Alongside these developments, the definition of history was assuming a distinctly scientific flavour. Termed 'positivism,' this trend of scholarship highlighted the polarization of fact and fiction; while history was deemed the recorded representation of factual reality, fiction was correspondingly considered the domain of literature. Continuing until the early twentieth century, history was understood strictly in terms of an objective science — subjectivity had no place in this approach to understanding the past. However, trends in historiography and philosophies of history and language, represented by Ranke, Collingwood, Levi-Strauss, Derrida, and Foucault, have since seriously scrutinized this demarcation between history and literature. Intent on exploring the modes of expressing reality, they have called attention to 'the extent to which the discourse of the historian and that of the imaginative writer overlap, resemble, or correspond with each other.'[80]

While nineteenth and twentieth-century historians claimed to be representing a factual presentation of the past, White and others have suggested that the writing of history can never be objective and will always share a close relationship with the discipline of literature. The telling of past events is usually conducted in a narrative tone, with major historical figures acting as characters and historical developments serving as quasi-plots. This emphasis on subjectivity in the role of historiography is especially important when considering the nature of seventeenth-century historical sources themselves. Can we accurately assert that early modern authors of historical sources shared their nineteenth-century counterparts' insistence that history was the province of objectivity while literature was only used to express the imagination and fantasy? Renaissance Humanism certainly made no such distinction with works like Francis Bacon's "Division of History and Learning" from *De augmentis scientiarum* discussing history as the midway point between philosophy and poetry, or reason and imagination.[81] Humanists collectively studied poetry, prose, history, philosophy, rhetoric, and languages with little sense of discernment. In Roe's case, we have an Englishman, well trained in Humanist thought, presenting a portrait of an utterly foreign cultural entity. To what extent can we trust Roe to ignore his Renaissance upbringing and report his experiences in an 'objective' capacity? Theoretically, was it even possible for Roe, limited by language and experience, to present anything Mughal as 'objective'? It is debatable whether Roe could recognize, or be interested in recognizing, the distinction between subjective and objective descriptions.

Nietzsche tells us that the real value of history lies "in inventing ingenious variations on a probably commonplace theme, in raising the popular melody to a universal symbol and showing what a world of depth, power and beauty exists in it."[82] Similarly, Collingwood postulated a "constructive imagination" whereby the historian fills any serious gaps of 'what happened' with his or her own deductions; as a result, histories written in the twentieth century can be incongruently modern in their application of terminology, concepts, and analyses to past societies.[83] But what about the historical source itself? Traditional historians suggested that narrative accounts are insights into a past reality and many students of history have looked, and will continue to look, upon a narrative as a factual portrayal of 'what really happened.'[84] There are underlying assumptions in this approach to source studies. First, there is a supposition that historical records are capable of providing a comprehensive and holistic understanding to the researcher. In doing so, historians offer a reconstruction of a past era, reign, or society by comparing and juxtaposing various sources. However, a number of problems present themselves at this point. Are the sources being used accurate? Are they biased? Are they properly translated? Most important, can the historian rely on sporadic written texts for a detailed knowledge of another 'reality'? The other latent assumption of the 'what really happened' approach is that the author of an historical source aspires towards objectivity in his or her own account. Historians of the nineteenth and twentieth centuries, conditioned by a prevalent sense of what is objective and what is not, have presupposed that early modern authors shared their belief that the "objective phenomena of observed nature are the ultimate constituents of reality."[85] Whether or not Thomas Roe was keen to subscribe to this objective approach while recording his experiences in India is highly debatable. But to better understand these theoretical considerations, it would be helpful to understand some possible motives for Roe to compile *The Embassy*.

William Foster, the nineteenth-century editor of *The Embassy*, tells us that "besides the fair copy made for his own use, Roe had others prepared from time to time to send to England."[86] In addition to these copies, Roe also dispatched letters to James I, Thomas Carew (1595-1635), and Thomas Smythe (1558-1625) of which portions are included in Foster's compilation. According to standard EIC procedure, Roe also presented a copy of his journal to the Company Board of Directors as a future reference source. However, the scope of Roe's readership widened significantly in 1622 when the geographer and editor of *Hakluytus Posthumus: or Purchas His Pilgrimes*, Samuel Purchas (1575-1626), requested permission from the EIC to use Roe's journal.[87] There are two important points worth considering here. First, we need to remember Roe's educational background and personal relationship with the influential figures of the English literary Renaissance. His self-fashioning as poet, historian, and philosopher, suggests that Roe might have been eager to see his account widely distributed. Having copies made in India and dispatched to his friends, as well as donating copies to the EIC, points towards such ambitions. The second point, dealing with what exactly Roe hoped to accomplish by writing and distributing this travel account, is more complicated. Anyone reading *The Embassy* will be struck by its dichotomous nature. On one hand, we have long passages describing his impressions of the king, ongoing political events, and the relationships within the court. On the other hand, we find lengthy sections discussing economic affairs: shipping of English goods, collecting on negligent accounts, or the current status of other zones of commercial activity, such as the exporting of silk from Iran. Realizing that his benefactors, the EIC, expected a detailed account of the economic state of affairs in India, yet still motivated to present a monumental reference source for historians, it seems possible that Roe wrote his journal to appease both the Company's expectations and his own personal Humanist ambitions. Moreover, it is the speculation here that Thomas Roe sought to write and publish a historical source worthy of future scholarly interest. In this age of exploration and travel, writing a travelogue and intending it to be distributed as a region or nation's history was not uncommon; in the early seventeenth century, the line between such 'travel literature' and proper history was easily crossed.[89]

If one examines the court minutes of the East India Company on 27 February 1622, an interesting note is found,

> ...one Purchas that wrote of the Religions of all Nacions hath now vndertaken a greate volume of all there voyages and did desire to haue a sight of some of the Companies Iournalls that might give him lighte for the setting downe the Companies voyages into the east Indies, *wherein he desires to see but the Historicall part and will medle with nothinge elce; Particularly he desires to see Sir Thomas Roes Iournall.* (italics mine)[89]

The implications of this request are not insignificant. Purchas, just beginning his compilation and generally interested in all EIC travelling accounts, took pains to specifically cite the text he was most interested in: *The Embassy of Sir Thomas Roe*. Interestingly, this petition comes only four years after Roe's return from the Indian subcontinent. How exactly Purchas learned of the "historicall" significance of *The Embassy* so quickly is difficult to establish but it seems that, in addition to consulting the Company's copy, Purchas also had a chance to meet with Roe and examine the ambassador's original journal.[90] This suggestion of a possible friendship or an awareness of one another is not implausible. Samuel Purchas, prior to initiating his massive compilation of travel literature, had served as chaplain to George Abbot, the Archbishop of Canterbury during much of the reign of James I. In addition to being his courtly benefactor, Abbot was a close and dear friend to Roe and many of the letters we find in *The Embassy* are addressed to him. As the title of his collection suggests, Purchas was continuing the efforts of his predecessor, Richard Hakluyt, who had spent much of his life dedicated to chronicling the age of exploration. Interestingly, Hakluyt was also a member of the South Virginan Company and part of a group of merchants organizing and funding expeditions to the Virginias. Given that Roe was a member of the Royal Council for Virginia during this period, as well as a shareholder in the chartered Company of Adventurers and Planters of the City of London for the First Colony in Virginia, it is probable that Hakluyt and Roe knew each other between 1606 and 1608. Roe's undoubted familiarity with Hakluyt's *Principall Navigations* and his later acquaintance with Purchas suggests that he might have planned a political and historical narrative of the Mughal empire well before his departure. Moreover, there is also evidence pointing towards such "historicall" ambitions while he was compiling the journal itself between 1615 and 1619. In a letter written to Lord Carew on 17 January 1616, Roe advised his friend, "if you be also weary of reading, I am glad. I shall desire your Lordship to let Master Hackwell reade the Iournall; for I promised him one, but I had not leasure to write it."[91] William Hackwill (1574-1655) was not an EIC agent or Board member but an "olld acquayntance" and one of London's most notable antiquarians and legal historians.[92] In addition to actively publishing tracts on political and legal issues, two of Hackwill's most well known works were *The Antiquity of Laws of This Island* and *Of the Antuiquity of the Christian Religion in This Island*.[93] In his reply to Roe, Carew writes "Lett me entreat you, to be carefull to make the mappe of the Mogolls territorie, as you haue intended; itt will be a worke worthiye of your selfe, and adorne your trauell and iudgement, and leaue to the world a lasting memoirie when you are dust."[94]

Roe could certainly appreciate the novelty of the Indian subcontinent for Englishmen. Cargoes of exotic Indian textiles, Persian silks, and Indonesian spices were being unloaded at the docks of London; sailors and merchantmen were relating what would have been wondrous, almost fantastic, sights and images. However, with the exception of a few captains' logs and a small number of EIC financial reports, there was very little published information about the 'East Indies.' If we consider his Humanist training and education, it seems unlikely Roe intended for his account to consist of a series of parochial economic reports. Rather, he aspired to present a description of Mughal India which would be eagerly received by the scholars and the general elite of metropolitan London. As he wrote in a letter to Lord Pembroke, he wanted to reduce his observations "into a meethood, and though this kingdome almost concerne not Europe, yet the Historye may, as well as some of those that are farther remooued by tymes past, and for subiect perhaps as woorthy."[95] Such Humanist leanings are seen later during the 1620s when, acting as English ambassador to the Ottoman empire, Roe obtained an extremely rare copy of the *Codex Alexandrinus* from the Greek Patriarch in Istanbul and later presented it to James I. The conclusion here is three-fold: a) Roe meant for his journal to supersede economic significance and be valued as an historical account; b) his Humanist background motivated him to make *The Embassy* available to the public; and c) he possibly did so by informing his colleague Samuel Purchas of its potential contribution who could then have it published and distributed.

The ramifications of this conclusion are interwoven with the earlier hypothesis of whether or not Roe intended an 'objective' or 'realistic' presentation of India. It was conjectured how Renaissance thought did not rigidly delineate history and literature. This is partially illustrated by later discussions of how Jacobean productions of Roman tragedy and comedy served as blueprints for proper government and kingship. Furthermore, English poets integrated history and poetry since, as Woolf observes, "the poetic and dramatic forms offered the writer ready-made subjects without binding him to relate the literal truth in the manner of the chronicler."[96] This use of popular myths and images is important here because Thomas Roe was acting as an intermediary between a strange and mysterious Mughal reality and the contemporary readership of England. This relationship between the Mughal Empire, Thomas Roe, and the Jacobean public has two significant features. First, we know that the Humanist tradition did not acknowledge a discrepancy between literary and historical styles of expression. Consequently, many of Roe's "factual representations" employ literary devices and methods of that period. Second, and more important, it is possible that Roe looked to conventional myths, plots, and paradigms to "familiarize" the Mughal Empire for seventeenth-century Englishmen. The original mystery or bizarreness is hence diluted and foreign cultural features can take on a familiar aspect, not so much in the details but in their "functions as elements of a familiar kind of configuration."[97]

It is the speculation here that Thomas Roe catered to 'subjective' observations and depictions in a sincere attempt to 'realize' this alien political and cultural entity. By endowing unfamiliar institutions and events with recognizable qualities, Roe could transcend the difficulty of transposing another 'reality' in a written text. But this leads us to ponder the role of language in such a written transmission. Predictably, his narrative could not have described Indo-Islamic characteristics with precise Mughal terminology or definitions. Incapable of using the proper Persian nomenclature as well as lacking a detailed knowledge of Mughal/Islamic institutions, Roe was forced to turn to European, specifically English, terminology to convey his impressions. As philosophers like to remind us, such terminology is rarely value free and is almost always wrought with cognitive baggage. Figurative language, or tropes, such as this can consist of metaphors, metonymies, and synecdoches and are rich with cultural biases and preconceptions. Moreover, Roe also used particular images which would have been instantly recognizable to the English reader. Specifically termed as an "extended metaphor," the use of a familiar image in historical narratives "does not give us either a description or an icon of the thing it represents, but tells us what images to look for in our culturally coded experience in order to determine how we should feel about the thing."[98] Consequently, Roe's use of Jacobean terminology and extended metaphors is capable of establishing an "Anglified" perception of the Mughal Empire. The Mughal system of kingship, government, court practices, and other salient features henceforth loses its original identity. This book is dedicated to understanding how Roe related his experiences and why he used certain well known Jacobean images in doing so. To appreciate the depth of this "Anglified" portrayal, however, we have to know more about early seventeenth-century England itself. Specifically, we have to investigate those features of Jacobean society which Roe was most familiar with and which would have most likely influenced his perception of a foreign political and cultural entity: literature, court culture, diplomacy, and politics.

NOTES

1. The first "slave dynasty" was established by Qutb al-Dîn Aibak in 1206 and continued through his successors, Iltutmish (1210-35), Nasîr al-Dîn Mahmûd (1246-66), and Balban (1266-90).
2. Typical taxes included the *khirâj* (land tax on conquered territories), the *zakât* (religious tithe), the *jizya* (non-Muslim, or *zimmî* tax), and the *khamsa* (1/5th of war booty). Over-taxation was conspicuous during the reign of 'Alâ al-Dîn Khaljî. As the historian Barânî tells us, these measures "operated to the ruin of the country and the decay of the people." It should be noted that Barânî is slightly biased in his interpretation of 'Alâ al-Dîn Khaljî's tax reforms; his native district, Barân, suffered heavily due to over taxation by the sultân's functionaries. Ziyâ al-Dîn Barânî, *Târîkh-i Fîrûz Shâhî*, in *The History of India, As Told By Its Own Historians*, Vol. III, eds. H. M. Elliot and J. Dowson (London: 1875), p. 468.

3. Malwâ was ruled by a Khaljî dynasty, highlighted by the reign of Mahmûd Khaljî (1436-69), until it was annexed by the ruler of Gujarât in 1531. Gujarât's period of independence was best characterized by the reigns of Ahmad Shâh (1411-41) and Mahmûd Bigada (1459-1511). This state was subsumed by Akbar in 1572. Probably the most famous of these territories was the thoroughly orthodox Bahmanid Kingdom of the Deccan which, under the leadership of men like Ahmad Shâh (1422-35) and Humâyûn (1457-61), subjugated much of the Hindu kingdom of Vijayanagar. After the collapse of the Bahmanids, the Deccan was divided into five, mostly *shî'î*, independent territories: Birar, Bîjâpûr, Ahmadnagar, Golkundâ, and Bidâr.
4. Shortly after Ibrâhîm's accession, various Afghân nobles orchestrated a revolt and supported a claim to the throne by his brother, Jalâl. While this coup was quickly dispersed, it was soon followed by another rebellion, led by the former governor of Qarâ Mânikpûr, Islâm Khân. Soon afterwards, Ibrâhîm ordered the arrest and execution of any dissenting elements among the Afghân nobility; fearing for their lives, notables like Dariyâ Khân, Khân Jahân Lodî, and Husain Khân Farmûlî joined ranks and openly rebelled against their overlord.
5. Control over Samarqand was bitterly contested between 1501 and 1503, culminating with the Battle of Archian in June 1503, when Shîbânî Muhammad Khân delivered a rather overwhelming defeat to the young Bâbur.
6. Initially, Bâbur was allied with the aging Sultân Husain Baiqarâ of Herât; however, Shîbânî Muhammad Khân's conquest of this city in 1506 effectively nullifed this arrangement. Thereafter, Bâbur worked in conjunction with the Arghûn brothers, Shâh Beg and Muhammad Muqîm, in recovering Qandahâr in 150. their duplicity, however, soured this relationship and Bâbur soon found himself a temporary ally in Abû Sa'îd Qazâq.
7. The *khutbah*, the proclamation of the ruler's name during Friday prayer (*jum'ah*), had long since been considered a symbolic demonstration of a ruler's sovereignty in a particular area. Moreover, the *shî'î khutbah* called for a condemnation of the first three *khalîfah* (Abû Bakr, 'Umar, 'Usmân), a statement obviously offensive to *sunnî* sensibilities.
8. Initially, Bâbur arranged an alliance with Daulat Khân which, in turn, had allowed for the *pâdshâh* to conquer Jâlandhar and Sultânpûr. Although these *jâgîrs* were initially allocated to Daulat Khân, his suspect behavior forced Bâbur to transfer control of these cities from the Afghân noble to his son, 'Âlam Khân. 'Âlam Khân proved no more trustworthy than his father and, after a brief return

to Kâbul, Bâbur realized his proposed conquest of Delhî would have to be done alone.
9. Zâhir al-Dîn Muhammad Bâbur, *Bâbur nâma*, Vol. II, trans. A.S. Beveridge (New Delhi: 1970 (reprint)), p. 174, Abû al-Fazl 'Allâmî, *Akbar nâma*, Vol. I, trans. H. Beveridge (New Delhi: 1993 (reprint)), pp. 243-47.
10. When Tîmûr died in February 1405, every mature member of his family retained some form of landholding or important administrative position. Although his grandson, Pîr Muhammad ibn Jahângîr, was appointed as successor, Chingîzîd succession law allowed Khalîl Sultân ibn Mîrân Shâh, another grandson, as well as Shâh Rukh, Tîmûr's son, to make bids for the throne. It would be four years of bloody conflict before the succession issue was settled.
11. While Badakhshân was administered by Mîrzâ Sulaimân, Kâmrân governed Kâbul and Qandahâr; the other two brothers, 'Askarî and Hindâl, were given *jâgîrs* in India. 'Allâmî, *Akbar nâma*, Vol. I, p. 287.
12. His original name was Farîz but while serving the governor of Bihâr, Bihâr Khân, he slew a tiger on a hunting expedition and was henceforth known as Sher Khân. After his displacement of Humâyûn, he was proclaimed Sher Shâh.
13. One of Sher Shâh's most impressive measures was to order an accurate survey of all agrarian land in northern India; by estimating the exact size and yield of these lands, the government could expect a consistent rate of tax collection.
14. Matters were not helped by the fact that Sûr territories were further divided when each of Islâm Shâh Sûr's sons were allotted a part of the empire.
15. 'Allâmî, *Akbar nâma*, Vol. II, pp. 58-69.
16. Bairâm Khân's proclivity for shî'ism, evident in his appointment of a fellow *shî'î* theologian as *sadr*, deeply offended the established *sunnî* orthodoxy who correspondingly rallied around the *khân-i khânân's* enemies.
17. These revolts were led by 'Alî Qulî Khân, Bahâdur Khân, Ibrâhîm Khân, and Iskandar Khân. 'Allâmî, *Akbar nâma*, Vol. II, pp. 376.
18. Muhammad Sultân Mîrzâ's father had originally been a fief holder in Tîmûrid Khurâsân. After his death, his son entered the service of Bâbur and his family would continue to be loyal servants of the Mughal royal house under Humâyûn. The sons of Muhammad Sultân Mîrzâ, however, "raised the standard of rebellion" from their fiefs in Sambal in 1567. `Allâmî, *Akbar nâma*, Vol. II, pp. 413-14.
19. Kunwar Refaqat Ali Khan, *The Kachwahas Under Akbar and Jahangir* (New Delhi: 1976), p. 45.

20. Bengâl was in a state of uprising for much of the 1580s due to the harsh governing policies of Muzaffar Khân Turbatî. The Qâqshâls, a settled Chaghtâ'î tribe, captured the city of Gaur and assassinated the Bengâlî governor while the *jâgîrdâr* of Jaunpûr, Mansûr Farankhûdî, also rejected Mughal overlordship. Through the military pressure and conciliation of Akbar's nobles Shâh Bâz Khân and 'Azîz Koka this movement was eventually subdued.
21. It was discovered that Muhammad Hakîm, Akbar's step-brother, had been in contact with the Uzbekî insurgents and encouraged to invade Hindûstân, which he did in the early 1580s. Defeated at Kâbul by Akbar's son, Prince Salîm (the future Jahângîr), and forced to flee to Uzbekî territory, Muhammad Hakîm never attempted another claim to the Mughal throne.
22. Akbar had personally led a campaign into Gujarât in the early 1570s and, after brief battles at Ahmadâbâd and Sûrat, the territory was formally annexed. Akbar, unable to summarily execute Muzaffar Shâh II, reduced the former ruler to a peasant's subsistence. He escaped in 1578 and five years later returned to Ahmadâbâd with a sizable force. A quick string of successes left Muzaffar Shâh with possession of Ahmadâbâd, Khambat, and Baroda. This however, only lasted until the arrival of Akbar's newly appointed governor, Mîrzâ 'Abd al-Rahmân, at the head of a large army.
23. Kashmîr and the immediate area to the north had long since been an area of instability for the Mughals. In 1585, Akbar entrusted the capable Râjah Mân Singh with the task of subduing any centrifugal elements. After the elimination of the Raushânîyya, a heterodox group of religious subversives, Râjah Mân Singh's generals, Zain Khân and Râjah Bîr Bar went on to subjugate the Yûsufzai tribe. This was soon followed by an organized expedition against the rebellious tributary ruler of Kashmîr, Muhammad Yûsuf Khân.
24. Proving his tactical skills in Gujarât, Mîrzâ 'Abd al-Rahmân was transferred to Multân in 1590 and ordered to reduce the independent territories of Sindh and Balûchistân. After the governor's conquest of Thatta, Akbar once again thought assimilation was the best policy and ordered that the former ruler, Mîrzâ Jânî Beg, be allowed to continue as the local *jâgîrdâr*.
25. Qandahâr, at this point, had been a Safavid possession. However, due to internal difficulties with the Qizilbâsh and foreign aggression from the Uzbeks, Shâh 'Abbâs was unable to prevent Akbar's siege and ultimate conquest of Qandahâr in 1595.
26. In addition to spice, other commodities included gold, silver, silk, textiles, cinnamon, porcelain, indigo, and slaves. There are a number of detailed studies of Portuguese trade in the Indian Ocean, including A. R. Disney's *Twilight of the Pepper Trade* (Cambridge,

Mass.: 1978), Bailey W. Diffie and George D. Winius, *Foundations of the Portuguese Empire, 1415-1580* (Minneapolis: 1977) and C.R. Boxer's *The Portuguese Seaborne Empire, 1414-1825* (London: 1969) and "The Portuguese in the East (1500-1800)" in *Portugal and Brazil: An Introduction*, ed. H.V. Livermore (Oxford: 1953).
27. 'Allâmî, *Akbar nâma*, Vol. III, p. 37.
28. One of the principal Jesuit accounts of the Mughal empire is Monserrate's *Mongolicae Lagationis Commentarius* which is available in translation as *Commentary of Father Monserrate, S.J. on his journey to the Court of Akbar*, trans. J.S. Hoyland (London: 1922).
29. Bâbur, *Bâbur nâma*, Vol. II, pp. 241-43. For a good analysis of Bâbur's memoirs, see Stephen Dale "Steppe Humanism: The Autobiographical Writings of Zahir al-Din Muhammad Babur, 1483-1530," in *International Journal of Middle East Studies*, Vol. 22 (1990), pp. 37-58.
30. This macro, comparative approach, especially regarding the three empires of the Mughals, the Safavids, and the Ottomans, was first systemized in Marshall Hodgson's paradigmatic work, *The Venture of Islam*, 3 Vols. (Chicago: 1974).
31. In 1555, there were roughly fifty-five nobles; by 1580, there were 222. See Iqtidar Alam Khan, "The Nobility Under Akbar and the Development of His Religious Policy, 1560-1580," in *Journal of the Royal Asiatic Society* (1968), pp. 29-36.
32. 'Allâmî, "*Â'în-i Akbarî*, Vol. I, trans. H. Blochmann (New Delhi: 1994 (reprint)), pp. 327-86. See also 'Alllâmî, *Akbar nâma*, Vol. III, p. 129, p. 686, p. 847.
33. 'Allâmî, "*Â'în-i Akbarî*, Vol. I, pp. 425-32.
34. Norman P. Ziegler, "Some Notes on Rajput Loyalties During the Mughal Period," in *Kingship and Authority in South Asia*, ed. J.F. Richards (Madison: 1978), pp. 231-35 and John F. Richards, *The New Cambridge History of India*, Vol. I•5: *The Mughal Empire* (Cambridge: 1993), pp. 22-23.
35. 'Allâmî, *'Â'în-i Akbarî*, Vol. I, pp. 353-54, pp. 361-63.
36. 'Allâmî, *'Â'în-i Akbarî*, Vol. I, pp. 376-78.
37. The most famous example is the career of Allâhvardî Khân, a Georgian convert who was appointed commander-in-chief and governor of the lucrative Fârs region in 1598; this proved to be a hereditary arrangement as his son, Imâm Qulî Khân, was allowed to retain this land holding.
38. The Jannisary corps, comprised entirely of former European slaves, was the most valued military institution of Istanbul.
39. For the Persian context, see A.K.S. Lambton's work, "Justice in the Medieval Persian Theory of Kingship," in *Studia Islamica*, Vol. 17 (1962), pp. 91-119, *Theory and Practice in Medieval Persian*

Government (London: 1980), and "Quis costodiet custodes? Some Reflections on the Persian Theory of Government," in *Studia Islamica*, Vol. 5 (1955), pp. 125-48; Vol. 6 (1956), pp. 125-46. Peter Hardy does an excellent job of contextualizing the Perso-Islamic model of kingship in India with "Unity and Variety in Indo-Islamic and Perso-Islamic Civilization: Some Ethical and Political Ideas of Ziyâ' al-Dîn Baranî of Delhi, of al-Ghazâlî, and of Nasîr al-Dîn Tusî Compared," in *Iran*, Vol. 16 (1978), pp. 127-35. Another good article is K.A. Nizami's "Aspects of Muslim Political Thought in India During the Fourteenth Century," in *Islamic Culture*, Vol. 52 (1978), pp. 213-40.

40. In the case of the Safavids, the composition of the government was initially dominated by Qizilbâsh *amîrs*. However, within ten years of Isma'îl's accession, these Türkmen found themselves displaced from certain positions of power. See Roger Savory, "The Principal Offices of the Safawid State During the Reign of Isma'îl I (907-30/1501-24)," in *B.S.O.A.S.*, Vol. 23 (1960), pp. 91-105. Frustrated to the point of rebellion, much of the reign of Isma'îl's successor, Tahmâsp, was spent trying to keep the Qizilbâsh in check. See Martin Dickson, *Shah Tahmâsp and the Uzbeks (The Duel for Khurasan with 'Ubayd Khan: 930-946/1524-1540)*. Unpubl. Diss.phil. (Princeton: 1968).

41. M. Athar Ali, "Akbar and Islam (1581-1605)," in *Islamic Society and Culture: Essays in Honour of Professor Aziz Ahmad*, eds. M. Israel and N.K. Wagle (Delhi: 1983), p. 127.

42. 'Allâmî, *Akbar nâma*, Vol. III, p. 364.

43. It was not until the reign of Shâh Sultân Husain (1694-1722) that the *shî'î 'ulamâ* were able to reappropriate the responsibility of *ijtihâd* from the *Shâh*. In the opinion of the great Iranologist, V. Minorsky, this is one of the reasons accounting for the 'decline' of the Safavid state.

44. 'Allâmî, *Akbar nâma*, Vol. III, p. 831.

45. Muhammad Hâshim Khâfî Khân, *Muntakhab al-lubâb*, ed. W. Haig, Vol. I (Calcutta: 1909-25), pp. 220-21.

46. Salîm responded positively to the overtures of Bir Singh Deo, the head of a rebellious clan of Mewarî Râjpûts, in organizing the waylaying and assault on Abû al-Fazl's expedition marching north from the Deccan. This event is detailed in several Mughal chronicles including Khvâjah Kâmgâr Khân, *Ma'âsir-i Jahângîrî*, in *History of India As Told By Its Own Historians*, Vol. VI, eds. H.M. Elliot and J. Dowson (London: 1875), pp. 442-44, Nûr al-Dîn Muhammad Jahângîr, *Tûzuk-i Jahângîrî*, Vol. I, trans. A. Rogers, ed. H. Beveridge (Delhi: 1968 (reprint)) p. 32, and Sujan Rai Khatrî,

Khulâsat al-tavârîkh, ed. Muhammad Zafar Husain (Delhi: 1918), pp. 433-34.
47. In addition to being Prince Salîm's son, Khusrau was also 'Azîz Koka's son-in-law and Râjah Mân Singh's nephew.
48. Khâfî Khân, *Muntakhab al-lubâb*, Vol. I, pp. 233-34.
49. Jahângîr, *Tûzuk-i Jahângîrî*, Vol. I, p. 16.
50. Jahângîr's fondness for nature heavily influenced miniature painting. It is during this period that the 'naturalist' trend reached its peak. Milo C. Beach, *The Grand Mogul: Imperial Painting in India 1600-1660* (Williamstown: 1978), p. 25. For a good insight into these features of Jahângîr's lifestyle see M.A. Alvi, *Jahangir - The Naturalist* (New Delhi: 1968).
51. Muhammad Bâqir Najm-i Sânî, *Advice on the Art of Governance: An Indo-Islamic Mirror For Princes: Mau'izah-i Jahângîrî*, trans. and ed. S.S. Alvi (Albany: 1989).
52. Khusrau actually managed to escape the rout but was soon captured by Mughal sentries while trying to get to Kâbul. Jahângîr, *Tûzuk-i Jahângîrî*, Vol. I, pp. 64-7.
53. See Niels Steensgaard, *The Asian Trade Revolution of the Seventeenth Century: The East India Companies and the Decline of Caravan Trade* (New York: 1974), p. 27.
54. Jahângîr, *Tûzuk-i Jahângîrî*, Vol. I, pp. 70-1, pp. 85-6, Mu'tamad Khân, *Iqbâl nâmâh-i Jahângîrî*, in *The History of India As Told By Its Own Historians*, eds. H.M. Eliot and J. Dowson, Vol. VI (London: 1875), p. 17-18, Khâfî Khân, *Muntakhab al-lubâb*, Vol. I, p. 255.
55. Jahângîr, *Tûzuk-i Jahângîrî*, Vol. I, p. 86.
56. Jahângîr, *Tûzuk-i Jahângîrî*, Vol. I, p. 111, pp. 122-23, Mu'tamad Khân, *Iqbâl nâmâh-i Jahângîrî*, pp. 27-30.
57. Jahângîr, *Tûzuk-i Jahângîrî*, Vol. I, p. 155.
58. Jahângîr, *Tûzuk-i Jahângîrî*, Vol. I, p. 161.
59. Jahângîr, *Tûzuk-i Jahângîrî*, Vol. I, pp. 178-80. Khâfî Khân, *Muntakhab al-tavârîkh*, Vol. I, p. 262.
60. Jahângîr, *Tûzuk-i Jahângîrî*, Vol. I, p. 221, Mîrzâ Ibrâhîm Zubairî, *Basâtîn al-salâtîn* (Bombay: 1968), pp. 271-72.
61. Jahângîr, *Tûzuk-i Jahângîrî*, Vol. I, pp. 273-76, Mu'tamad Khân, *Iqbâl nâmâh-i Jahângîrî*, pp. 76-77, Khâfî Khân, *Muntakhab al-lubâb*, Vol. I, p. 279.
62. Jahângîr, *Tûzuk-i Jahângîrî*, Vol. I, p. 274.
63. 'Allâmî, *Â'în-i Akbarî*, Vol. I, pp. 572-73.
64. Jahângîr, *Tûzuk-i Jahângîrî*, Vol. I, p. 22.
65. Irfan Habib, "The Family of Nur Jahan During Jahangir's Reign - A Political Study," in *Medieval India - A Miscellany*, ed. K.N. Nizami, Vol. 1 (Delhi: 1969), p. 80.

66. Habib, "The Family of Nur Jahan," pp. 90-94.
67. Steensgaard, *The Asian Trade Revolution*, p. 141.
68. Stephen F. Dale, *Indian Merchants and Eurasian Trade, 1600-1750* (Cambridge: 1994), p. x.
69. Dale, *Indian Merchants and Eurasian Trade*, pp. 21-26.
70. Steensgaard, *The Asian Trade Revolution*, pp. 400-1.
71. William Hawkins arrived in India on 24 August 1608. He was able to negotiate with the Mughals on a limited scale but left three years later. Henry Middleton's mission came in 1611 which was soon followed by Thomas Best's squadron of ships in September of 1612. In 1614, Nicholas Downton arrived off the coast of Sûrat and defeated the Portuguese in a small scale naval battle. See Holden Furber, *Rival Empires of Trade in the Orient, 1600-1800* (Minneapolis: 1976), pp. 39-41.
72. K.N. Chaudhuri, "Foreign Trade: 1. European Trade with India," in *The Cambridge Economic History of India*, Vol. 1, eds. T. Raychaudhuri and I. Habib (Cambridge: 1982), p. 386.
73. Steensgaard, *The Asian Trade Revolution*, p. 114.
74. Early EIC reports include William Hawkins, *Captain William Hawkins his relations of the occurents which happened in the time of his residence in India, in the countrie of the Great Mogoll, and of his departure from thence; written to the Companie* in *Hakluytus Posthumus or Purchas his Pilgrimes*, ed. MacLehose, Vol. 3 (London: 1905), pp. 1-50, Henry Middleton, *Account of the Sixth Voyage set forth by the East India Company in three ships* in *Hakluytus Posthumus or Purchas his Pilgrimes*, Vol. 3, pp. 115-94, William Finch, *Observations of William Finch, merchant, taken out of his large Journall* in *Hakluytus Posthumus or Purchas his Pilgrimes*, Vol. 4, pp. 19-77, Nicholas Withington, *Extracts of a tractate, written by Nicholas Withington* in *Hakluytus Posthumus or Purchas his Pilgrimes*, Vol. 4, pp. 162-74, Richard Steele and John Crowther, *A Journal of the Journey of Richard Steel and John Crowther* in *Hakluytus Posthumus or Purchas his Pilgrimes*, Vol. 4, pp. 266-79, Nicholas Downton, *Nicholas Dounton, Captain of the Peppercorne, a ship of two hundred and fifty tunes and Lieutenant in the sixth voyage to the East Indies set forth by the said Companie, his journall or certain extracts thereof* in *Hakluytus Posthumus or Purchas his Pilgrimes*, Vol. 3, pp. 194-304, and Thomas Best, *Journal of the Tenth Voyage of the East India* in *Hakluytus Posthumus or Purchas his Pilgrimes*, Vol. 6, pp. 119-47. Letters dispatched by EIC agents and factors can be found in F.C. Danvers and William Foster's edited work, *Letters Received by the East India Company From its Servants in the East* (London: 1902).

75. Actually, Roe had miscalculated the relative value of the English pound versus the Mughal currency and it was only after did Roe realize that this original offer was a fair one.
76. William Foster, "Introduction," in *The Embassy of Sir Thomas Roe to the Court of the Great Mogul 1615-1619 As Narrated in His Journal and Correspondence*, Vol. I, ed. W. Foster (London: 1899), p. 2. It should be noted that this edition includes many documents, like Roe's royal commission, which the later Jalandhar (1993) edition does not. The remainder of references for *The Embassy* in chapters 2 through 5 correspond with the pagination of the Jalandhar edition.
77. See "Royal Commission to Sir Thomas Roe," in *The Embassy of Sir Thomas Roe*, Vol. II, pp. 549-50.
78. This suggestion was first put forward by Roger Merriman in 1936 with *Six Contemporary Revolutions* (Oxford: 1938). Since then, the issue of 'the seventeenth century crisis' has been intensely debated from a number of political, social and economic angles. See H.R. Trevor-Roper, "General Crisis of the Seventeenth Century," in *Crisis in Europe, 1560-1660, Essays from Past and Present*, ed. T.H. Aston (London: 1965), E.J. Hobsbawm, "The Crisis of the Seventeenth Century," in *Past and Present*, Vol. 5 and 6, and N. Steensgaard's excellent article in G. Parker and L. Smith's edited collection of essays: *The General Crisis of the Seventeenth Century* (London: 1978).
79. *Instruccions for Sir Thomas Rowe, knight, autorised by vs vnder our Great Seale of England to repaire as our Ambassadour to the Great Magoar* in *The Embassy of Sir Thomas Roe to the Court of the Great Mogul, 1615-1619, As Narrated In His Journal and Correspondence*, ed. W. Foster, Vol. II (London: 1899), p. 552.
80. Hayden White, "The Fictions of Factual Representation," in *Tropics of Discourse: Essays in Cultural Criticism*, ed. H. White (Baltimore: 1978), p. 121.
81. D.R. Woolf, *The Idea of History in Early Stuart England* (Toronto: 1990), p. 151.
82. Friedrich Nietzsche, *The Use and Abuse of History*, trans. Adrian Collins (Indianapolis: 1957), p. 37.
83. R.G. Collingwood, *The Idea of History* (Oxford: 1946), p. 239.
84. Hayden White, "Interpretation in History," in *Tropics of Discourse: Essays in Cultural Criticism*, ed. H. White (Baltimore: 1978), p. 51.
85. S.K. Heninger, "Framing the Narrative," in *Perspective as a Problem in the Art, History, and Literature of Early Modern England*, eds. M. Lussier and S.K. Heninger (Lewiston: 1992), p. 4.
86. William Foster, "Introduction," in *The Embassy of Sir Thomas Roe*, p. lxxi.
87. Foster, "Introduction", p. lxii.

88. Denys Hay, *Annalists and Historians: Western Historiography from the VIIIth to XVIII Century* (London: 1977), p. 134.
89. February 22, 1622. Excerpt from *A Calendar of the Court Minutes of the East India Company*, ed. E.B. Sainsbury, Vol. I (London: 1907).
90. Foster, "Introduction", p. lix
91. Roe, *The Embassy of Sir Thomas Roe*, Vol. I, p. 114.
92. George Lord Carew, *Letters From George Lord Carew to Sir Thomas Roe, Ambassador to the Court of the Great Mogul, 1615-1617*, ed. John Maclean (London: 1860), p. 106.
93. *Compact Edition of the Dictionary of National Biography* (Oxford: 1975), p. 866.
94. Carew, *Letters from George Lord Carew*, p. 123.
95. Roe, *The Embassy of Sir Thomas Roe*, p. 326.
96. Woolf, *The Idea of History*, p. 77.
97. Hayden White, "The Historical Text as Literary Artifact," in *Tropics of Discourse: Essays in Cultural Criticism*, ed. H. White (Baltimore: 1978), p. 86.
98. White, "The Historical Text as Literary Artifact," p. 91.

2

SIR THOMAS ROE AS *LITTERATEUR*

Thomas Roe was born and raised in an area of Europe which had only recently adopted the principles of Renaissance Humanism developed in fourteenth and fifteenth-century Italy and Spain. Northern Humanism, or Christian Humanism, was different in many respects from its Mediterranean counterpart. While Italian scholars like Picco della Mirandola, Marsiglio Ficino, Poggio Bracciolini, and Lorenzo Valla had been fascinated with a pure, unadulterated restoration of Roman and Greek pagan culture, northern sixteenth and seventeenth-century Humanists had alternate methods, approaches, and interests. Since the mid-sixteenth century, Christian Europe had been divided over the role of the Vatican, its ecclesiastical hierarchy, and the principle of apostolic succession. Catholic theologians held that the first and true Christian church was established by the apostle St. Peter in Rome; moreover, they insisted that the theology developed by Church fathers like St. Jerome and St. Augustus was sound and that every Christian must acknowledge and accept the authority of the Catholic Church and its early writings. By the 1520s, Luther had made his stand at Worms and many other Swiss and German theologians were now scrutinizing the Church of Rome's claim of infallibility and its monopoly of scriptural interpretation.

Endeavoring to undermine the historical claims of the Vatican, Humanist scholars like Melancthon, Montaigne, and d'Etaples began reading and retranslating the original Hebrew and Greek biblical texts. Even within the Catholic Church itself, a reform movement developed with men like Desiderius Erasmus trying to restore the Church to a less ostentatious, more simple institution. Protestant theologians took their interest in the Classical age one step further. Arguing that the principles of Christianity had been corrupted by the Church of Rome shortly after the time of the Savior, scholars began extolling the pre-Christian virtues of pagan philosophers, historians, poets, and playwrights such as Aristotle, Tacitus, Ovid, and Euripides. Originally Humanists examined the Classical texts for metaphors and analogies dealing with Christian principles and doctrines, but by the late sixteenth century Roman and Greek culture had assumed a paradigmatic position in European thought. Histories, collection of verses, philosophical tracts, and play scripts were now considered the ultimate blueprints for a perfect society. Predictably, every educational institution dedicated itself to the study of Greek and Latin and the works of major Classical philosophers, poets, and historians were approached with a rigorous analogical agenda.

In the late sixteenth and early seventeenth century, England was at the height of this mania. John Colet and Sir Thomas More had earlier worked extensively in scholastic theology and philosophy, and the early seventeenth century was characterized by the writings of politician, political theorist, and scientist, Sir Francis Bacon. His *Advancement of Learning* and *Novum Organum* can be considered two of the most instrumental texts in English Renaissance thought. Due to the efforts of these men, the writings of the Ancients had become the political, legal, and cultural guidelines for Jacobean society. Theater companies were reenacting the stories of Caesar and Anthony; London lawyers and parliamentarians were delving into Roman law annals to find historical precedents; poets were resurrecting and applying Classical metre and rhyming patterns. It is within this educational and social milieu that Thomas Roe's future perception and phenomenological outlook was formed.

A son of Robert Roe, prominent haberdasher and landowner, Thomas was baptized in March 1581 in Low Leyton, Essex. His father died in 1587 and his mother was eventually remarried to Sir Richard Berkeley of Stoke Gifford, located near Bristol.[1] Roe was fortunate enough to live in Rendcomb Manor of Gloucestershire as Sir Richard's stepson and soon became familiar with gentry etiquette and self-presentation. In fact, he was introduced early on to court protocol when Sir Berkeley hosted Queen Elizabeth and her entourage for a short duration in 1592.[2] As was standard practice for sons of gentry, Roe began his formal education at the age of twelve; Sir Berkeley enrolled his stepson in Magdalen College at Oxford where he received instruction in Latin, rhetoric, mathematics, logic, and metaphysics. In 1597, he left Magdalen College and continued his education at Middle Temple of London, where only "gentlemen of blood" were admitted. The four Inns of Court (Middle Temple, Inner Temple, Lincoln's Inn, and Gray's Inn) were combined with the eight Inns of Chancery to form, in effect, a third university in England. Here at what was commonly referred to as "the Inns," Roe became fascinated with verse, poetry, epigraphs, play writing, and the phenomenon of masque performances.[3] The Inns in fact were considered a finishing school—a place to interact with the "creame o'th kingdome" and to experience the glories of the great capital city.[4] Roe was an active member and participant in the exclusive literary circle of The Mermaid Tavern Club; here, future figures such as John Donne, Christopher Brooke, and Hugh Holland debated and discussed wit and rhetoric over "the quintessence of the Spanish, French, and Rhenish grape." With the likes of Ben Jonson, John Marston, and William

Shakespeare also in attendance, The Mermaid Tavern hosted frank and lively discussions and arguments on various companies' recent dramatic productions. As Finkelpearl comments, young men attended such clubs as "a group with certain shared assumptions and something like a prevailing ethos."[5]

It was also during this period that Roe was introduced to Jonson, soon to be one of the most influential playwrights of the Jacobean period. By the turn of the century, Roe had also established himself in a group of "small poets," including Sir Henry Goodyer and Sir Edward Herbert. This network of London wits, spearheaded by Jonson and John Donne, wrote each other consistently between 1605 and 1615 and often circulated copies of their verse and prose work.[6] Jonson knew other members of the Roe family more intimately; Roe's grandfather had been an intimate friend and mayor of London and Roe's cousin, Sir John Rowe, is reported to have died of the plague in Jonson's arms.[7] After serving in Shakespeare's Lord Chamberlain's Company, Jonson began drafting his own plays, often in collaboration with another young and upcoming playwright, Marston. Nonetheless, Roe and Jonson continued the friendship from their earlier days at The Inns and the Mermaid Tavern Club and were fond of exchanging letters written in verse, a forum of correspondence Roe liked to use with his close acquaintances. A 9 November 1603 verse epistle to Jonson cleverly uses similes and synonyms to lightly satirize the theme of great men whose standing raises them above the poor and insignificant. Roe's strong inclination for the Humanist principles of the equality of man and the horrors of injustice is discernible in a couplet written to Jonson which the playwright was still able to quote fifteen years later,

> Forget we were thrust out; it is but thus:
> Gods threaten kings, kings lords, as lords do us.
>   ...trust and believe your friend...[8]

Roe went on to reassert his fondness for Jonson with the sentiment that "friends are our selves," and cautioned the young author against self-analysis and anxiety: "Let for a while the time's unthrifty rout/Condemn learning and your studies flout."[9] This warmth was reciprocated by Jonson who thought Roe to be a scrupulous young man destined for a great career:

> Thou hast begun well ROE...
> He that is round within himselfe and streight
> Need seeke no other strength, no other height;
> Fortune upon him breakes her selfe, if ill,
> And what would hurt his vertue makes it still.
> ...Be always to thy gather'd self the same:
> And studie conscience, more than though would'st fame.
> Though both be good, the latter is worst
> And ever is ill got without the first.'[10]

Jonson's esteem can be partially explained by his respect for Roe's literary acumen. This time of the early 1600s was the formative period of Jonson's career. In 1603, he became the masque playwright for the royal court and started staging personal productions for King James I. Apropos of the recent neoclassical trend, many of his satires paralleled Jacobean society in their recreations of the royal courts of ancient Greece and Rome. To what extent he might have discussed these matters or consulted with Roe is not clear but we do know that two of Jonson's most popular plays, *Sejanus* (1605) and *Volpone* (1607), were published with prefaces that included epigraphs penned by Roe himself. The beginning of *Sejanus* begins with 'Th.R's' short dedication to Jonson,

> To his learned and beloued Friend
>   vpon his aequall worke.
> Seianvs, great, and eminent in *Rome*,
> Rays'd aboue all the *Senate*, both in grace
> Of *Princes* fauour, authority, place,

And popular dependance; yet, how soone,
Euen with the instant of his ouerthrowe,
Is all this Pride and Greatnesse now forgot,
(Onely that in Former grace he stood not)
By them which did his State, not Treason knowe!
His very Flatterers, that did adorne
Their neckes with his rich *Meddales,* now in flame
Consume them, and would loose euen his Name,
This was his *Romane* Fate. But now thy Muse
To vs that neither knew his Height, nor Fall,
Hath rays'd him vp with such memoriall,
All that future States and Times his name shall vse.
What, not his Good, nor Ill could once extend
To the next Age, thy Verse, *industrious,*
And learned *Friend,* hath made illustrious
To this: Nor shall his, or thy fame haue end.
           Th.R.[11]

The story of Sejanus, one of tragedy, corruption, and betrayal in the time of Tiberius, was a well-known one among educated Englishmen. Jonson's choosing to re-enact the rise and fall of Sejanus apparently appeased Roe's Humanist tastes: "But now thy Muse/To vs that neither knew his Height, nor Fall/Hath rays'd him vp with such memoriall/All that future States and Times his name shall vse." Likewise, Jonson also published one of Roe's dedications in his publication of *Volpone,* a satirical comedy set in Venice which is modeled on the ancients' theory of kingship:

Ionson, to tell the world what I to thee
Am, 'tis *Friend.* Not to praise, nor vsher forth
Thee, or thy worke, as if it needed mee
Send I these ri'mes to adde ought to thy worth:
So should I flatter my selfe, and not thine;
For there were truth on thy side, none on mine[12]

Roe's relationship with this playwright and early works must be considered significant. Jonson's productions, both comedic and tragic, were immensely popular with the theater-going crowd of London. In addition to his notoriety as the personal playwright of King James I, his energetic efforts while producing conventional stage plays, such as *Cynthia's Revels* (1602), *Sejanus* (1603), *Volpone* (1607), *The Silent Woman* (1609), and *The Alchemist* (1610), earned him a position in the 1600s as "the honored guest of a crowd of noble friends and a king among his fellow poets and playwrights."[13]

Another important development resulting from Roe's tenure at "The Inns" was his close friendship with the poet and divine John Donne. Donne was renowned for his synthesis of intellectual and theological issues with lyrical beauty and, along with Milton, can be considered one of the dominant figures of seventeenth-century English poetry. The first period of his writing, between 1590 and 1601, was a period of passion and cynicism, evident in his *Elegies* and *Songs and Sonnets*. After being appointed secretary to Thomas Egerton, Keeper of the Great Seal, Donne started interacting with the political and literary elite of London. His talents were highly applauded and by 1615 Donne was considered the premier poet of England. Besides writing poems of dedication and praise for various court personalities, he also began introducing a more meditative, somber tone to his verse in this period. In 1603, Donne wrote a letter in verse to Roe, referring to some pleasant memory (now hopelessly obscured), and is interesting mainly for the familiarity of its address to "Dear Tom", a surprising intimacy given that Roe was several years his junior.[14] The two exchanged correspondence throughout this period while Roe was serving as gentleman-in-waiting for James I's daughter, Elizabeth. In 1609, it was rumoured that Thomas Roe was having an affair with one of the Queen's ladies-in-waiting, Cecilia Bulstrode. When she passed away on August 4, Donne visited the inconsolable Roe in London but left "Sir Tho. Roe so indulgent to his sorrow, as it had been an injury to have interrupted it with my unusefull company."[15] Donne so cherished his colleague, he later wrote "I have bespoke you a New Year's gift, that is, a good New Year, for I have offered your name with my soul heartily to God in my morning's best sacrifice." Interestingly, Donne continues the letter by asking "if for custom you will do a particular office in recompense, deliver this letter to your Lady now, or when the rage of 'The Mask' is past."[16] Donne seems to be making a direct reference to Ben Jonson's recent masque production of *The Hue and Cry after Cupid* in the court of James I in 1607. Although Roe would spend most of his professional career stationed in India, Turkey, and Sweden, they continued their relationship through a long and healthy correspondence until Donne's death in 1631. In 1622, while Roe was serving as ambassador to Istanbul, Donne wrote to his colleague and offered spiritual comfort for certain slanders of which Roe had been the victim in the Jacobean court:

> Outward thorns of calumny, and mis-interpretation do us least harme; Innocency despises them; or friends and just examiners of the case blunt or breake them. Finde thorns within; a woundinge sense of sin; bringe you the thorns, and Christ will make it a Crown; or do you make it a crown, when two ends meet and make a circle (consider yourself, from one mother to another, from the womb to the grave), and Christ will make it a crown of glory. Add not you to my thorns by giving any ill interpretations of my silence or slackness in writing; you, who have so long accustomed to assist me with your good opinion and testimonies and benefits, will not easily do that; but if you have at any time declined towards it, I beseech you let this have some weight towards re-rectifying you, that the assiduity of doing the Church of God that service which I am thought to be able to do, possess me, and fills me.[17]

Of course, by the 1620s Donne had shifted away from the esoteric themes of love and friendship and was now wholly dedicated to writing sermons and hymns as a minister in the Church of England. Later letters such as this focused mostly on political and doctrinal topics with occasional references to circulating plays and published writings. Roe's connection with such a literary personality has to be considered significant when contemplating his tools of expression and description; his ability to establish and build such an intimate friendship with the likes of John Donne suggests Roe was not without his own literary talents. Roe's Humanist education, the literary circles he moved with, and close friendships with *litterateurs* like Jonson and Donne suggest that Roe was not only aware of the literary world but actually participated in it on a limited scale. The ramifications of this conclusion only become clear if the language and style of the early seventeenth-century English playwright and poet is understood. This, combined with highlighting the relevant issues and concerns of the Jacobean court, can help us analyze the tone and subject matter of Roe's later journal.

The year 1603 not only represented a major change in dynastic succession but also a shift in Westminster court dynamics. Influential elements of England, including ecclesiastics, courtiers, nobility, and ministers of parliament, had previously admired Queen Elizabeth's ability to astutely gauge any given situation and implement the necessary practical policies of state. Faced with parliamentary demands for continued reform of the Church and an aggressive foreign policy with Catholic Europe, combined with an alliance with Protestant Holland and Germany, Elizabeth prudently avoided commitments to parliament and adopted a strategy of vacillation. With Elizabeth's designation of James VI of Scotland as her successor, many Englishmen viewed the future leadership with some hesitation and anxiety. It was generally feared among the ruling elite that James was too inexperienced with the mechanics of English politics, and his upsetting experiences with the heavily Calvinist Scottish Kirk might threaten inroads accomplished by the English Protestant movement.[18] On the other hand, James's moderate religious policy, combined with his intense dedication to the concept of divine monarchy, was seen as a potential stabilizer to what had been a tumultuous sixteenth century for England.[19] James's approach to rule was largely rooted in his experiences as the young king of Scotland. The execution of his mother, Mary Queen of Scots, and his fiery debates with the egalitarian Scottish Calvinists hardened his belief in legitimacy and monarchical infallibility. Calvinist ecclesiastical structure, with its rejection of the Church of England and the king of England as the supreme head of the church, was anathema to his deeply entrenched perception of monarchical power. Within one year of his accession, the new king of England called the Hampton Court Conference to discuss a recently submitted puritan petition calling for continued reform. He appeased the conservative majority of church officials and courtiers by finally declaring that religious issues were a "settled matter" which he had no wish to disrupt.[20] James's views on monarchical prerogative and the concept of Divine Right find early elucidation in two works penned as king of Scotland, *Basilikon Doron* and *The Trew Law of Monarchies*. The opening verse of *Basilikon Doron* waxes poetic on the virtue of kingship,

> God giues not kings the stile of Gods in vaine,
> For on his throne his Scepter doe they sway:
> And as their subjects ought them to obey
> So Kings should feare and serue their God againe.
> If then ye would enjoy a happie reigne
> Observe the statutes of your heauenlie King.[21]

His theory of divine kingship is further espoused in *The Trew Law of Monarchies*, "...the kings are called Gods by the propheticall King David, because they sit upon God his Throne in the earth, and have the count of their administration to give unto him." Furthermore, "by the

Law of Nature the King becomes a naturall Father to all his Lieges at his Coronation; And as the Father of his fatherly duty is bound to care for the nourishing, education, and vertous government of his children; even so is the king bound to care for all his subjects."[22] Although his convictions regarding the divine origin of royal prerogative eventually became a source of contention with the House of Commons in later parliaments, James's language and style of monarchy fostered interesting responses in areas of architecture, numismatics, art, literature, drama, and prose. Jonathan Goldberg meticulously details the shifts in English architecture, art, and coin designs during the first decade of the seventeenth century; his observations warrant the conclusion of James being keen to resurrect Roman classicism in its purest form to supplement his personal "style of gods."[23] However, it is the structural and stylistic changes within the dramatic arts that merit attention here. The Roman heritage of theater and public performance was a new, attractive source of style and subject matter for English playwrights. The seedling Elizabethan interest in Classical drama eventually blossomed into a full-grown passion during the reign of James I. Classical histories, legends, and biographies were read and transformed by playwrights into popular theatrical productions. Particularly, the poets and playwrights educated at the Inns looked to Classical literature as a repository from which to borrow ideas for the creation of a native drama.[24] Not only were these plays becoming increasingly popular with the elite, there was now a new demand at the pedestrian level for this form of entertainment and its distinctly 'Roman' flavour.

Many Renaissance literature scholars (Tennenhouse, Goldberg, Sharpe) have established the close relationship between dramatic expression and concurrent political issues and social concerns. Moreover, they interpret early seventeenth-century playwrights' scripts as being occasionally deliberate commentaries on English polity.

Historiographically, these cultural historians turn away from traditional sources of expressing protest (political tracts, pamphleteer literature) and look to the Jacobean stage as a viable means of investigating popular reactions to court politics, machinations, and systems of government. As Goldberg comments, "the theatre, that tragic scaffold, was a place for self-knowledge precisely because it mirrored state, because its representations duplicated public life."[25] While this approach is certainly valid, it is largely founded on the premise of 'art imitating life.' By assuming the reverse supposition, i.e. 'life imitating art,' some other observations become possible.

It is the contention of this discussion that, due to the recent inundation of play and masque performances, Jacobean courtly language partially assimilated dramatic analogies and terminology. Holderness supports the assertion of how drama has an active, occasionally dominant, role in the making of history; moreover, the court of James I, with its propensity for Roman and masque plays, became an institution which was as much cultural as political. He seals his point by stating: "the business of a Tudor or Stuart court might have been understood more as transactions in the symbolic language of authority than in the material details of implementing power."[26] These recent studies on court culture propose the idea of the Renaissance court being key to understanding early seventeenth-century English expression both at an elite and common level. In other words, the court and its participants can be interpreted as creators and diffusers of popular motifs, language, and terminology. The court was a profoundly historical institution and simultaneously the source of a particular symbolic language, a language potent enough to penetrate and influence the general culture at all levels.[27] The aforementioned relationship between Jacobean court and drama, with their exchanging of vocabulary and motifs and mutual adoption of Roman classical trends, was most likely directly observed by Roe during his education at The Inns with his circle of literary friendships. If not a direct participant, Roe was at least a spectator to a milieu where "stagecraft collaborates with statecraft in producing spectacles of power."[28]

The early modern paralleling of the English king with the protagonist of a play, with the stage as the court and the audience as his subjects, was a common theatrical device. As Greenblatt notes, "royal power is manifested to its subjects as in a theatre, and the subjects are at once more absorbed by the instructive, delightful, or terrible spectacles and forbidden intervention or deep intimacy."[29] While playwrights sought to establish the actor as king, it was not uncommon for the monarchy to see the relationship inversely. "We princes are set on stages in the sight and view of all the world," Elizabeth once remarked.[30] Given the popularity of theatre during the early seventeenth century and James's propensity to actually participate in court masque plays, not surprisingly the metaphor of king and actor became a popular one during the Jacobean period. The king himself realized this relationship and expressed so in his *Basilikon Doron*,

> Kings being publike persons, by reason of their office and authority, are as it were set upon a publike stage, in the sight of all the people; where all the beholders eyes are attentively bent to looke and pry in the least circumstance of their secretest drifts: Which would make Kings the more carefull not to harbour the secretest thought in their minde, but such as in the owne time they shall not be ashamed openly to avouch...[31]

Here we can discern James's disdain for being a "publike" figure forced to contend with the problems of inner intention and outward appearance. James continually struggled to reconcile the polarized nature of responsible rule; while bound by law to maintain some sense of accessibility to his subjects, the king hoped nonetheless to imbue the English people with a sense of awe and unapproachability,

> It is a trew old saying, That a King is as one set on a stage, whose smallest actions and gestures, all the people gazingly doe behold: and therefore although a King be never so praecise in the discharging of his Office, the people, who seeth but the outward part, will ever iudge of the substance, by the circumstance; and according to the outward appearance, if his behaviour bee light or dissolute, will conceive pre-occupied conceits of the Kings outward intention...[32]

This theme of mystique is not uncommon with James I and repeated instances of "the mysterie of the Kings power" appeared in his speeches and writings.[33] He believed his royal prerogative to be an enigma, an inner sanctum from which all others were excluded, and one of his favourite admonitions to ambitious Members of Parliament was "incroach not upon the Prerogative of the Crowne." This fervent belief that he was shrouded in some unquestionable, ineffable mystery, combined with his taciturn approach to public appearances, led to an isolation of both the monarchy and courtly elements. This trend was best exemplified by the growth of the masque performance phenomenon. The masque was the arrival of a number of nobles dressed in elaborate disguise to mark a particular occasion and to honour their monarch; the duty of the masque writer was to provide an accompanying fictional plot to explain the disguised arrival.[34] While these performances were often presented for the benefit of the king, it was not uncommon for James and other members of the royal family to assume corresponding roles in the production. Here, the monarch would supersede analytical similes or metaphors and literally enact the concept of a "player-king."[35] The relationship between court culture and theater was not highly polarized; subject matter, terminology, and motifs was readily exchanged and adapted. In fact, the line dividing 'reality' and 'imagination,' such as the division between the actor and the king, became blurred to the point where, in the opinion of the James I himself, the two were interchangeable. We also see this association between politics and drama in the writing of the great Humanist scholar, Sir Francis Bacon. In his *Novum Organum*, he describes the existence of four "idols" which distort or mould popular sociopolitical perceptions. The fourth idol, the idol of theater, describes the entrenchment of defective systems of polity and philosophy, "for we regard all the systems of philosophy, hitherto received or imagined, as so many plays brought out and performed, creating fictitious worlds."[36]

There are far too many conventional plays of the Jacobean era to examine here. However, there are a number which, cursorily examined, provide key insights to understanding early seventeenth-century dramatic expression. Predictably, many playwrights had agendas beyond simple entertainment. They, and sympathetic courtiers, considered plays excellent vehicles by which they could comment and, in some cases, criticize the behavior of both court and king. In addition to the increasingly idiosyncratic statements on the mystery of divine kingship and his affinity for self-isolation, James I's handling of patronage and finance was becoming an issue of some scrutiny and alarm. After assuming the throne of England, James initiated a program of patronage that shocked the established gentry. During the 1590s, records place the number of knights at 550; after three years of rule, James had tripled it.[37] A comparison of Elizabethan and Jacobean patronage practices hints at the scope of James's generosity: despite ruling twice as long, Elizabeth only created 878 knights and 18 peers whereas James bestowed 1900 knighthoods, 200 baronets, and 65 peerages.[38]

Financially, the situation was even more dire. In spite of inheriting a debt of £400,000, James inaugurated his reign with staggering expenditures. He established three households (for himself, his wife, Anne, and his son, Henry) which doubled household expenses from £40,000 to £80,000 in the first year of his reign.[39] Financial crisis precipitated the proposed Great Contract of 1610, engineered by James's trusted official Lord Cecil, which sought to reverse the crown's insolvency. Due to the king's reticence to relinquish certain monarchical prerogatives as well as court factional opposition to Cecil, the Contract was opposed and defeated in the 1610 Parliament. Annual royal disbursements soared from £300,000 to £500,000; by 1612, the year Lord Cecil died, the royal debt reached £600,000.[40] To complement the three households, as well as the large number of royal estates he had acquired (there were ten), James was forced to increase his spending for court officials and household staff. By 1614, fees and annuities dispensed from the Exchequer to support this infrastructure went from £27,000 (1603) to £104, 860.[41] As MP John Hoskyns, a colleague and friend of Thomas Roe's, stated, "the royal cistern had a leak, which, till it were stopped, all our consultations to bring money unto it was of little use."[42]

To further complicate matters, James's court was, like many contemporary Renaissance counterparts, racked with favouritism and factional competition. It soon became obvious there was a network of patrons and clients co-ordinating political activity. Simply put, the two main competing groups were centered around the family of the Howards, known as the "Spanish" faction, and the "French" faction, which included the Duke of Lennox and other Scots who had come to England with James in 1603.[43] As the titles suggest, these groups' designs revolved around foreign policies conducive to either Spain or France. Furthermore, proximity to the king was considered key for securing political appointments and offices. As a result, competition for the king's attention was fierce and often conducted in clandestine fashion. Favouritism was best illustrated in George Villiers's, the Duke of Buckingham, meteoric rise despite numerous accusations of ineptitude and inexperience; nonetheless, Villiers prospered thanks to his good, possibly intimate, relationship with James I. These events and trends were the obvious sundry characteristics of James I's court and many playwrights took it upon themselves to write and stage productions which, in couched language and veiled allusions, were subtle warnings to the king and his immediate circle of favourites. The majority of such productions were based on famous Roman figures and events; specifically, the years 1603-24 witnessed an emphasis on tragedy as the dominant motif for playwrights. Defined loosely as "the fall of princes: (the) misfortune of the highly placed," tragedy reveled in insane despots, heightened rhetoric, bloody images, terrorized innocents, and revenge.[44] Referred to as a "Senecan" motif, its purpose was to present terrible spectacles which strove to subtly reveal man's inner nobility, a virtue often lost or temporarily swept aside in violent circumstances.[45] Jacobean playwrights occasionally orchestrated their tragedies to parallel ongoing events and situations in the court and the production would end with a soliloquy lamenting the lost age of just monarchs and untainted courtiers. In cases of plays making blatant allusions to the Jacobean court, the authorities were swift and uncompromising. John Dary's *The Isle of Gulls*, performed in 1606, presented the main character Duke Basilius (a reference to James's work, *Basilikon Doron*) vacationing in the countryside while his principal minister, Dametas, was left to dispense gifts and patronage to a greed-racked court.[46] Recognizing Duke Basilius as James and Dametas as Lord Cecil, royal authorities closed down the production team and the *Act to Restraine Abuses of Players*, a bill designed to censor any threatening drama text, was passed in May of 1606.[47] Political and personal satire became so daring that Samuel Calver warned, "the plays do not forbear to present upon their Stage the whole Course of this present Time, nor sparing either King, State, or Religion, in so great Absurdity, and with such Liberty, that any would be afraid to hear them."[48]

While acting companies had, to some extent, prospered under Elizabeth, it was during the Jacobean era when plays became the dominant cultural medium for the ruling elite. In fact, upon his accession, James I appropriated all three existing acting companies (Admiral's, Worcester's, and Lord Chamberlain's) as his personal servants.[49] Thus in 1603, the majority of English drama companies became His Majesty's Servants and entered into the closest relationship a theatrical team could possibly have with a monarch and royal court.[50] Under the close scrutiny of the king's agents, popular Senecan tragedies were still written and performed for Jacobean audiences. Specifically, Jonson's *Sejanus* tackled these issues of ineffective rule, factional competition, and rampant political corruption in an organized state. Jonson, true to the Humanist tradition, based his script on the *Annals* of the Roman historian Tacitus to portray the decay eroding Caesar Augustus' government; the character of Macro, ally of Sejanus, is used as an agent to uncover this moral stagnation.[51] In England, Tacitism was linked with the Senecan revival and became a philosophical and historical means by which playwrights and courtiers expressed discontent.[52] The device of using an impartial observer to reveal such elements of vice and avarice was popular among Jacobean playwrights. Termed the "disguised Duke plays," Marston's *Malcontent* (1602) and *The Fawn* (1604), Shakespeare's *Measure for Measure* (1603), Middleton's *The Phoenix* (1603) and Sharpham's *The Fleer* (1606) all present a leading figure winding his way through the various strata of society uncovering abuse after abuse. As Tricomi states, "within this satiric perspective, the corruption of government and of men in high places, including judges, courtiers, and nobility, looms large."[53] Degeneration of government became a prevalent image in Jacobean drama with corruption originating with the King and then passing on through the aristocracy and court elements.

The popularity of such plays points to an increasing political awareness among early seventeenth-century Englishmen. More importantly, it is the process of understanding *realpolitik* through the dramatic lens that interests us here. While parliamentarians, lawyers, and political theorists certainly discussed the political state in direct, unambiguous language, this new forum of political expression and description was obviously becoming popular. Roe's education and early friendships provide us with a window into these larger trends taking place in Jacobean theatre and play writing. If we adopt the argument of scholars like Holderness of how drama can dictate popular language and perception, which is then disseminated to the public by the court, it can be conjectured that Roe was part of a medium which increasingly looked to theatrical dimensions (language, plots, characters, motifs) to express itself, not only culturally but politically as well. His close relations with men like Donne and Jonson, friendships in which Roe was respected for his literary talents, presents a gentry man and courtier reasonably versed in this new cultural and political *lingua franca*. As he wrote in a letter to his former patron, Queen Elizabeth of Bohemia, the theatre "makes our statesmen see the good use of them...for if our heads had been filled with the loves of Piramus and Thisbe...we should never have cared who made peace or war, but on the stage."[54]

"Affinitye With a Theater": Pre-Generic Plot Structures in Jahângîr's Court

When Roe initially set sail eastwards, he was venturing into an area of the world which was relatively little known by Europeans. Seventeenth-century conceptions of Africa and

Asia were largely rooted in those built up during the early Middle Ages; while the Holy Land and northern Africa had been substantially documented due to economic and military encounters, knowledge of lands further east was to some extent still shaped by popular imagination and fantasy. These territories, specifically those outside the boundaries of the Judeo-Christian macro-tradition, were a subject of intrigue, if not outright terror. Knowledge of subjects like ethnography, botany, and zoology was so rudimentary that seventeenth-century English contemporaries believed the outer peripheries of the world to be inhabited by prehistoric 'wild' men, carnivorous plants, and a number of kinds of mythical beasts. As Roe himself wrote in a letter to his friend and patron, the Archbishop of Canterbury, "places farr remote, having somewhat of woonder in the distance, cause much expectation in them selves of strange matter among the vulgar."[55] Probably the most sustained oral tradition of the Middle Ages, however, was the myth of Prester John, supposedly a powerful European monarch established somewhere in the deep parts of Abyssinia. By the early sixteenth century, this folk tale had hardened into fact; cartographers were including his territorial boundaries, merchants speculated on the amount of gold he was exporting from the mines of Africa, and adventurers dreamed of joining his ranks to wage holy war against the Moorish infidel. When the Turkish threat reached its peak during the mid-sixteenth century, Portuguese and Spanish sailors navigating the coast of Africa were actually instructed to seek out information on this European overlord in the hopes of co-ordinating a two-front offensive on the Ottoman empire. Moreover, in the sixteenth century there were rumours circulating that Prester John was, in fact, residing in India.[56] The possibility of discovering this elusive monarch was also on the mind of Sir Thomas Roe when the *Lion* was navigating the eastern coast of Africa in August of 1615. While anchored off the island of Johanna,

Roe's expedition met an experienced Madagascar trader, Mu`allim Ibrâhîm, who happily provided some valuable nautical and geographical advice. Apparently during some point of their conversation, Roe inquired as to any information about this mysterious potentate but, as Roe writes, "Off Prester Jhon he knoweth noe more then that he is a great prince and a Capharr (*kafîr*)."[57] This interest in Prester John's whereabouts continued during his voyage and, three weeks later, he described how the King of Socatra "hath some knowledge of Prester John, confessing him the greatest prince in the world."[58]

This particular curiosity of Roe's is interesting because it reflects on some of the popular imagery associated with non-European rulers during the age of expansion. As is in the case of King Prester John, Europeans viewed contemporary Asian heads of state with a certain awe and anxiety. Rumours of fabulous wealth and power, combined with news of unspeakable atrocities and cruelty, were commonly circulated and believed. Europe had long since absorbed the earlier legends of Chingîz Khân and Tîmûr and, by the seventeenth century, rulers of the east were considered synonymous with barbarity, wealth, and tyranny. Due to their remoteness, these men also took on a mystical, ineffable quality that only enhanced the extent of their potential power and hegemony. The dehumanizing effect of this mystification was augmented by a tendency to personify Asian ruling institutions; these personifications had a permanent, almost immortal, quality. For instance, Europeans did not, or could not, differentiate the reigns of Bâbur, Humâyûn, Akbar and Jahângîr: in their imagination there was only 'the Great Mogul,' an institution in itself characterized by despotism, fantastic wealth, and intrigue.

We see similar developments with other Muslim political states where the *shâhs* of Safavid Iran, Isma`îl, Tahmâsp, and `Abbâs, were simplified into "the Grand Sophy" or "the Persian," and the *sultâns* of Istanbul became "the Turk." One only has to consider the Elizabethan genre of oriental dramatic tragedies to realize some of England's popular conception of such rulers. In Marlowe's *Tamburlaine* (1587), the blood thirsty conquests of Tîmûr are recounted; in Thomas Lodge and Robert Greene's joint production of *A Looking Glass For London and England* (1594), we have a recreation of the chaos pervading ancient Nineveh of Babylonia. It is in this vein that we must understand Roe's initial perceptions of the Mughal ruling elite. The first noble personality he encountered was in Burhânpûr while en route to the court of Jahângîr in Ajmîr; here, he was ushered into the presence of Prince Parvaiz, the king's second son, who "satte, high in a Gallerie that went round, with a Cannipe over him and a Carpett before him, in great but barborous state." Invited to speak with Parvaiz, Roe "passed on, till [he] came to a place rayled in, Right vnder him, with an assent of 3 steepes...wher stood round by the side all the great men of the Towne with their handes before them like slaues." The scenery was obviously impressive "with a Rich Cannapie, and vnderneath all Carpetts" but Roe had his misgivings about Parvaiz. He had already heard that the prince only "hath the name" and it was the *Khân-i Khânân*, Mîrzâ `Abd al-Rahîm, who actually "governs all." But it is during his description of Parvaiz's court that Roe makes his most interesting statement: "to discribe it rightly it was like a great stage, and the Prince satt above, as the mock kings doth thear."[59]

Of course we are reminded of James's thoughts on the similarity between actor and king and the popular concept of actor-king in Jacobean society. There is an additional qualitative element to Roe's observations whereby he impinges on Parvaiz's status by equating him with those "mock kings" of the English stage. Specifically, it is his intention to "discribe it rightly" that interests us here and we are drawn, once again, to the issue of how Roe expected to relate these experiences to his future readers. In the same vein as the previous discussion of "familiarizing"

Mughal India, we come to the concept of "emplotment" which H. White has described as "the encodation of the facts contained in the chronicle as components of specific kinds of plot structures."[60] Keen to "familiarize" the unfamiliar, chroniclers supplemented their explanations with a narrative element, essentially a form of story telling. This quasi-fictional approach to presenting history was by no means contrary to Jacobean practice as D. R. Woolf adequately demonstrates in his *The Idea of History in Early Stuart England*. No set of events is inherently tragic, epic, or comedic with a discernible beginning, middle, and ending. Reality is transformed into these qualitative adjectives of 'tragic' or 'epic' by human perception; this is, in fact, a moralizing process of what we see or experience and, as Lévi-Strauss cautions, history will "never completely escape from the nature of myth."[61]

Illustrations suggest that Roe, intricately versed in the subject matter and popular motifs of literature and drama, moralized or 'explained' his observations to accommodate popular Jacobean *mythoi* or plot structures. By comparing his first royal encounter, Prince Parvaiz, to the stage and its "mock kings," Roe invites the reader to indulge in those epic tales and tragedies so commonly known in early seventeenth-century England. Dramatic analogies like this associate the reader with a number of possible "pre-generic plot structures," established earlier by playwrights like Marlowe, Shakespeare, Jonson, Marston. These "plot structures" could vary but the setting was almost always a royal court. Whether they were set in first-century ACE Rome or in fifteenth-century Venice, these plots told the story of the inherent conflict, both comedic and tragic, found in such political arenas.

When Roe reached Ajmîr and was later summoned to the king's *darbâr*, or court, he finally came face to face with "the Great Mogull." After making "reverences", Roe was brought to the king's throne where he observed "the place is a great Court, whither resort all sorts of people." He commented on the location of Jahângîr "in a little Gallery ouer head" and also noticed a number of ambassadors and nobility "within the inmost rayle vnder [Jahângîr]." The visible wealth of this court, decorated with "Canopyes of veluet and silke" and "good Carpetts," only reaffirmed Roe's European conception of the "Great Mogull" as the pinnacle of opulence and extravagance. The *khâns, amîrs*, and other state functionaries stood on a raised platform by the first railing. These men were apparently then surrounded by the "people without in a base Court" but were positioned "soe that all may see the King."[62] This arrangement, to Roe's mind, was eerily familiar of Jacobean stage productions, so much so that he chose to write: "it hath soe much affinitye with a theatre...that an easy description will informe of the place and fashion." This instant association of the Mughal royal court with a dramatic production is not surprising given the popular imagery of the "player-king" among political and literary circles in Jacobean society. Moreover, Roe's description of the "manner of the king in his gallery" surrounded by his courtiers "lifted on a stage as actors" with the "vulgar below gazing on" is identical to how masque performances had been staged in the court of James I.[63] It appears that Roe was quite dedicated to this particular analogy.

In describing his first meeting with the emperor, Roe tells his patron Lord Carew that Jahângîr was "set aboue like a King in a play and all his nobles and my selfe below on stage couered wih carpetts—a iust theatre."[64] Likewise, in a letter to Prince Charles dated 30 October 1616, he writes "if Your Highness haue any vacancy from better recreations to caste your eies vpon one of the greatest theatres of the world, I could take pride in the paynes to relate to Your Highnes many rare varietyes..."[65] Roe's decision to enact the "player-king" image was not motivated out of some creative whimsical fancy; he had been striving to present an accurate and reliable "universall description of the state and customes of the land."

However, the implicit commentary underpinning these observations is significant. Roe's decision to use words like 'theatre' and 'actors' introduces a critical literary element to his portrayal of the Mughal court. At this juncture, the journal shifts from a dry geo-economic travelogue to a narrative with a potential plot. The establishment of such a narrative, which could be furnished with characters, plot, and conflict, was not meant strictly for story-telling purposes: it provided a framework of reference for Roe's Jacobean audience to facilitate their understanding of the Mughal court. More importantly, historical literature of the seventeenth century encouraged the employment of literary and dramatic devices; in the opinion of Humanist scholars, references or allusions to "pre-generic plot structures" provided a powerful and useful means of description.

Characters, of course, are critical to any narrative and immediately after Roe's interview with the emperor, Roe describes his meeting with Prince Khurram, and Khurram's aide-de-camp, Âsaf Khân, on 14 January 1615. Khurram promised a *farmân* ordering the redress of English grievances at Sûrat but its conspicuous absence "contrarye to all the Princes faire woords and his own assurances of justice" were beginning to alarm Roe. When he complained of this to Âsaf Khân, Roe found "he was the author of this device and an earnest disputer for the reasonablenes thereof." Roe apparently believed the circulating rumours of a factional alliance: "I saw now the faction...[Âsaf Khân] was a broken reede; the Prince gouerned by him...the beloued queene, ante to Sultan [Khurram's] wife, sister of [Âsaf Khân]." This narrative intensifies when Roe places himself in the center of this intrigue: "the King was my only refuge, from whom I was sure of justice if I complaynd, but I feard I should drawe upon me the hate of [Nûr Jahân]...and all that powrfull faction, against whom, though I might once preuayle, yet the advantage of tyme, language, and oportunitye, the power of a wife, sonne, and a fauorite, would produce reuenge."[66]

For much of the next six months, Roe met with leading Mughal nobles, Mîr Jamâl al-Dîn Husain, *sûbadâr* (provincial governor) of Bihâr, Muqarrab Khân, state functionary and former governor of Sûrat, Khvâjah Abû al-Hasan, the emperor's paymaster-general, Âghâ Nûr, the *kutwâl* of Âgrâ, Zû al-Faqâr Khân, governor of Sûrat until early 1616 and his replacement, Khvâjah Nizâm. During this time, Roe became familiar with the *ghusâl khânah*, or private baths, of the emperor, an institution that had become the Mughal forum for frank political discussions. According to Roe, during these meetings he became quite close to Jahângîr, a development that apparently alarmed the "faction." After being denied further interviews with the emperor, Roe "sawe by [Âsaf Khân] it was [Zû al-Faqâr Khân's] busines that putt this trick vpon mee, by the [Khurram's] order and [Âsaf Khân's] coniuence in the Kings name."[67] By September, Roe was convinced that "[Âsaf Khân] was our enemy, or at beste a false friend: that hee had faltered with mee in my busines with the King."[68]

The story of this elite alliance, or faction, has two main parts. The first theme relates Roe's discovery of and personal confrontation with this quartet consisting of Nûr Jahân (the emperor's wife), Âsaf Khân (Nûr Jahân's brother), I'timâd al-daulat (their father), and Prince Khurram. *The Embassy*, however, is also the story of Prince Khurram's rise to power in the Mughal political structure. As related in Chapter 1, he had subjugated what had essentially been a fifty-year rebellion in Mewâr in 1614 and, by 1616, was promising to settle the long-standing conflict with Malik 'Ambar and the kingdom of Ahmadnagar. Khurram's eldest brother, Parvaiz, had disappointed the emperor with his earlier Deccan campaign and the other brother, Khusrau, was in confinement for his attempted coup d'état a decade earlier. This absence of fraternal opposition opened the way for Khurram to secure prestigious titles and offices, including the governorship of Gujarât. Roe's presentation of Khurram's ascendancy, however, takes an interesting turn when the ambassador comments that "[Jahângîr] entends him not the kingdome" and that, in fact, the rebellious Khusrau was the heir-apparent because he "is both extreamly beloued and honored of all men, almost adored, and very iustly, for his most noble parts." Jahângîr, the patient yet naive ruler could not appreciate "that this sly youth [Khurram] doth more darken him by ambitious practices then the other [Khusrau] could by vertuous actions."[69] This theme of an honorable, popular claimant to the throne being pitted against the nefarious designs of a power-scheming opponent was a popular one in Jacobean theatre. Particularly, the plot of Ben Jonson's *Sejanus* tells a similar story of political machination and subterfuge in Tiberian Rome. Sejanus, sycophant and flatterer, becomes a protege of the Emperor Tiberius while the legitimate successor Drusus is increasingly displaced from the court thanks to Sejanus's intrigues. The plot crescendos when Sejanus, joined by his lover and Drusus's wife Livia, orchestrate a plan to poison the prince to ensure the ambitious courtier's nomination as emperor. Like all early seventeenth-century Jacobean tragedies, this play has the strong Senecan motif of political chaos and moral turpitude in its portrayal of Sejanus's tempting of the Fates and his ultimate fall.

Roe's description of Khurram and the Mughal court during the year 1616 should be understood in light of the author's familiarity with works such as Jonson's *Sejanus* which had, upon original publication, been prefaced by Roe's dedication to Jonson. In *The Embassy*, the juxtaposition of Khurram and Khusrau as contenders for the throne is no subtle thing. While Khurram is "Proud, Subtill, false, and barberously Tyranous," we are presented with an image of Khusrau as "both extreamly beloued and honored of all men, almost adored, and very justly."[70] Here, we have a striking familiarity with Jonson's characters of Sejanus and Drusus. Despite being "a riotous youth," the Roman nobleman Sabinus thinks Drusus "bears /Himself each day more nobly than other; /And wins no less on men's affections, /Than doth his father lose. Believe me, I love him; /And, chiefly for opposing to Sejanus."[71] Of Sejanus he warns: "Tyrants' arts /Are to give flatterers grace; accusers, power: /That those may seem to kill whom they devour."[72]

With his departure for the Deccan front imminent, Khurram apparently feared a reconciliation between the emperor and Khusrau and "by [Khusrau's] liberty all the glory and hopes of [Khurram's] faction would vanish and the iniury and ambition hardly bee pardoned."[73] At this juncture, Roe suspects Khusrau's life to be in danger since Prince Khurram *et alia* "resolued it was not possible for them to stand if the Prince Sultan [Khusrau] liued, whom the nobilitye loued, and whose deliuery or life would Punish their ambitions in tyme; therfore Practised how to bring him into their Power, that poyson might end him."[74] This development in Roe's narrative is roughly parallel with the designs of Sejanus, Livia, and Eudemus to assassinate Drusus: "Be resolute in our plot; you have my soul, /As certain yours as it is my body's. /And, wise physician, so prepare the poison, /As you may lay the subtle operation / Upon some natural disease of his."[75] When Khusrau was transferred to the charge of Âsaf Khân, the dramatic tension of Roe's narrative intensifies: "the whole Court is in a whisper" and the public reaction to this development was dark and resentful: "the Multitude, like it selfe, full of tumor and Noyce, without head or foote; only it rages but bendes it selfe vpon doe direct end."[76] Likewise, suspicion of Sejanus's poisoning of Drusus led to "fears, whisperings, tumults, noise" in the streets of Rome and, in the closing moments of the play,

> The eager multitude (who never yet
> Knew why to love or hate, but only pleased
> T' express their rage of power) no sooner heard
> The murmur of Sejanus in decline,
> But with that speed and heat of appetite
> With which they greedily devour the way
> To some great sports, or a new theatre
> ...
> Of their wild fury; first, they tear them down;
> Then fastening ropes, drag them along the streets[77]

Of course, Khurram never had to answer a riotous mob such as this for his alleged intrigues against his father and brother but Roe nonetheless predicts a devastating end: "a rending and tearing of these kingdomes by diuison when the King shall pay the debt to nature, and that all parts wilbe torne and destroyed by a ciuill war."[78] Roe apparently overestimated the popular support for Prince Khusrau since he would continue to be in the charge of Âsaf Khân until 1622 with little reaction from the populace.

In early November, the Mughal war machine, with every royal personality in attendance, began its departure from Ajmîr towards the Deccan. After traveling four miles, the royal camp pitched its tents at Dorâi "in forme of a fort with divers coynes and bulwarks."[79] Roe took this opportunity to meet with Khurram who, as governor of Gujarât, would have been instrumental to solving the dilemma of Zû al-Faqâr Khân's outstanding debt to the English trading agents at Sûrat. After discussing these matters with the Prince in his royal tent, Roe was offered "a cloth of gould cloak of [Khurram's]" to which Roe curiously added "When his Ancester Tamerlane was represented at the Theatre, the Garment would well haue become the Actor, but it is here reputed the highest of fauour to giue a garment worne by the Prince."[80] This direct reference to Christopher Marlowe's *Tamburlaine* 1587 is the only acknowledgment of an actual Jacobean theatrical production in *The Embassy* and represents an excellent example of Roe visualizing his perception of Prince Khurram by citing a popular piece of theater. The Jacobean reader would have been reminded of Marlowe's Prologue,

> From jigging veins of rhyming mother wits,
> And such conceits as clownage keeps in pay,
> We'll lead you to the stately tent of war,
> Where you shall hear the Scythian Tamburlaine
> Threatening the world with high astounding terms
> And scourging kingdoms with his conquering sword.
> View but his picture in this tragic glass,
> And then applaud his fortunes as you please [81]

Roe's comparison of Khurram to the "Scythian" conqueror becomes further significant if we recall one of Tamurlaine's monologues in which he describes how "The thirst of reign and sweetness of a crown /That cause the eldest son of heavenly of heavenly Ops /To thrust his doting father from his chair /And place himself in the empyreal heaven /Moved me to manage arms against thy state."[82] Central Asian bids for succession were often convoluted and bloody affairs, as was certainly the case for Tîmûr, and such characteristics would have made appealing subject matter for Elizabethan and Jacobean playwrights. Considering Roe's suspicion of Khurram as "sordidly ambitious," his reference to *Tamburlaine* in this sense might have been very deliberate.

A prominent figure in this account of Khurram's ascendancy is, of course, the Queen Begum, Nûr Jahân. Mentioned earlier, it was due to her recent marriage with the emperor that the "Khurâsânî" contingent was able to prosper within the Mughal political structure. Moreover, Roe perceived that her subtle manipulations of the emperor contributed to the fall of Khusrau and the subsequent rise of Khurram: "in all actions of consequence in a court, especially a faction, a woman is not only always an ingredient, but commonly a principall drugg and of most vertue." Her ability to procure *farmâns* and give royal orders proved "that [she] was not incapable of conducting business, nor herself voyd of witt and subtiltye."[83] In a letter to Sir Thomas Smythe, Roe writes: "for Sultan [Khurram] is an absolute by [Nûr Jahân's] power as shee, who is all."[84] This image of megalomaniacal royal consorts was a favourite one among Jacobean theatre audiences and one is tempted to think of personalities like Lady Macbeth: "Come you spirits /That tend on mortal thoughts, unsex me here; /And fill me, from the crown to the toe, topfull / of direst cruelty!"[85] Nûr Jahân's 'puppeteering' of the young Khurram against Khusrau was reminiscent of player-queens manipulating various courtier-pawns, like the vengeful Queen Tamora and her use of Demetrius and Chiron to assassinate Emperor Saturnius's brother, Bassianus, in *Titus Andronicus*. While playwrights often looked upon women as paragons of virtue and simplicity, one of the most popular images was the one borrowed from Judeo-Christian doctrine; seen as the direct cause for Adam's fall and humanity's resulting proclivity for sinful acts, women were often associated with inherent evil and subterfuge,

> It is the woman's part: be it lying, note it
> The woman's; flattering, hers; deceiving, hers
> Lust and rank thoughts, hers, hers; revenges,
> Ambitions, covetings, change of prides, disdain,
> Nice longing, slanders, mutability,
> All faults that have a name, nay that hell knows,
> Why, hers, in part or all; but rather all.[86]

Particularly it is their alleged ability to use feminine wiles and charm to unduly influence their husbands towards destructive decisions and/or policies; as Anthony said of the alluring Cleopatra: "I must from this enchanting Queen break off /Ten thousand harms, more than the ills I know / My idleness doth hatch."[87] Like Lady Macbeth's whispered counsels to her husband or the Queen's "betwixing" of

Cymbeline, Nûr Jahân "attemptes the king with the false teares of womans bewitching flattery."[88] The image of such females delicately eroding men's virtue and ability to think clearly is an ancient one. As the virtuous, yet naive, Adam was gently coaxed into tempting Fate, likewise we see characters like Macbeth ultimately undone by his wife's murderous ambitions. This motif is also readily apparent in Roe's description of the Mughal emperor, who is "gentle, soft, and of good disposition." However, he is unable to control this "faction that dare attempt anything" and he "giues...liberty beyond eyther the law of their owne condition or the limitts of policye and reason."[89] This theme of just rulers undone by their generosity and lack of cunning was a popular one on the London stage and we are reminded of King Duncan of Macbeth who "hath borne his faculties so meek, hath been /So clear in his great office, that his virtues /Will plead like angels trumpet-tounged against /The deep damnation of his taking off."[90] Roe sees the Mughal emperor as being "soe good of disposition," but fears "that he suffers ill men to gouerne." Jahângîr is a "gratious and iust prince, famous for wisdome and benenigitye toward strangers; and His Maiuestie will fynd in the end there are ill councellers and traytors to his peace."[91] From the perspective of the Jacobean stage, the outcome of such situations was never good and Roe feared a disastrous ending for Jahângîr; like Timon of Athens, Jahângîr would be "brought low by his own friends / Undone by goodness! strange, unusual blood, /Where man's worst sin is, he does too much good!"[92]

Subtler descriptions and observations, catering to generic plot structures and *mythoi*, are also found in this stage of the narrative. In a letter written to the Archbishop of conterbery, Thomas Roe reveals some deep-rooted and unsavoury characteristics,

> ...to show...what friendships it hath needes and affected; the ambitions and diuisions in the Present state, that like

impostumes lye now hidd, but threaten to breake out into the rending and ruine of the whole by bloody war; the Practices, subtiltyes, and carriages of factions and Court-secretts, falysly called wisdom, wherein I assume your Grace they are pregnant, and excell in all that art which the diuell can teach them.[93]

With the verb "to show," Roe enacts himself as the investigator who brings to light the "impostumes," "practices," and "subtiltyes" which "lye hidd" and "pregnant" underneath the facade of the Mughal political structure and we are reminded of that favourite motif among Jacobean playwrights, the theme of the "disguised Duke." Disguising an agent or the protagonist himself was a popular method by which plays were brought to a climax. In the case of Roman tragedies, Jonson's Macro is instructed by Tiberius to "to be our eye and ear" and "spy, inform and chastise" on Sejanus's movements.[94] Roe's exposure of the Mughal court's "many rare and Cunning Passadges of State, subtile euasions, Policiyes, answers, and adages"[95] is reminiscent of the theatrical techniques used in such plays made up "of whispers, of informers, toadies, flatterers and spies, who congregate in small impenetrabke groups."[96]

A Mughal Perspective of Jahângîr's Court: 1616

The rise to power of the "Nur Jahan junta" after 1611 is a popular feature of Jahângîr's reign among historians. Building conclusions on the observations recorded in *The Embassy*, in addition to commentaries provided in the Mughal chronicles *Iqbâl nâmah-i Jahângîrî* and *Ma'âsir-i Jahângîrî*, we are expected to see Jahângîr as a kindly yet ultimately inept emperor outdone by the intrigues and devices of his "monstrous" immediate family.[97] There can be little doubt that Jahângîr's failing health after 1622 led him to rely increasingly on his wife in matters of state and, as he himself admitted, "I gave the establishment and everything belonging to the government and Amirship of I'timâdu-daulat to Nûrjahân Begam, and ordered that her drums and orchestra should be sounded after those of the king."[98] However, the contention that Nûr Jahan, Khurram, I'timâd al-daulat, and Âsaf Khân operated in a co-ordinated fashion as early as 1615, in addition to being the exclusive recipients of Jahângîr's largesse, is problematic. As Nurul Hasan has argued, there is no evidence to suggest that these four worked conjunctively to supersede the policies of the emperor and, moreover, Hasan calls attention to how scholars have concentrated on the "junta's" rise in *mansabs* while curiously rejecting the significance of the numerous and substantial appointments for Mahâbat Khân, Khân A'zam, Khvâjah Jahân, Khvâjah Abû al-Hasan, and others.[99]

With respect to this early development of Nûr Jahân's power and prestige, the only available evidence comes from Sharif ibn Mu'tumad Khân's *Iqbâl nâmah-i Jahângîrî*.[100] In discussing the sixth year of Jahângîr's reign (1611), Mu'tamad Khân writes, "the Emperor granted Nur Jahan the rights of sovereignty and government" and "on all firmans...receiving the Imperial signature, the name of "Nur Jahan, the Queen Begam," was jointly attached." To punch the point home, he adds the *bayt*: "*bi-hukm-i Shâh Jahângîr yâft sad zîvar/ bi-nâm-i Nûr Jahân Pâdshâh Baigum zar.*"[101] Of course, diplomatic and numismatic evidence is contrary to this statement. While such *farmâns* dating from the later period of Jahângîr's reign do exist, imperial missives and coinage from the period of 1611-16 are conspicuously absent. Moreover, relying on *Iqbâl nâmah-i Jahângîrî* and *Ma'âsir-i Jahângîrî* for information about the Queen Begum is dangerous. These authors were commissioned by Shâh Jahân (r. 1628-1658) to complete the chronicles of his father's reign; in presenting these narratives, however,

Mu'tamad Khân and Khvâjah Kâmgâr Husainî had to delicately rationalize their patron's earlier rebellion in 1622. By depicting Nûr Jahân as a power-hungry royal consort attempting to undermine the pillars of Mughal sovereignty, Shâh Jahân's rebellion is transformed from an act sedition into a gesture of familial loyalty.[102]

Of course, we cannot expect these same sources to shed light on Khurram's "sordid ambitions" in the year 1616. Mu'tamad Khân's only reference to the prince in this year is to mention: "*bih Shâh Khurram mumtâz sakhtând wa mansab-i ân hazrat bîst hizâr wa dah hizâr savâr ... muqarrar gasht.* (Shâh Khurram was distinguished and his *mansab* and *savâr* was changed to 20,000 and 10,000 [respectively]."[103] The emperor's memoirs, *Tûzuk-i Jahângîrî*, are also silent on the prince's supposed domination of the emperor. Jahângîr describes in 1615 how,

> [Khurram] paid his respects [and] laid before me a celebrated ruby of the Rânâ...which the jewelers valued at 60,000 rupees...among the offerings of Bâbâ Khurram was a little crystal box of Frank work, made with great taste, with some emeralds, three rings, four Iraqi horses, and various other things, the value of which was 80,000 rupees.[104]

The prince was very much in the emperor's favour during this period of 1615-16; as the emperor narrates, "the more [Khurram] expressed his reverence and respect for me, the more my tenderness increased towards him."[105] There can be little doubt that Khurram was an ambitious young man and, like many princes, dreamed of the day when he would assume the penultimate title of *pâdshâh*. Roe's belief that Khurram's elevated status in the empire was earned through sycophancy and intrigues, however, does not accurately reflect the events and developments of the last two years. Jahângîr's oldest son, Parvaiz, had seriously bungled the 1612 Deccan campaign and rumours of his excessive drinking were now openly circulating in the

Mughal court. The prudence of relying on Khusrau as a future candidate was also questionable; the last time the emperor had ordered his release, the prince had rebelled in a matter of days. With one prince ensconced in drink and revelry and the other imprisoned for plots and rebellions, Jahângîr predictably turned to Khurram as the only available heir-successor. Khurram, unlike his brothers, was a prudent young man with a keen strategic mind. His methodical elimination of the Mewârî rebellion in 1614 had demonstrated an ability to appreciate the multi-faceted necessities of running a military campaign. His astuteness in such matters, as well as being able to command loyalty from a large cross-section of the military elite, earned him the strategic command of the Deccanî front in 1616. Jahângîr's decision was the right one, and within one year, Mughal armies had reversed the recent successes of Malik 'Ambar and were now in control of most of the Ahmadnagarî kingdom. In matters of succession, Tîmûrid tradition was simple and straight-forward: control of the empire went to the most capable candidate, and, at this stage of Jahângîr's reign, the logical choice could only have been Prince Khurram. With respect to two of the other members of Roe's "faction," Âsaf Khân and I'timâd al-daulat, they are described by the emperor and Mu'tamad Khân only in terms of their merit and contribution to the state. Jahângîr states that I'timâd al-daulat was appointed as *vakîl* because of his "previous service and great sincerity and ability."[106] When one noble, Sâbit Khân, took to "unbecoming speeches" about I'timâd al-daulat and Âsaf Khân, he was severely reprimanded and later punished by Jahângîr for failing to comply.[107] Âsaf Khân's loyalty is alluded to during his grandiose reception of Jahângîr in 1616 in which the *amîr* had arranged for a carpet of "velvet woven with gold brocade," valued at 10,000 rupees, to cover half of the route from the royal palace to his house.[108]

With respect to the axial feature of Roe's 1616 narrative, the pitting of the dearly loved Khusrau against the sly and cunning Khurram, we have little supporting evidence. Khusrau's character, "full of curtesye and affability," can be more accurately explained by Roe's belief that Khusrau was amenable to Christian doctrine and European trade. Roe's estimation that "he loues and honours ... Christians," is difficult to substantiate; effectively imprisoned since 1607, it seems highly unlikely that Khusrau would have had the opportunity to fraternize with European trading agents. In fact when Roe met the imprisoned prince in February 1617, Khusrau himself admitted that he "neuer heard of any ambassador nor English."[109] Regarding the rivalry between the two princes in 1616, it would be reasonable to assume that Khurram indeed felt threatened by his brother. According to Tîmûrid rules of succession, Khusrau would be released and allotted a portion of the Mughal empire after their father's death. Jahângîr's approval of Âsaf Khân's request to assume charge of the imprisoned Khusrau was probably at Khurram's instigation and was most likely done in a bid to keep closer tabs on his rival. His mysterious death of colic pains (*qanânj*) six years later while under his brother's charge only underscores the brutal reality of Mughal polity. These developments, nonetheless, would have been consistent with Tîmûrid and Perso-Islamic traditions; confinement and, occasionally, murder of siblings was a common occurrence in the courts of Kâbul, Samarqand, and Isfahân.

Like any narrative, Roe's account of the Mughal court from 1615 to 1619 has its climaxes and *dénouments*. We cannot, and should not, look upon historical accounts such as this as an objective reporting of the past. From a theoretical perspective, the historical narrative will always be a phenomenon which employs certain literary techniques. Protagonists and antagonists, developments of plots, the rise and resolution of conflict are inherent features of the recording of history. In the case of *The Embassy*, we only find an intensification of this relationship between history and literature. Roe's literary background, and the skills he gleamed from it, needs to be better acknowledged and understood if historians are going to rely on his observations as a viable historiographical source. If we are not more discriminating about our use of *The Embassy*, we ourselves might believe the Mughal empire's "greatnes, compared and weighed iudiciously, is like a play, that serues more for delight and to entertayne."[110]

NOTES

1. Michael Brown, *Itinerant Ambassador: The Life of Sir Thomas Roe* (Lexington: 1970), p. 5.
2. Michael Strachan, *Sir Thomas Roe, 1581-1644: A Life* (London: 1989), p. 1.
3. Strachan, *Sir Thomas Roe*, p. 2.
4. Philip J. Finkelpearl, *John Marston of the Middle Temple: An Elizabethan Dramatist in His Social Setting* (Cambridge: 1969), p. 11.
5. Finkelpearl, *John Marston of the Middle Temple*, p. 31.
6. W. David Kay, *Ben Jonson: A Literary Life* (London: 1995), p. 99.
7. Charles H. Herford and Percy Simpson, *Ben Jonson*, Vol. I (Oxford: 1954), pp. 224-25.
8. Rosalind Miles, *Ben Jonson: His Life and Work* (London: 1986), p. 80.
9. Miles, *Ben Jonson*, p. 80.
10. Herford and Simpson, *Ben Jonson*, Vol. XI, p. 319.
11. Herford and Simpson, *Ben Jonson*, Vol. XI, p. 315.
12. Herford and Simpson, *Ben Jonson*, Vol. XI, p. 319.
13. *Compact Edition of the Dictionary of National Biography* (Oxford: 1975), p. 866.
14. Edmund Gosse, *The Life and Letters of John Donne*, Vol. I (Gloucester: 1959), p. 121.
15. Gosse, *The Life and Letters of John Donne*, Vol. I, p. 232.
16. This letter was written in December of 1607. Gosse, *The Life and Letters of John Donne*, Vol. I, p. 182.
17. Gosse, *The Life and Letters of John Donne*, Vol. II, p. 174.
18. The Scottish Kirk, the head ecclesiastical institution, had obvious problems with James's conception of divine monarchy.
19. The furor over the Protestant Reformation, Queen Mary's stringent Catholic policies between 1553 and 1558, and the war with Spain were some of the key issues for England in this period.

20. For a good discussion of the Hampton Court Conference and the general state of church reform during the reign of James I, see Patrick Collinson, "The Jacobean Religious Settlement: The Hampton Court Conference," in *Before the English Civil War*, ed. H. Tomlinson (London: 1983).
21. The *Basilikon Doron* was written as an instructional manual on kingship for James's son, Henry.
22. Charles H. McIlwain (ed.), *The Political Works of James I*. Reprinted from the Edition of 1616 (Cambridge: 1918), pp. 54-55.
23. Jonathan Goldberg, *James I and the Politics of Literature* (Baltimore: 1983), pp. 44-46.
24. A. Wigfall Green, *The Inns of Court and Early English Drama* (New Haven: 1931), p. 19.
25. Goldberg, *James I and the Politics of Literature*, p. 150.
26. Graham Holderness, "Endgames," in *Shakespeare Out of Court: Dramatization of Court Society*, ed. G. Holderness (New York: 1990), p. 238.
27. Holderness, "Endgames," p. 238. Other sources adopting a similar approach include Peck's edited work, *The Mental World of the Jacobean Court*, Tricomi's *Anticourt Drama in England, 1603-1642*, and Goldberg's *James I and the Politics of Literature*.
28. Leonard Tennenhouse, *Power on Display: The Politics of Shakespeare's Genres* (New York: 1986), p. 15.
29. Stephen Greenblatt, "Invisible Bullets: Renaissance Authority and its Subversion," in *Glyph*, Vol. 8 (1981), p. 57.
30. J.E. Neale, *Elizabeth I and Her Parliaments, 1584-1601*, Vol. II (London: 1965), p. 119.
31. McIlwain (ed.), *Political Works of James I*, p. 5.
32. McIlwain (ed.), *Political Works of James I*, p. 43.
33. Goldberg, *James I and the Politics of Literature*, p. 56.
34. Jerzy Limon, "The Masque of Stuart Culture," in *The Mental World of the Jacobean Court*, ed. L.L. Peck (Cambridge: 1991), p. 209.
35. Linda L. Peck, "The Mental World of the Jacobean Court: An Introduction," in *The Mental World of the Jacobean Court*, ed. L.L. Peck (Cambridge: 1991), p. 7.
36. Sir Francis Bacon, *Novum Organum or true suggestions for the interpretation of nature* (London: 1844), p. 19.
37. In fact, James actually knighted 432 men on his accession day. Linda L. Peck, *Court Patronage and Corruption in Early Stuart England* (Boston: 1990), p. 32.
38. Cecile C. Hanley, *Jacobean Drama and Politics*, Ph.D. Dissertation (Ann Arbor: 1972), p. 8.

39. Albert H. Tircomi, *Anticourt Drama in England, 1603-1642* (Charlottesville: 1989), p. 7.
40. D.H. Loades, *Politics and the Nation* (London: 1972), p. 339.
41. Peck, *Court Patronage*, p. 34.
42. Loades, *Politics and the Nation*, p. 338.
43. Peck, *Court Patronage*, p. 53.
44. John Cox, *Shakespeare and the Dramaturgy of Power* (Princeton: 1989), p. 171.
45. Cox, *Shakespeare and the Dramaturgy of Power*, p. 173.
46. Tricomi, *Anticourt Drama in England*, pp. 34-36.
47. Tricomi, *Anticourt Drama in England*, p. 46.
48. Sir Ralph Winwood, *Memorials of Affairs of State in the Reigns of Queen Elizabeth and King James I*, ed. E. Sawyer, Vol. I (London: 1725), p. 271.
49. Graham Holderness, "Introduction: Theatre and Court," in *Shakespeare Out of Court: Dramatization of Court Society*, ed. G. Holderness (New York: 1990), p. 132.
50. Graham Holderness, "Introduction: Theatre and Court," p. 132.
51. Ben Jonson, *The Selected Plays of Ben Jonson*, Vol. I, ed. J. Proctor (Cambridge: 1939), p. 3.
52. Kay, *Ben Jonson: A Literary Life*, p. 69.
53. Tricomi, *Anticourt Drama in England*, p. 14.
54. This letter was written in October of 1630. Two decades earlier, Roe had been Elizabeth's gentleman-in-waiting prior to her marriage to the Prince of the Palatinate. Malcolm Smuts, *Court Culture and the Origins of the Royalist Tradition in Early Stuart England* (Philadelphia: 1987), p. 90.
55. Roe, *The Embassy of Sir Thomas Roe* (Jalandhar: 1993 reprint), p. 104.
56. C.F. Beckingham, "The Quest for Prester John," in *Between Islam and Christendom: Travelers, Fact, and Legend in the Middle Ages and the Renaissance*, ed. C.F. Beckingham (London: 1983), p. 300.
57. Roe, *The Embassy of Sir Thomas Roe*, p. 14.
58. Roe, *The Embassy of Sir Thomas Roe*, p. 22.
59. Roe, *The Embassy of Sir Thomas Roe*, pp. 70-72.
60. White, "The Historical Text as Literary Artifact," p. 83.
61. Claude Lévi-Strauss, *The Savage Mind* (Chicago: 1966), p. 187.
62. Roe, *The Embassy of Sir Thomas Roe*, p. 87.
63. Roe, *The Embassy of Sir Thomas Roe*, p. 87.
64. Roe, *The Embassy of Sir Thomas Roe*, p. 91.
65. Roe, *The Embassy of Sir Thomas Roe*, p. 269.
66. Roe, *The Embassy of Sir Thomas Roe*, p. 97.
67. Roe, *The Embassy of Sir Thomas Roe*, p. 167.
68. Roe, *The Embassy of Sir Thomas Roe*, p. 230.

69. Roe, *The Embassy of Sir Thomas Roe*, p. 244.
70. Roe, *The Embassy of Sir Thomas Roe*, p. 244.
71. Ben Jonson, *Sejanus*, Act I: Scene i, in *The Complete Plays of Ben Jonson*, ed. F. Schelling, Vol. I, (London: 1910), p. 313.
72. Jonson, *Sejanus*, Act I: Scene i, p. 312.
73. Roe, *The Embassy of Sir Thomas Roe*, p. 256.
74. Roe, *The Embassy of Sir Thomas Roe*, p. 245.
75. Jonson, *Sejanus*, Act II: Scene i, p. 329.
76. Roe, *The Embassy of Sir Thomas Roe*, p. 257.
77. Jonson, *Sejanus*, Act V: Scene x, p. 396.
78. Roe, *The Embassy of Sir Thomas Roe*, pp. 244-45.
79. Roe, *The Embassy of Sir Thomas Roe*, p. 286.
80. Roe, *The Embassy of Sir Thomas Roe*, p. 294.
81. Christopher Marlowe, *Tamburlaine*, ed. J.W. Harper (London: 1971), p. 7.
82. Marlowe, *Tamburlaine*, Act II: Scene vii, lines 12-16.
83. Roe, *The Embassy of Sir Thomas Roe*, p. 325.
84. Roe, *The Embassy of Sir Thomas Roe*, p. 338.
85. William Shakespeare, *Macbeth*, Act I: Scene iv, in *The Complete Works of Shakespeare*, ed. W.J. Craig (London: 1900), p. 1104.
86. Shakespeare, *Cymbeline*, Act II: Scene v, in *The Complete Works of Shakespeare*, p. 943.
87. Shakespeare, *Anthony and Cleopatra*, Act I: Scene ii, in *The Complete Works of Shakespeare*, p. 891.
88. Roe, *The Embassy of Sir Thomas Roe*, p. 245.
89. Roe, *The Embassy of Sir Thomas Roe*, p. 245.
90. Shakespeare, *Macbeth*, Act I: Scene vii, in *The Complete Works of Shakespeare*, p. 1105.
91. Roe, *The Embassy of Sir Thomas Roe*, p. 279.
92. Shakespeare, *Timon of Athens*, Act IV: Scene ii, in *The Complete Works of Shakespeare*, p. 808.
93. Roe, *The Embassy of Sir Thomas Roe*, p. 272.
94. Jonson, *Sejanus*, Act III: Scene iii, p. 358.
95. Roe, *The Embassy of Sir Thomas Roe*, p. 245.
96. Anne Barton, *Ben Jonson, Dramatist* (Cambridge: 1984), p. 100.
97. A number of secondary works have subscribed to this view, including Prasad's *History of Jahangir* (Allahabad: 1920), Ikram's *Muslim Rule in India and Pakistan* (Lahore: 1961), and Findley's *Nur Jahan* (Oxford: 1993).
98. Jahângîr, *Tûzuk-i Jahângîrî*, Vol. II, p. 228.
99. Nurul Hasan, "The Theory of the Nur Jahan 'Junta' - An Examination," in *Proceedings of the Indian History Congress, Trivandrum Session*, Vol. 21 (1958), pp. 324-35.

100. The sections of Khvâjah Kâmgâr Ghairât Khân's *Ma'âsir-i Jahângîrî* pertaining to Nûr Jahân's ascendancy is essentially a duplication of Mu'tamad Khân's work.
101. Mu'tamad Khân, *Iqbâl nâmâh-i Jahângîrî*, ed. Maulana Maulavi Muhammad Rafi' Sahib Fazil Divband (Allahabad: 1931), p. 60.
102. Hasan, "The Theory of the Nur Jahan 'Junta'," p. 326.
103. Khân, *Iqbâl nâmâh-i Jahângîrî*, p. 94.
104. Jahângîr, *Tûzuk-i Jahângîrî*, Vol. I, pp. 285-86.
105. Jahângîr, *Tûzuk-i Jahângîrî*, Vol. I, p. 351.
106. Jahângîr, *Tûzuk-i Jahângîrî*, Vol. I, p. 199.
107. Jahângîr, *Tûzuk-i Jahângîrî*, Vol. I, p. 278.
108. Jahângîr, *Tûzuk-i Jahângîrî*, Vol. I, p. 320.
109. Roe, *The Embassy of Sir Thomas Roe*, p. 342.
110. Roe, *The Embassy of Sir Thomas Roe*, p. 270.

3

SIR THOMAS ROE AS COURTIER

Perception, of course, is a multi-faceted mental process. When encountering an unfamiliar society or culture, we have a large and wide-ranging repository of personal cultural images and experiences from which similarities and analogies can be drawn. While one might unconsciously rely on a particular theme or motif, much like a musician would be prone to concentrating on a culture's approach to metre or melody, the cultural observer is certainly not restricted. Analogical perception can be conducted, consciously or unconsciously, on a number of levels: political, religious, economic, etc. The heterogeneous nature of perception became fully evident during the early modern era as Renaissance humanists began involving themselves in the exploration and 'discovery' of new civilizations. For instance when the French Huguenot Lefèvre encountered the Brazilian Tupi culture in the mid-sixteenth century, he paralleled their proclivity for cannibalism with the Eucharist and the Catholics' eating of Christ's blood and body; in the same narrative, he draws an analogy between the Portuguese terrorization of the Tupis and the Catholic persecution of Protestants during the French Wars of Religion.[1] Of course these analogies were quite deliberate and tend to reflect on the manipulation of encountered cultures for political and religious agendas. The massive documenting efforts of the Jesuit orders during their prosyletization and conversion drives in the New and Old World is a good example of such ulterior motives. What is important here, however, is to acknowledge that humanists were especially adept at pointing out similarities and differences between an encountered culture and that of Europe's; their education and training spanned a large number of areas and disciplines, thus enlarging the potential for cultural comparison and contrast.

In the case of Sir Thomas Roe, we can see this multi-layered recording of perceptions at work. While we have already discussed the extent to which Roe's narrative was influenced by his interaction with the Jacobean literary world, there are other areas of his career, with a corresponding body of experiences and presuppositions, which were equally influential. Already alluded to earlier, Roe was fascinated with the nobility surrounding the emperor and, as a result, much of *The Embassy* is dedicated to presenting what he believed to be the salient features of the Mughal court and its relationship with Jahângîr. Why he might have been so interested is not difficult to explain: Roe had spent close to fifteen years operating as a courtier himself under James I. We are then drawn back to the earlier discussed concepts of "familiarization" and "cultural encodation." If Roe facilitated his rendition of Mughal court politics with popular literary allusions, is it not possible that he looked to other areas of his education and career to supplement his portrayal of Mughal polity? Previously we discussed how the early seventeenth century was an era of politicization for both the elite and commoners of England. A number of controversial issues were coming to the forefront and being debated at every strata of society. MPs were beginning to fidget under the constraints of Stuart absolutism, popular preachers were screaming about clandestine Catholics both in the court and the countryside, and rival courtier groups were publicly accusing each other of criminal misdeeds and corruption. To what extent did Roe's familiarity with these issues, and specifically the terminology, tropes, and images associated with them, carry over into his written account of the Mughal empire ?

We pick up the details of Roe's biography immediately after his education at the Inns and his subsequent friendships with Donne *et alia*. At the turn of the sixteenth century, London was the fastest growing city in Europe. The influx of dispossessed peasantry, the growth of domestic and overseas mercantile activity, and the city's status as the administrative and governmental center of England all contributed to London's fantastic demographic boom.[2] One of the other important factors explaining London's sudden growth was the rising number of landed rural gentry coming to the metropolis in search of careers as lawyers, mercantile company shareholders, government officials, and professional courtiers. As a man of reasonable wealth and substantial education, it was only logical that Thomas Roe's next step after matriculation was to join the exodus to London and the outlying boroughs. Roe opted for the courtier route and quickly secured an appointment as Esquire to the Body of Queen Elizabeth in 1601. It is probable that this service began with a form of apprenticeship, such as acting as one of the twelve Gentlemen of the Privy Chamber, before he assumed the special responsibilities of an Esquire of the Royal Body. Explaining Roe's unruffled entry into courtier circles is not difficult; besides inheriting a sizable portion of his father's estate, the Roe family was reasonably well-connected in London. As mentioned, his grandfather, Sir Thomas, was Lord Mayor in 1568 and his uncle Henry would assume the same position in 1608.[3] Moreover, his step-father, Sir Richard Berkeley, had been appointed Lord Lieutenant of the Tower of London in 1596. Roe's orders as Esquire to the Queen were to guard the monarch's "person by night, to set the watch, and to give the word and to keep good order in the whole house by night, as the Lord Chamberlain and his officers are to do by day."[4]

While the Queen's failing health dictated a rather static political atmosphere from 1601 to 1603, Roe would have certainly been privy to the negotiations and arrangements regarding who was to succeed the childless Elizabeth. After several months of diplomatic dispatches and envoys to and from the north, the Queen formally nominated the King of Scotland, James VI, as her successor. After Elizabeth's death and James I's arrival in 1603, Roe maintained his status as courtier by being appointed a gentleman-in-waiting for Princess Elizabeth, James's only daughter.[5] Lord Harington, after receiving a Privy Seal charging him with the protection and education of the king's daughter, established a lavish household at Combe Abbey located near Coventry. For two years Roe lived at this abbey and served as the princess's gentleman-in-waiting. In 1605, Roe's tenure as a resident courtier was interrupted when he was assigned to the earl of Nottingham's entourage being sent to Spain to conduct peace negotiations. This ambassadorial mission, discussed in further detail later on, was successful and an Anglo-Spanish peace was finally secured after nearly seventy years of enmity. The massive English entourage concluded its one month mission in Spain and set sail back home. Roe, however, decided to remain in Europe and spent the rest of 1605 serving in a number of English garrisons across the Netherlands.[6]

After his return from continental Europe, Roe expanded his interest to exploration by being appointed as a member of the Royal Council for Virginia on 9 March 1606. The Virginia Colony, established by Sir Walter Raleigh in 1585, and again in 1590, offered attractive trade possibilities for many of the courtier and mercantile elements of London. In addition to serving on the Royal Council, consisting of powerful court personalities like Sir Thomas Smythe and Sir Edwin Sandys, Roe also became a shareholder in the chartered Company of Adventurers and Planters of the City of London for the First Colony in Virginia. Eventually a new council for the Company was set up and headed by the Earls of Southampton, Pembroke, Lincoln, Exeter, and Lord Carew, Roe's lifelong friend.[7] Interaction with these men allowed Roe, as an aspiring courtier, to witness firsthand the court and its patronage system. While traditional English historians such as Trevor-Roper and Zagorin separate and isolate the royal court from parliament and other governmental machinery, revisionists like Conrad Russell suggest that all governmental and business matters were conducted under the larger umbrella of court politics and patronage.[8] Moreover, there is a twentieth-century assumption that such patronage policies were somehow unique or uncommon in a seventeenth-century setting. James I's reign has been characterized as morally and financially stagnated; specifically, historians look to the Stuart king's extravagant gift-giving as an explanation of the crown's economic crisis. Further, James was considered particularly prone to favouritism, evident in the arrival of the Scottish courtiers in the English court and their subsequent rise under the auspices of their former king. An emphasis was placed on the crown's cannibalising of patronage, i.e. selling various honors, titles, licenses, and offices, to regenerate the royal coffers.[9] However, a new generation of court historians (Levy, Smuts) have argued how the language and behavior of the Jacobean courtiers was consistent with early modern administration.

While acknowledging that there was increasing pressure to curb such corrupt practices, scholars have stressed the existence of a general understanding among the ruling elite of how patron-client relations were to be conducted; furthermore, critics of royal patronage did little to challenge this understanding. Early modern political theorists saw the king as a guarantor of justice and dispenser of favour. Royal largesse significantly expanded under the Tudors as Henry VIII and Elizabeth I both implemented healthy policies of selling offices and dispensing court positions. This concept of symbiosis was largely based on the Stoic philosopher Seneca's *On Benefits*, an influential text among

Jacobean humanists with their newfound affinity for anything Roman.[10] The basic idea was that, in return for a gift or bounty, a subject reciprocated with unyielding loyalty and service. This type of reward was essential to the king because he could thereby reinforce the reciprocal bonds established between the Crown and the political elite.[11] James's advice manual, *Basilikon Doron*, refers to this definition,

> The more frequently that your court can be garnished with them (gifts); thinke it the more your honour; acquanting and employing them in all your greatest affaires; sen it is, they must be your armies and executors of laws...as may make the greatest of them to thinke, that the chiefest point of their honour, standeth in striuing with the meanest of the land in humilitie towards you, and obedience to your laws.[12]

Operating on the principle of using "trew liberalitie in rewarding the good, and bestowing frankly for your honour and weale," James believed that duty and servitude would naturally follow from the grateful recipients.[13] Considering there was no central or local bureaucracy directly administered by parliament or king, nor a standing army, the function of gift-giving and office sales was central to the maintenance of the monarchy. As Holderness comments, "court members saw themselves as part of a court which was a microcosmic model of the universe of which the king was the creator and controller."[14] The significant increase in the created number of offices and the expansion of landed gentry resulted in vigorous competition; as a result, control of access to the Jacobean court was deemed a valuable commodity. To participate in the court one was forced to navigate a complicated system of court patronage; in this, one engaged the services of a broker who could guarantee adoption by a major patron in the court.[15] Predictably, corruption like this did not go unnoticed and court observers, believing avaricious societies to be marked for apocalyptic judgment, were quick to criticize. Contemporary John Chamberlain described the competition as "the court fever of hope and fear that continuously torments those that depend upon great men and their promises."[16] An anonymous discourse discusses how "the courtier knoweth the secrets of Court, judgeth them not, but useth them for his particular advantage. He is a great dissembler, for he that knoweth not how to put on that vizard is not fit to live in the courts of princes."[17] Smuts reminds us, however, that the majority of great courtiers were not politicians in the modern sense: men strictly interested in pursuing official appointments and exerting control over the state's patronage resources. They were peers or royal favourites who saw political power as a natural extension of high birth and personal influence. Rivalry among them took place not only in the Council Chamber but in all environments where they might influence the king, and often through activities that we would not readily associate with high politics.[18] It should be noted that one of the underpinning features of the Jacobean courtier system was securing appointments through bribery and gift-giving. Ambitious gentry could guarantee landed aristocracy status through simply buying a title. Moreover, royal appointments to important offices, such as lieutenantcies and Justices of the Peace, were facilitated by generous 'donations' to courtiers who happened to enjoy some proximity to the king.[19]

Roe's involvement in court politics intensified as he developed a close relationship with James I's son, Prince Henry; as heir-apparent, Henry was touted by the anti-Spanish faction as the future champion and defender of the Protestant cause. With the increasing involvement of state governments in the expansion of overseas commerce and empire building, the New and Old Worlds were now seen as a new frontier for continuing the century-old conflict between Catholic and Protestant Europe. When Sir Walter Raleigh returned from his exploration of Guiana in the late 1590s, there was excited talk in the royal court of El Dorado, a city made of gold with fantastically wealthy citizens. To Prince Henry and the anti-Spanish faction, Guiana was seen as the key to the reversal of the Spanish empire in the Americas. By virtue of his close relationship with hispanophobes like the Earl of Carlisle and the Archbishop of Canterbury, it would seem reasonable to conclude that Roe was himself a staunch Protestant nationalist who, like many of colleagues, sought a policy of isolating and containing the powerful Habsburg empire. This, combined with the promise of lucrative profits, best explains Roe's decision to throw his lot in with Prince Henry, Robert Cecil, and other prominent courtiers organizing the South American trading venture. The Guiana expedition of 1610 proved to be an utter failure. Roe himself was part of the crew which spent nearly a year sailing amongst a maze of estuaries and rivers along the coast of South America before deciding to cut their losses and returning to England.

Interpreting Roe and his involvement in the Guiana project as simply another private mercantile enterprise would be a bit inexact; this expedition was also highly reflective of the court and courtier politics in the early seventeenth century. Although friendship with Spain was the primary ambition of His Majesty's foreign policy, Roe nevertheless associated himself with a venture which was conceived and commanded by persons close to the anti-Spanish faction. The opposing "Spanish" faction had been doing its best to pressure both court and king towards positive relations with Spain. Consisting of courtiers like Henry Howard, the Lord Privy Seal, Charles Howard, the Earl of Nottingham, and Thomas Howard, the Lord Chamberlain, the Spanish Faction exercised some dominance between 1603 and 1612, highlighted by the negotiated peace with Spain in 1604. Their efforts were constantly frustrated by the French faction, comprising the Duke of Lennox, the Earl of Carlisle, the Earl of Pembroke, the Archbishop of Canterbury, George Abbot, and James's wife, Queen Anne.[20]

The organization of joint-stock companies, like the East India and Levant Companies, was initially free of political influences; the trading magnates of Jacobean London were adamant that their trading institutions were not to be used as vehicles for establishing an overseas empire. As they had learned from the Portuguese, controlling and redirecting the flow of overseas commodities opened up debilitating areas of expense: forts, local bureaucracies, ship-building yards, etc. Nonetheless, the Spanish and Portuguese were deeply antagonistic to the arrival of the English in the East Indies, the Caribbean, and North America and companies like the EIC were forced to fight tooth and nail for their trading niches. Despite the recent peace, English anti-Catholic sentiments were still running high and any reversal of Iberian trading fortunes in the New and Old World was certainly allowable, if not outright encouraged. The growing polemic of anti-popery in court and parliament, combined with the occasional naval battle in the Indian Ocean or off the coast of Barbados, eventually politicized joint-stock company commercial expeditions. Allowing this, the Guiana venture of 1610 was not only a personal financial venture for Sir Thomas Roe but also a valuable lesson in the niceties of Jacobean foreign policy and their relationship with factional court dynamics.

Historiographically, it was once popular to present Jacobean government as neatly divided between court and parliament; courtiers were seen as crypto-Catholics and staunch advocates of Stuart absolutism, while the parliamentarians were juxtaposed as the Puritan-minded opposition dedicated to establishing responsible representative government. This surgical approach to court and parliament composition conveniently situated the majority of the court among the pro-Spanish or French factions, and the House of Commons was juxtaposed as the driving force behind public demands for a political union with north European Protestant powers. There is little doubt that divided camps did exist in parliament and court, and foreign policy would have been a major galvanizer of such factional groups, but the nature of early seventeenth-century court politics was much more fluid and dynamic. While lines were drawn among courtiers and parliamentarians on points of foreign policy, other debated issues contributed to courtiers and MPs frequently and unabashedly crossing factional boundaries. How else can we explain the careers of men like the parliamentarian Thomas Wentworth ? Initially an ardent critic of James I's policy of conciliation towards Catholic France and Spain, Wentworth would eventually become the same Earl of Strafford who proposed the use of Catholic Irish troops to suppress the agitated 1640 Parliament during the reign of Charles I! Moreover, believing in the tenets of absolutism did not necessarily entail supporting a pro-Catholic domestic and foreign policy. Some of James I's closest supporters, including Archbishop Abbot, were the leading proponents of increasing legislation against Catholic recusancy in conjunction with adopting a hostile stance towards the Spanish Habsburgs. Even Roe's immediate circle of friends and patrons tends to reflect the amorphous nature of Jacobean court affiliations. On one hand, his access to the court was made possible by men who were staunch advocates of Stuart absolutism, including Archbishop Abbot, the Secretary of State, Sir Ralph Winwood, and the Lord Exchequer Lord Carr. On the other, he still managed to continue his friendships with Sir Edwin Sandys, Nicholas Fulbrooke, and Sir Dudley Digges, men who had dedicated their parliamentary careers to reversing what they considered arbitrary rule.

After the disaster of the Guiana expedition, Roe decided to return to Princess Elizabeth's service since no aspiring courtier could afford to be away from the court, the source of all patronage and sponsorship. 1611 proved to be a dynamic year in Jacobean foreign policy, the effects of which would change Roe's life forever. In September, the Duke of Savoy suggested a double marriage between his two eldest children and those of James I. Meanwhile, King Philip III of Spain was secretly inquiring whether Princess Elizabeth would convert to Catholicism and marry him. The Prince of Wales, Henry, was violently opposed to a marriage treaty with either of these 'popish' rulers and advocated negotiations with the Elector Palatine, Frederick. Calls for an alliance with a Protestant power were echoed throughout the English court since Spain, having recently signed the Truce of Antwerp with the Netherlands, was now free to pursue designs elsewhere in Europe.[21] The international Protestant cause had many advocates among the servants of James I: Thomas Roe, Archbishop Abbot and court peers like the Earl of Pembroke.

Anti-catholicism was a pervasive element in seventeenth-century English society and the early reign of James I was certainly no exception. The alleged Gunpowder Plot of 1605, in which Guy Fawkes 'confessed' to a fantastic Catholic plot to blow up the Parliament, only reinforced reactions against any proposed alliances with France or Spain. In May 1612, articles for the marriage between Frederick and Elizabeth were drawn up, and in October the Elector Palatine landed at Gravesend to escort his bride to the Bohemian court. Unfortunately for Roe, his immediate sponsor, Prince Henry, died on 6 November. This, combined with the recent death of another important patron, Robert Cecil, Earl of Salisbury, deprived Roe of two of his most critical court contacts. The Howard faction, temporarily set back by James's decision not to appoint one of their supporters to the office of secretary, moved quickly. In 1613, the divorce between Lady Frances Howard, the Earl of Suffolk's daughter, and the Earl of Essex enabled Lady Frances to marry the king's favourite, Robert Carr (now the Earl of Somerset). The aforementioned dynamism of the Jacobean court is no better evident in Roe's decision to associate himself with the rising star of Carr, "the king's minion," who soon filled Cecil's shoes as the principal advisor to James I until his imprisonment in 1615.[22] Nonetheless, Carr and the Howards' agenda of blocking the marriage alliance with the Palatinate was unsuccessful and Elizabeth and Frederick were married on 14 February 1613. As Elizabeth's gentleman-in-waiting, Roe was obliged to escort Queen Elizabeth to the Palatinate the following April.

Although the details of this diplomatic event are discussed later, it was during his short stay at Spa, Holland following the wedding that we learn of an interesting episode where Roe participated in a intense religious debate with Father Thomas Wright, the Jesuit-trained theologian appointed to the Apostolic Nuncio of Cologne. Wright's career is certainly an interesting one. After being imprisoned for subversion in 1597, he was released and banished from England in 1603. After secretly returning, Wright was appointed by the Privy Council to represent the infamous Guy Fawkes in 1605. He spent the next three years working for toleration of Catholics in England but was eventually forced to flee to Holland. After meeting at Spa, the two men, one Catholic and the other Protestant, debated various topics, including the remission of sins, the saliency of Calvinist doctrine, transubstantiation, and papal infallibility. The discussions were recorded and later published in 1614 by the Irish Catholic James Nixon under the title *Quatuor Colloquia*. William Trumbull, the British representative at the court of Liège, sent a copy to one of Roe's court allies, the Archbishop of Canterbury. The archbishop replied, "Sir Thomas Roe is a proper gentleman, and goeth among the number of the writs, so that when they [the Jesuits] choose him for a disputer against Wright and can make no greater triumph of it than in the pamphlet they do, it goeth very hard with them." Nixon's biased presentation of the Roe-Wright debate at Spa forced Thomas's cousin, William Roe, to publish *Epilogus ad Quatuor Colloquia*, or "Epilogue to the Four

Conversations of Dr. Wright, held in bad faith; and recorded not in good faith by James Nixon of Ireland, and dedicated to William Stanley, a man of no faith, our enemy. Published on behalf of the author's friend and relation, Sir Thomas Roe." William Roe applauds his cousin in the preface, "Although my relation Sir Thomas Roe was not accustomed to such disputes on religion, still so great is the sharpness of his intellect and the strength of his faith that your Dr. Wright wasted his labour and hopes on him. This is quite certain from this fragmentary and deceptive narrative of yours."[23] Whether or not the accounts of the debate were entirely accurate is unclear but it did promote Roe's reputation as a champion of the Protestant cause and only further strengthened the bond between himself and the archbishop.[24]

Another important feature of Roe's courtier career was his subsequent tenure as a Gentleman of James I's Privy Chamber.[25] Traditionally, most courtiers coveted a position in the Privy Chamber, the forum in which bureaucratic agencies like the Secretaryship and the Exchequer conferred and debated policy with the king. However the initial years of James I's reign saw significant changes in the relative importance of the Privy Chamber and the Bedchamber. Alluded to earlier, there was a significant degree of trepidation among Englishmen with the coronation of a Scottish king to the English throne. Predictably, James attempted to secure lucrative offices for the Scottish courtiers, most notably the Duke of Lennox who had accompanied him to London from Edinburgh. Alarmed at the introduction of this "barbarous" Scottish element to Westminster, English courtiers did their best to frustrate and block James's efforts. James stacked the staff of his Bedchamber with Scots and, in doing so, began allocating to this institution many of the administrative power previously held by the Privy Chamber. The Privy Chamber was relegated to formal, ceremonial duties, while the Bedchamber became the focus of the monarch's private life.[26] This newly restricted access to the king's person only contributed to favouritism trends in the Jacobean court. However, a telling feature of this development in political dynamics and court structure is the shift towards personal contact with the monarch; the formal, administrative ethos of the relationship between the Privy Chamber and the monarch was being abandoned and replaced with a system which operated more on the principle of personal access. This certainly blended well with the Senecan theory of kingship and its emphasis on the monarch being the sole fount of appointments and largesse. Roe's appointment as James's Gentleman only lasted one year; perhaps the aforementioned de-evolution of the Privy Chamber influenced Roe's decision to become a Member of Parliament in 1614 (a development discussed in chap. 5). Nonetheless, during this year Roe was able to leave the provincial confines of Combe Abbey, where he had once fondly attended on Princess Elizabeth, and move to the political hub of England—Westminster. Roe's duties, as discussed, would have been strictly ceremonial, but he performed them efficiently enough to impress the king. Eighteen months later, he would be nominated as England's first ambassador to the Mughal empire.

Factions and Favourites: Roe's Depiction of the Mughal Court and Indo-Islamic Administration

Not unlike some of the circulating European rumours and imagery of Asian potentates, there were also popular preconceptions regarding an Asian ruler's court and nobility. Under the umbrella of unyielding absolutism, the courts of Tîmûr, Chingîz Khân, and the Great Turk were considered arenas of extreme cruelty, intrigue, and more than a little debauchery. The nobility under such rulers were nothing more than peons, doing little to usher in any of the democratic developments supposedly taking place in early modern Europe, and the administration was designed for one purpose: the ruthless extraction of wealth through taxation. Thomas Roe's familiarity with this imagery, evident in popular playpieces like Marlowe's *Tamburlaine*, has already been discussed. Moreover, his interaction with overseas merchant institutions was now introducing the enterprising Jacobean to stories, fables, and reports of overseas rulers and their courts. While en route to India through the Atlantic and Arabian Oceans, Roe had his first encounters with Asian court systems; although somewhat primitive in design and ambition, these courts reflect some of Roe's preconceptions. During a rest-stop in Molalia off the coast of Africa, the crew of the expedition went ashore to meet the local *sultân*. 'Umar ibn 'Âdil was "akinne to Mahomette, not unlike to be descended of such an imposturous race; his cloathes not vnlike the Gouernors but somwhat better stuffe; his manners differing much, being with lesse grauitie and state; somewhat a light foole, and yeary hastie to be druncke, with wyne carried by the English."[27] When the EIC trading fleet later temporarily anchored off the city of Socotra, Roe himself remained on board and "gleand the most probable reports" from the landing party led by Captains Keeling and Newport. Despite not being a first-hand observer, Roe apparently felt comfortable enough to describe how the Socotran *sultân* "reignes soe absolutely that noe man can sell any thing but him selfe" and that his subjects "dare not speake without lycence' and 'kisse his foote, and these doe all his worke and make his aloese."[28] The fleeting, and rather judgmental, nature of these perceptions suggests that Roe had his reservations about Asian systems of rule. These feelings were more than likely rooted in the centuries-old European romantic discourse towards Islamic, specifically Ottoman, despotism. Roe could not (or would not) disassociate himself from these trends, obvious in the description of his first encounter with a Mughal royal family member. We have already examined his remarks for their literary potential, but his portrayal of Prince Parvaiz in his "great but baborous state" in the *dîvân-i 'amm* of Burhânpûr, where the "great men of the towne with their handes before them like slaves," rings of the popular European imagery of Asian courts. These motifs would continue throughout *The Embassy* but were ultimately insufficient for Roe's intended "universall description."

While no doubt coloured by the imagery of his European contemporaries, Roe was still a trained scholar and humanist who strove to convey his impressions and understandings. The daunting unfamiliarity of the mechanisms, language, and systems used in the Mughal court, however, was a formidable barrier for the Jacobean ambassador. Roe's tenure as Esquire to Elizabeth I (1601-03), Gentleman-in-Waiting for Princess Elizabeth (1603, 1612-14), and Gentleman of the Privy Chamber under James I (1612-14) had introduced him to a number of Jacobean court mechanisms. Key features included a symbiotic system of patronage between the monarchy and its subjects, a network whereby an aspiring courtier curried favor through bribes and gift-giving, and, a number of interest groups who were roughly defined by their international allegiances and were constantly contending for James I's countenance. Further to the premise of Roe "familiarizing" the Mughal experience, we detect a recurrence of these traits and others when examining Roe's remarks on the Mughal court.

Of course, Roe's initial perceptions of the Mughal court on 10 January 1616 were strictly visual and rather fleeting; his lack of Persian and the overwhelming novelty of his new ambassadorial station made any initial significant understanding of the institution impossible. Interestingly, he must have made a substantial effort, probably through enquiries to other Englishmen, to understand the Mughal system of noble and land appointments. In a letter he wrote to Lord Carew only one week after his arrival in Ajmîr, Roe gives a description of how "the great men about [Jahângîr] are not borne Noble, but Fauorities raised; to whom hee giueth wonderfull meanes" and that they are ranked "by Horses; that is to say; Coronels of twelue thousand Horses, which is the greates: so descending to twentie Horses." These "Coronels" were *mansabdârs*, or "holders of rank," who were expected to equip a requisite contingent of armed cavalrymen (*savâr*) and had a personal numerical rank (*zât*).[29] Roe makes note that these appointments were not hereditary and that the emperor was free to revoke a *mansabdâr's savâr* and *zât*: "as they die, and must needs gather, so it returneth to the King like Riuers to the sea, both of those he gave to, and of those that haue gained by their owne industry." With respect to how appointments are secured, Roe believes that "they all rise by presenting him, which they striue to doe both richly and rarely, some giuing a hundred thousand pounds in iewels at a time."[30] While his assessment of this system is rudimentarily sound, the theme of nobles seeking *mansabdârî* appointments strictly through gifts and cash is problematic and worth examining; Roe's oversimplification of the Mughal administrative system, and more specifically its familiarity with certain Jacobean court terminology and procedures, is persistently reinforced throughout *The Embassy*. In another letter, he relates that "all men ryse to greater and greater seignoryes, as they rise in fauour, which is only gotten by frequent presents, both rich and rare."[31] Jahângîr is presented as a king whose countenance is impossible without some form of gift-giving: "for presents I had none, and the King neuer takes any request to hart except it come accompaned, and will in playne tearmes demand yt."[32] Mughal *mansabdârs* being described, not as nobleborns, but as "Fauorites raised" is reminiscent of the English court where favourites, like Robert Carr and George Villiers, prospered as a result of their personal relationship with James I. Moreover, Roe's understanding of *zât* and *savâr* as gifts, or "wonderfull meanes," which the nobility are not "bound to keepe or raise at all" can be construed as a parallel interpretation of James I's patronage policies. The manner in which nobles "all rise by presenting him, which they striue to doe both richly and rarely" implies an exchanging of titles and ranks for gifts, a well-documented characteristic of the financially strapped Jacobean monarchy.

Predictably, court dynamics, and specifically the means of self-advancement, are a popular topic for Roe. As an ambassador hoping to garnish certain advantageous trading concessions, access to the inner sanctum of the Mughal political scene was critical for Roe but, as Âsaf Khan told him, "[he] was a stranger and knew not the pace of the court."[33] Roe's training as a courtier was a Jacobean one and it should be not surprising that he looked to his own experiences as a potential guide while serving in the Mughal court. In one of his many letters to the EIC, Roe instructs his sponsors on their future policies in the Indian subcontinent. Much of the letter discusses the holistic trade practices in the Indian Ocean, however in a postscript Roe suggests,

> The best way to doe your busines in this Court is to find some Mogol that you may enterteyne for 1000 rupees by the yeare as your solicitor at Court. Hee must bee authorised by the King, and then hee will better serue you then ten Ambassadors. Vnder him you must allowe 500 rupees for another at your Port to follow the Gouernor and Customers and to aduertise his Cheefe at Court. These two will effect all....[34]

This observation is consistent with Linda Peck's discussion on Jacobean court patronage where access to resources at the early Stuart court was controlled by major patrons.[35] The Jacobean practice of engaging intermediaries, or "broakers," is referred to periodically by Roe as the best recourse for aspiring courtiers and ambassadors. For instance, by October of 1616 he realized that the Mughals were hesitant to shrug off the economic influences of the Portuguese *Estado da India*. Believing that the continued presence of the Portuguese would only impede the success of the EIC, Roe went to the home of Prince Khurram, the Gujarât governor, to convince him of the advantages of trading exclusively with the English. During the conversation, Roe placated Khurram "for respect for his Highnes I addressd my selfe to him, both to acquaynt him with the Propositions, to desier his fauour, and to obteyne his Mediation to present mee to the King at Night."[36] Roe apparently believed that, like the Jacobean court, there could be a number of potential conduits; earlier he had approached Âsaf Khân who told Roe that "hee would write on the morrow to ['Abd Allâh Khân] and to two other frends he had there, who should be solicitors for the English."[37] Roe's hope of using Khurram, Âsaf Khân, and 'Abd Allâh Khân as means of breaching the Mughal king's inaccessibility is interesting. While these verbal exchanges certainly took place, one should be careful in assuming that there was an implicit understanding between the English ambassador and the Mughal officers. As will be discussed, the Mughal emperor and his surrounding elite had no interest in issues of trade. Confining themselves to the simple extraction of taxes and port tariffs, Mughal officers treated any participation in the actual regulation of trade with complete disdain. To solicit a Mughal state functionary as great as Khurram or Âsaf Khân for the purposes of representing an insignificant nation's commercial interests was a doomed enterprise. It seems likely that Roe approached these men with the hopes of obtaining "fauour" and "Mediation" but did not realize the extent to which such Jacobean court procedures were inapplicable.

The Mughal court was not a permanent fixture like its counterpart in Westminster. Akbar and Jahângîr had built a number of royal palaces across the Indo-Gangetic Plain in Lahore, Âgrâ, Fâtihpûr Sikrî, Delhî, Ajmîr, and Mandû. Rarely occupying a city's palace for more than three years at a time, the Mughal emperors preferred to periodically shift the court and its royal entourage as their Tîmûrid ancestors had done in the upper reaches of Central Asia. Ostensible motives for court nomadism could vary, inclement weather or a strategic need to be near an ongoing campaign, but the underlying rationale was to ensure a constant visual display of imperial power in the varying regions of the Mughal empire. Likewise the features and functions of the Mughal court differed significantly from that of James I. The English court, being a place where matters of state were discussed, was highly restricted even among relatively trusted officials, but the Mughal court, specifically the *savâr-i 'âmm* (public hall), was much more accessible. Of course, there were locations in the Mughal court, the *ghusâl khânah* (private baths) and the *dîvân-i khâss* (special audience chamber), where access was strictly controlled, but for the most part trusted nobles and courtiers were free to come and go in the main Mughal court, or *darbâr*. To Roe's credit, he makes an effort to use the appropriate terms, like *ghusâl khânah* and *darbâr*, but some of his other descriptions include some intricate Jacobean references which colour, if not distort, the overall impression of the Mughal court. In one instance, Roe writes to the EIC how, after the company's first delivery of royal gifts, "Contentment outwardly appeared, but I will acquaynt you with the Cabinettes opinion, by which you may Judg. Three exceptions were taken by the King and his Priuadoes."[38] Here, the Mughal administration is styled as a "cabinette," an obvious use of English governmental nomenclature. Moreover, this term is reinforced by Jahângîr's counsel being depicted as *privadoes*, a Spanish term meaning "intimate friends" which had been used by Jacobean contemporaries to designate the pro-Spanish Howard faction close to King James I. On another occasions Roe refers to Jahângîr's functionaries as *cavalleros* and *fiadors*, meaning "gentlemen' and 'sureties" respectively.[39] The consistent use of these and other Iberian terms (*scrivano* (scribe), *procuador* (procurer), *soldado* (soldier) and *serraglio* (harem) is an extremely interesting feature of *The Embassy* and worth examining in more detail.

One might argue that such terminology is more reflective of the Spanish court of Philip III, but we have to remember that a healthy Spanish lobby group was operating in the Jacobean court during Roe's tenure as a courtier. The efforts of the Howards to arrange a diplomatic marriage with the Spanish Hapsburgs, and to generally orient English foreign policy towards the Mediterranean, were some of the most hotly contested issues of the early seventeenth century. The reaction of stalwart Protestants like Prince Henry, Archbishop Abbott, and a majority of the House of Commons was predictably belligerent. Besides openly obstructing the Howards' agenda, the anti-Spanish contingent also adopted a belligerent hispanophobe rhetoric to describe the overly 'popish' trends of the Jacobean court. Probably the principal target of this anti-Catholic court rhetoric was Gondomar, the Spanish ambassador who was well-known for his fraternization with the king and certain members of the court. An anonymous pamphleteer warned the king that Gondomar is "maister of your cabinett without a key, and knowes your secrets before the greatest part and most faithful of your councel."[40] Another nameless petition describes the hispanophile Howard family and their supporters as that "Jesuitical Hispanized Faction of Falsehood, Hipocrisy, Sedition and Treason."[41] Why Roe decided to use this same rhetoric and its accompanying terminology to describe the composition and personalities of the Mughal court is intriguing. As James I was surrounded by a faction which sought to strengthen relations with Philip III, likewise we see the Mughal court divided into two groups over the issue of a pro-Iberian foreign and commercial policy.

As Roe familiarized himself with the court proceedings, he grew to believe that "the Portugalls haue Crept into this Kingdome, and by what Corners they gott in." Typical of his hostile Catholic stance, Roe lamented the "enterance of the Jesuits, their entertaynment, Priuiledges, Practises, endes, and the growth of their Church, wherof they sing In Europe so loud Prayses and glorious successes."[42] He was also convinced that the Jesuit "faction," led by Jerome Xavier (grandson of St. Francis Xavier), was misrepresenting and frustrating English ambitions: "for [they] dive deepe into your secretts and blaze them."[43] The combination of the Portuguese presence in the Mughal court and the military threat of the *Estado da India's* ships, was obviously worrisome to Roe. In a letter to the Portuguese Viceroy of Goa, he warned: "wishing Your Excellence to remember what the wronges offered by your nation did cost you; how many millions, both men and crownes, in the days of the blessed and famous Queen Elizabeth."[44] English nationalism was no small part of this animosity; Roe and any other seventeenth-century Englishman would never lose an opportunity to remind the Spaniards of their disastrous routing off the coast of England in 1588. The Iberian presence in the Indian subcontinent was obviously being undermined by the arrival of the north Atlantic trading companies but the brutal policing policy of the *Estado da India* in the Arabian Ocean was also beginning to erode relations with the indigenous rulers. All ships were expected to purchase and carry a pass (*cartaze*) which listed the eligible ports of trade and types of cargo to be carried; violating the stipulations of the *cartaze* could result in a seizure by Portuguese authorities.[45] Particularly offensive to the Mughals was the strict control of all *hajj* traffic to Mekkah and when the Portuguese boarded and looted the *Rahîmî*, a royal vessel, in 1613, relations visibly degenerated. Muqarrab Khân, the governor of Sûrat, was ordered to besiege the Portuguese-held port of Damân and the Jesuit church at

Âgrâ was closed down.[46] But Roe's anxieties about the Portuguese influence were justified to a certain extent. Three months before his arrival, tensions had dissipated and a preliminary peace treaty was organized between Muqarrab Khân, Father Xavier of the Jesuit Order, and Gonçalo Pinto da Fonseca of the *Estado da India*. Subject to final approval by the emperor, this treaty called for the banishment of the English and the Dutch from Mughal territories. By October 1615, it was clear that the Mughals were holding off on committing themselves to the Portuguese; as Captain Kerridge wrote, "the expected peace with the Portugalls is confidently broken of."[47] Not surprisingly, Roe's commentary on the Portuguese was also influenced by his own providential Calvinist views: God "doth chastise [the Portuguese], and [their] pride sees it not...All these considered, mee thincks the Heauenes conspire the fall of the Portugall in this quarter."[48]

Much like the divided court of James I, with the "seditious Iesuiticall and Spanish" Howards cavorting with known Catholic elements, we see the Mughal *darbâr* dominated by a group linked with the aforementioned Jesuits and Iberian trading agents. Not surprisingly, this group are the same individuals, Prince Khurram, Âsaf Khân, Nûr Jahân, and I`timâd al-daulat, responsible for subverting Jahângîr's authority and supposedly engineering the removal of Khusrau. The Mughal ruling elite were certainly no fools and realized that a policy of vacillation towards the Portuguese and the English would be advantageous. Using the English to displace the heavily-entrenched Portuguese in Gujarât, the Mughals were also refraining from a full commitment to the EIC in the hopes of soliciting gifts and increased economic concessions. In Roe's estimation, this was motivated out of weakness; as he wrote King James I, "they feare the Portugall, they fear vs, and betweene both patch vp a frendship."[49] However, the English ambassador lay the blame for his inability to procure the much-coveted bilateral trading agreement squarely on the shoulders of the "pro-Portuguese" faction. Led by the now infamous Khurram, *The Embassy* recounts how "the Prince dislikes vs, and though he fauour no Christian, yet the Portugall [he favours] the most" and that "it was our misfortune that this gouernment is fallen into the Princes hands, who hates all Christians...his faction is strong."⁵⁰ Âsaf Khân, Khurram's aide-de-camp, had engaged the EIC "into this miserye, knowing him to be a protector of [the Portuguese] and a slaue to their bribes."⁵¹ Roe confronted Khurram on these matters on 14 October 1616 and attempted to argue the dangers of continuing his alliance with the Portuguese but found "no disposition in this Prince to breake with them." When Roe pressed his case further, Khurram "answered with scorne that his father nor hee needed our assistance: he ment not warr with the Portugall for ous sakes, neyther would euer deliuer any fort to vs."⁵² Mughal accounts are silent regarding this court intrigue between nationally-aligned factions. References to the Portuguese and English can be found in documents contemporary to Roe, but these are few and far between and can hardly substantiate the portrayal of a European-dominated Mughal court.⁵³

Monarchical Status and the Nobility in Mughal India

Understanding court features and dynamics in the Mughal setting is impossible without appreciating Indo-Islamic perceptions of kingship. The underlying foundations of the emperor's prerogative and right to rule are key to, not only the workings of the court and the surrounding administration, but to the entire ethos of the empire. While Muslim Indian statesmen had been deeply influenced by orthodox *sunnî* political thought, they had largely adopted the pre-Islamic Sassanian model of kingship which had been resurrected by the twelfth-century Perso-Islamic world. The theoretically egalitarian approach of *sunnî* Islam in determining who was to rule an Islamic state was eventually subsumed by the ancient cult of hereditary monarchs which had been so popular in ancient Iran and Central Asia. The Mughal approach to kingship and its role in the Indian context, however, was somewhat unique and can be accounted for by a number of variables: a predominantly Hindu populace, deeply rooted ties to the Tîmûrid dynasty, and an amalgamation of *sunnî* and *shî'î* definitions of authority. Nonetheless, Mughal monarchical authority is an area of some debate; motives aside, historians of pre-modern India have presented a wide spectrum of interpretations on this matter with conclusions varying from arbitrary despotism to enlightened Muslim rule. Scholarship, however, is in agreement that the Mughal ruler exercised almost unlimited power in every significant department of the empire: governance, revenue, judiciary, army, etc. The extent of these prerogatives, combined with the relative success of the Mughals in the sixteenth and seventeenth centuries, has raised several questions. How was the emperor able to maintain his status as the epicenter of the empire? How were the Hindus harmonized to the idea of Muslim minority rule? How did the Mughal *pâdshâh* reconcile the wide-ranging prerogatives of his office with the strict dictates of the *Sharî'ah*, whereby the Muslim community theoretically wields the power to approve or reject individual rulers?[54] By examining the prototype of the model emperor, designed by Abû al-Fazl for Akbar, we can begin to appreciate the Mughal rationalization of these questions. Furthermore, we can analyse the extent to which Jahângîr adhered to Akbar's framework for monarchy by looking at sources from the period of 1605-27.

The principal source for understanding Akbar's rationale of kingship is the *Akbar nâma*; this history is supplemented by the incredibly valuable *Â'în-i Akbarî*, an appendix of imperial regulations and guidelines. The architect of this manual, Abû al-Fazl, was well-trained in political analysis, philosophy, mysticism, and the science of rhetoric and, as Akbar's principal advisor and right-hand man, was central to all state matters and policies. At this stage of Akbar's reign, conquests had significantly expanded the parameters of the state and the empire now incorporated a diversity of indigenous ethnic groups. Also, Abû al-Fazl needed to design a system of defence against the legitimate claims and challenges from the Central Asian *mîrzâs*, described as "Akbar's collateral Timurid princes."[55] These developments, combined with the unprecedented need to extrapolate the emperor's influence to newly-acquired, yet distant, territories, contributed to the designing and streamlining of the Mughal emperor as the "Perfect Man" and supreme authority. This authority was extrapolated from the secular realm into the profane when Akbar announced the *mazhar* decree of 1579, appropriating the right to make certain religious judgments from the *'ulamâ*. However, the traditional argument of Akbar claiming monarchical infallibility[56], has recently been challenged by Khaliq Nizami who believes the *mazhar* allowed the emperor only a "certain power of *ijtihâd*...for administrative considerations and the welfare of mankind."[57] The *Â'în-i Akbarî* reiterates previous Muslim theorists' arguments regarding the need for authoritative rule: "if royalty did not exist, the storm of strife would never subside, nor selfish ambition disappear. Mankind being under the burden of lawlessness and lust, would sink into the pit of destruction"; furthermore, "protection of subjects means a worship for household of sovereignty."[58] This theme of the ruler being ultimately responsible for ensuring a stable society and protecting his subjects from both internal and external threats was not new; a number of previous political theorists, including al-Ghazâlî and al-Tûsî, had made this a key feature in their models of Perso-Islamic kingship. Realizing the intricacies and subtleties underpinning a ruler's title, Abû al-Fazl ignored using *sultân* and advanced the term *pâdshâh*. He explained the etymology by equating *pâd* with stability and possession while *shâh* represented origin and lord; hence, *pâdshâh* designated a superior king, or emperor.[59] Furthermore, Akbar and his *vazîr* worked diligently to establish a metaphor between the emperor and the empire, whereby resistance to Akbar was synonymous with a challenge to the sanctity of the entire imperial system.

The pivotal characteristic of Abû al-Fazl's ideology, however, was the reiteration of legitimacy through affirming the "divinely illumined right of the Emperor to rule mortals with lesser qualities."[60] In the preface to *Â'în-i Akbarî*, royalty is described as "a light emanating from God and a ray from the Sun, the illuminator of the universe, the argument of the book of perfection, the receptacle of all virtues. Modern language calls this light *farr-i îzidî* (the divine light) (the sublime halo) and the tongue of antiquity called it *kiyân khura*. It is communicated by God to kings without the intermediate assistance of any one."[61] Abû al-Fazl asserted the divine right of Akbar's rule by tracing a series of lineages, starting with Adam, through the Biblical prophets, to the first Turco-Mughal figure, Mughâl Khân.[62] This transmission of divine illumination continues with Bâbur, whom Abû al-Fazl describes as "the carrier of the world-illuminating light (*hâmil-i nûr-i jahân âfruz*)," to Akbar.[63] Having established the invulnerability of his claims, the "divine light" argument was protracted to ratify Akbar's monarchical infallibility. Abû al-Fazl supersedes the religio-legal constraints on Muslim leadership by asserting that "[Akbar] is a king whom on account of his wisdom, we call *zû funûn* (possessor of sciences), and our guide on the path of religion. Although kings are the shadow of God on earth, [Akbar] is the emanation of God's light. How then can we call him a shadow?"[64] Abu al-Fazl's theory of divine largesse imbued the emperor with the necessary qualities and virtues to govern successfully—trust in God and prayer, devotion, and, most important, a paternal love for his subjects.[65] This emphasis on hereditary transmission of divine power is, of course, directly borrowed from *shî'î* and *sûfî* theologies, whereby the community is led by a series of family-related temporal and spiritual masters guided by the holy spirit (*ruh-i quds*). The *shî'î* doctrine of divine knowledge was also assimilated: "many sincere inquirers from the mere light of his wisdom, or his holy breath, obtain a degree of awakening which other spiritual doctors could not produce by repeated fasting and prayers for fourty days."[66] Whether Abû al-Fazl's ideology was influenced by the prevalent *sûfî tarîqahs* of northern India, or the large *shî'î* number of Persian *émigres* in the court, is difficult to say. More than likely, it was a combination of the two traditions. Akbar, seeking "elements of unity in Indian cultural life," looked to religious syncretism as a means of stabilizing his heterogeneous empire.[67]

This monarchical ideology defined the relationship between the Mughal emperor and his elite. The exclusiveness of the *pâdshâh*'s position, as guarantor of justice and stability, symbol of religious authority, and beneficiary of God's will, predictably centralized his role in state maintenance. And while the emperor was regarded as the symbol of unity and potency, the nobility were seen as a potential source of disintegration and anarchy.[68] By no means was this view exclusive to the Mughals; Barânî's *Fatawa-i jahândârî* of the Delhi Sultanate period warns rulers to "follow the traditions of the Real King of kings in selecting virtuous persons for appointment as your confidential officers and partners in your supreme command."[69] Fully aware of the danger posed by competitive noble elements, especially remote ones, Akbar looked to both his constructed ideology and previous Turkic traditions. Abû al-Fazl's adoption of *shî'î/sûfî* principles of leadership is clear: the sacred nature of his station dictated that "at the sight of it (the Divine Light) everyone bends the forehead of praise to the ground of submission."[70] Since "he [Akbar] is now the spiritual guide to the nation," to resist or rebel against the emperor was tantamount to agitating a divinely-endowed universal order.[71] However, this alone could not dissuade sedition and Akbar organized his empire to secure a close bond with his noble elite.[72]

Using the term "patrimonial-bureaucracy," Stephen Blake has advanced an interesting argument of how the Mughals were deeply influenced by Mongol patrimonial models of government. Specifically, he asserts that "patrimonial domination [like that of the Mongols] originates in the patriarch's authority over the household. It entails obedience to a person, not an office."[73] This system, in turn, was revived, modified, and implemented by Akbar to guarantee the loyalty of his nobility and his personal participation in all facets of government. Moreover, this intense loyalty to the individual ruler, and not the institution, lent itself to the charismatic ethos borrowed from the *shî`î imâmî* tradition. The *mansabdârî* system, essentially the imperial allotting of rank and payment to competent nobles, represented a reciprocal relationship between Akbar and his officers as well as a means of social and political control.[74] *Mansabs* were conferred on *amîrs* and *khâns* in return for loyal, consistent service in both the military and the administration. By stipulating a) when and how much *mansabdârs* were promoted, and b) that powerful rank-holders were to be kept relatively close to the imperial court, Akbar fashioned his empire on this "extended-household" model. Moreover, loyalty and subservience to the patriarchal figure of the emperor were theoretically the only means of advancement.[75] The *Â`în-i Akbarî* states that nobles were obliged to report to the emperor regularly and serve on a series of rotational guard duties; furthermore, strict ordinances outlined proper behavior and demeanour for nobles in the emperor's presence.[76] This code of behavior, as Richards notes, was founded on the principle of *khânazâd*, or "devoted, familial hereditary service to the emperor."⁷⁷ Richards further contends that this principle has it roots in the Turkic institution of military slavery because nobles, serving in either military or administrative capacities (sometimes both), were referred to as *khânazâd*, or "offspring of a slave."⁷⁸ Mughal imperial governing was then essentially an extrapolation of the Mongol household-oriented pattern of rule. In this, we see the emperor as a divinely-sanctioned patriarch figure who dictated close relations with the extended members of his household through the *mansabdârî* system. Furthermore, the identification of the nobility as *khânazâd*, combined with the king's status as the "light of God," guaranteed a submissive, yet intensely loyal, military and administrative elite.

Documentation suggests Jahângîr closely followed both his father's ideology and the governmental innovations he introduced in the sixteenth century. A number of Akbar's elite nobles continued to serve under Jahângîr after 1605 (Mîrzâ 'Abd al-Rahîm, 'Abd Allâh Khân, Mahâbat Khân, Râjah Mân Singh) and, as the meticulous entries of the *Tûzuk-i Jahângîrî* demonstrate, he was a faithful distributor of healthy *mansab* appointments. The tone and language of his memoirs also points to a ruler who believed very much in the idea of public governance. With the numerous celebrations (*Naurûz*, birthday) and public weighings, the emperor seemed to enjoy the public's attention. Regular public displays of the imperium, to Jahângîr's mind, reinforced the "patrimonial" identity of the Mughal emperor; hand-in-hand with this emperor-cum-*pater* concept, Jahângîr strove to reiterate the divinely endowed nature of his office. This relationship between God and the Mughal ruler is alluded to in the emperor's reaction to Khusrau's rebellion in 1606, "[the rebels] overlooked the truth that acts of sovereignty and world rule are not things to be arranged by the worthless endeavors of defective intellects. The Just Creator bestows them on him whom he considers fit for this glorious and exalted duty, and on such a person doth He fit the robe of honour."[79]

Other sources, specifically advice manuals written by *arbâb-i qalam* (people of the pen), suggest that theories of kingship deviated little after the death of Akbar. Sânî's *Mau'izah-i Jahângîrî* describes how the imperium governs "the lives, possessions, properties, and honor of the people."[80] This theme is continued in the later *Mazhar-i Shâhjahânî* by Yûsuf Mîrak who considers sovereignty to be the only means of protecting humanity against oppression.[81]

The emperor's embodiment of "Divine light" was also a popular motif during the reign of Jahângîr and many sources point towards its continued use. The synonymous nature of light and kingship in the Perso-Islamic world was, of course, one of the many cultural features assimilated from the Sassanian tradition. The sun was a powerful symbol in ancient Persian Zoroastrianism and its view of a polarized light and dark universe; solar images were readily identified with kingship and were affixed to Sassanian emblems of sovereignty such as crowns, scepters and royal daises. In the Islamic context, this metaphor of light and kingship was modified slightly so as to identify the sun with God, or *Allâh*. By the sixteenth century, dynasties like the Mughals and the Safavids had formed a political ideology which was essentially an amalgamation between the Islamicized Sassanian metaphor of sun and kingship and the *shî'î* theory of divine designation (*nass*). Thus it is no surprise that on his day of accession, Jahângîr took the "title of honour (*laqab*) Nûr al-dîn, inasmuch as my sitting on the throne coincided with the rising and shining on the earth of the great light."[82] Mughal dynastic rule came at a point in Perso-Islamic history when using sun-emperor or light-kingship metaphors were enjoying their highest popularity among poets, *munshîs*, and political theorists. Jahângîr's personal recognition of this ideology is seen in a poem he recites in his memoirs,

O God, Thy essence has shone from eternity
The souls of all the saints receive light from Thine,
O king, may the world ever be at they beck,
May thy Shâh-Jahân ever rejoice in thy shade
O Shadow of God, may the world be filled with thy light
May the Light of God ever be thy canopy.[83]

The prominent role of light and light-related terminology ("shone," "shade," "canopy"), combined with the reference here to the 'shadow of God,' suggests that the principles of Abû al-Fazl's *Â'in-i Akbarî* were very much in vogue in the early seventeenth century. The supernatural, quasi-*pîr* qualities of the Mughal emperor, hinted at by Abû al-Fazl, take on added significance when discussing Jahângîr. Akbar's supposed forest encounter with the *sûfî shaikh* Salîm Chistî in 1568, and Chistî's foretelling of Jahângîr's birth, was a favourite legend in the Mughal annals. The legacy of this Chistîyya *shaikh* and his prediction, and possibly Prince Salîm's upraising in a rather religiously heterodox court, help us understand Jahângîr's later relationship with the various *sûfî tarîqahs*. He spent Friday evenings associating with "learned and pious men, and with dervishes and recluses" and, on more than one occasion, he donated time and money to various *sûfî* projects.[84] His regular patronage of *sûfî* masters (Khvâjah Qâsim, Shaikh Pîr, Shaikh 'Alâ al-Dîn, Shaikh Husain Jâmî, and Shaikh Ahmad Lâhorî) plus a healthy correspondence reveal an emperor intricately aware of the tenets of *tasawwuf* and its' manifestations into the different *silsilahs*. The divine properties of Jahângîr's office and his own familiarity with *sûfî* discourse contributed to a reinforcing of his own mystical qualities. In an *'ariza dâsht* (petition), the court *munshî* Khânazâd Khân addressed the emperor as *rûshan-i zamîr murshid-i kâmil salâmat qiblah-i dîn va dunyâ salâmat va pîr-i dastgîr qablah murâdat salâmat* (health to the enlightened [royal] mind, the perfect spiritual advisor, the *qiblah* of sacredness and profanity, the *pîr* and saint [who] provides wishes.").[85] An interesting series of inscriptions found in a ruined palace's vault in the old imperial center of Ajmîr bears the following ode,

> The king of seven climes, of lofty fortune, whose praise cannot be contained in speech,
> The lustre of the house of king Akbar, emperor of the age, king Jahângîr,
> When he visited this fountain through his bounty, water began to flow and dust turned to elixir
> The Emperor gave it the name Chashma-i Nûr from which the water of Immortality acquires its relish.[86]

The record states that this palace, arranged around a splendid fountain, was constructed at Jahângîr's behest in 1615 and is referred to in his memoirs.[87] The spectacular outcome of Jahângîr's visit, where water spontaneously erupted from the fountain and dust was transformed into elixir, is reminiscent of the miraculous power wielded by *pîrs* and *îmâms*. Miracles, or *karâmat*, were not unfamiliar to the Mughal emperors; Abû al-Fazl recounts how Akbar "takes the water with his blessed hands, places it in the rays of the world-illuminating sun ... many sick people had been restored to health by this divine means."[88] As the court poet Sherî jokingly remarked: *pâdshâh imsâl da'watî nabwat kardih ast/ gar khudâ khvâhad digar sâlî khudâ khvâhad shudan* ("This year the king has declared himself as Prophet/In the following year, if God so wills, he will become god.").[89]

It appears that Turkic "household" rule also continued to serve as the model of government under Jahângîr. The emperor himself attests to the continuation of the *khânazâd* designation while discussing the recruitment and appointment of *mansabdârs*:

> If the details were to be described of all the commanders and servants' appointment by me, with the conditions and rank of each, it would be a long business. Many of my immediate

attendants and personal followers and nobles' sons, house born ones (*khânazâdân*) and zealous Rajputs, petitioned to accompany this expedition.[90]

In addition to alluding to his status as the central administrator, Jahângîr's reference to *khânazâdân* substantiates Richards's argument of an emperor perceiving his surrounding nobility with metaphorical terms like 'slave' and 'master' and, furthermore, how this understanding was preserved after Akbar's death. This 'slave' analogy, or *khânazâdân*, is found in a number of examples throughout Jahângîr's memoirs and other contemporary documents.[91] While the nobles were described as "the pillars of the country" (*arkân-i mamlakat*) upon whom the ruler relied heavily, it was commonly understood that the nobility were deeply indebted to the Mughal emperor on the basis of his very existence, "[the wise men] have also likened royal service to an ocean [and the employee] to a merchant embarking on a voyage—[the merchant] either accrues immense profit or becomes trapped in a whirlpool of annihilation."[92] Sânî's section 'On the Etiquette of Royal Service' of his mirror for princes manual provides a valuable noble's perspective on the relationship between an emperor and his ruling elite during the 1605-27 period,

> ...he [the noble] must never ignore the dues for these bounties and favors [granted to him]. He must concentrate his energies on showing them allegiance and he must serve them with utmost sincerity, conviction, and good will. He must not neglect in any matter the well-being of his benefactor. Had he a thousand lives, he must sacrifice them for one moment of his lord's peace of mind. He must throw himself in the most perilous situation for requital of the favors of his patron and for leaving his name [inscribed] on the record of Time for his devotion [to his master].[93]

The relationship between the Mughal emperor and his nobility was founded on a premise of symbiosis whereby the emperor, as the fount for all *mansabdârî* allotments and military appointments, expected unfailing loyalty and subservience from his elite. There is, however, another feature to this relationship which needs commenting on. Sir Thomas Roe had observed that the best route to preferment in the Mughal court was through the giving of "daylie bribes" to the emperor; these 'bribes,' in turn, resulted in advancement in the administrative structure. The use of the word 'bribe,' a term more useful for understanding the Jacobean Senecan approach to government disbursements, is inappropriate for the Mughal context. For instance, when Prince Khurram arrived at Mandû in 1617, Jahângîr described how "in proportion as he strove to be humble and polite, I increased my favours and kindness to him and made him sit near me. He presented 1,000 *ashrafis* and 1,000 rupees as *nazar* and the same amount by way of alms.(italics mine)"[94] This quote is particularly intriguing because it makes note of a) the salutation process required of nobles and princes and b) the mandatory presentation of *nazr*.

Discussed earlier, *The Embassy* depicts the Mughal court as an arena of factional competition, avaricious negotiations, and unabashed bribery. Nonetheless, a Mughal emperor's style of rule was founded on personal contact and expressions of commitment from the ruling elite. The physical act of prostrating oneself was of itself an acknowledgment of your loyalty, and nobles, regardless of station or rank, were expected to perform these necessary steps of salutation.[95] The guidelines for this act were set out in *Â`în-i Akbarî*:

> Men of deeper insight are of the opinion that even spiritual progress among a people would be impossible unless emanating from the king, in whom the light of God dwells; for near the throne, men wipe off the stain of conceit and build up the arch of true humility...His Majesty has commanded the palm of the right hand to be placed upon the forehead and the head to be bent downwards. This mode of salutation, in

the language of the present age, is called *kornish*, and signifies that the saluter has placed his head into the hand of humility, giving it to the royal assembly as a present, and has made himself in obedience ready for any service that may be required of him. The salutation, called *taslîm*, consists in placing the back of the right hand on the ground, and then raising it gently till the person stands erect...When His Majesty seats himself on the throne, all that are present perform the *kornish*, and then remain standing at their places, according to their rank, with their arms crossed, partaking, in the light of his imperial countenance, of the elixir of life, and enjoying everlasting happiness in standing ready for any service.[96]

The apparent formality of this procedure was not particular to Akbar's reign. Jahângîr describes the arrival of many nobles who performed "the dues of salutation" or "came to pay [their] respects (*kûrnish*)." Obeisance such as this was designed to reinforce the mutual sense of loyalty when in the presence of the emperor. The other feature, *nazr*, is also frequently referred to in the emperor's memoirs.[97] Roe's simple summation of this as the "giuing of trifles is the way of preferment," does not adequately reflect the importance of gift-giving in the building of political relationships. Furthermore, Roe's experience in Jacobean England, where bribery was a central means of upward social mobility, distorted his interpretation of this phenomena.[98]

Nazr originally described a pre-Islamic promise or vow after making a sacrifice to a god. The consecration "placed the person making the vow in connection with the divine powers, the *nadhr* was an '*ahd*, whereby he pledged himself. A neglect of the *nadhr* was a sin against the deity."[99] The procedure of *nazr*, as a symbolic gesture of devotion, is also mentioned in Qur'ânic scriptures.[100] In the Mughal setting, this gesture manifested itself in gold and silver rupees or other valuable items; the act of presenting a large gift was metaphoric of the donor acknowledging the king as the source of all his wealth and being. However

European travelers misunderstood the procedure as bribery or a periodic collection of tribute. Consequently, Roe's statement that "for such is the custome and humour of the King, that he will seize and see all, lest any Toy should escape his attention," is a misinformed judgment at best.[101] Later interpretations of Jahângîr's appetite for gifts also look to his memoirs for vindication, yet on many of these occasions they are specifically referred to as *nazr*.[102]

"The pride and falshood of these people attended only aduantage and were gouerned by priuate interest and appetite," concludes Roe in one of his last letters to the EIC.[103] As he later boarded the *Anne* in March of 1618 to return home, he seemed to be struggling with some level of resentment and personal frustration. Operating in a political forum not his own, it seems Roe by his own account experienced considerable difficulties in attempting to procure the EIC's wanted bilateral trading agreement. Part of this lack of success can be explained by Roe's inability to appreciate the differences between Jacobean and Mughal courtier systems. While this book has attempted to highlight some of these differences by examining the indigenous Mughal perspective on kingship, the court, and the surrounding nobility, another latent concern has been the manner in which Roe recorded his experiences. Jacobean Westminster and Mughal Ajmîr, according to *The Embassy*, do not seem that far apart. Both were dominated by a voracious court element; both were polarized over issues of foreign alignments; and both were defined by an uncontrolled patronage system of gift giving. The question begs itself: why did Roe feel so out of his element? I suspect the differences, as I have outlined, were greater than Roe expected or experienced. The underpinnings of the Mughal court system were rooted in a larger and more complex historical and political tradition that Roe was incapable of appreciating. Absorbing these new political features was impossible for Roe without first moulding them to fit a Jacobean model. His decision to implement certain familiar

Jacobean court terms and imagery, despite their inadequacy, was also motivated out of a need to facilitate an understanding on behalf of his future English audience. Writing for an environment where courtiers were increasingly thought of as avaricious "dissemblers," Roe's less-than-kind portrayal of the Mughal court ("a misserie unexpressable") and its participants ("ravens") begins to make more sense.[104]

NOTES

1. A good discussion of Lefèvre's *Rélation d'une voyage à Brésil* can be found in Frank Stringant's *Le Huguenot et le sauvage* (Paris: 1993).
2. The most comprehensive historical demographic study of England to date is E.A. Wrigley and R.S. Schofield's *Population History of England, 1541-1871: A Reconstruction* (Cambridge: 1989). Pertaining to the growth of London in this period, we have the work of F.J. Fisher, including "London's Export Trade in the Early Seventeenth Century," in *Economic History Review* (2nd Series), Vol. III, No. 2, and "The Development of the London Food Market," in *Economic History Review*, Vol. V.
3. Brown, *Itinerant Ambassador*, p. 4.
4. Strachan, *Sir Thomas Roe*, p. 5.
5. Brown, *Itinerant Ambassador*, p. 7.
6. Strachan, *Sir Thomas Roe*, p. 13.
7. Strachan, *Sir Thomas Roe*, p. 17.
8. See Conrad Russell, "Parliamentary History in Perspective, 1604-29," in *History*, Vol. 61 (1976), pp. 1-27.
9. Peck, *Court Patronage*, p. 4.
10. Peck, *Court Patronage*, p. 12.
11. Peck, *Court Patronage*, p. 14.
12. McIlwain (ed), *Political Works of James I*, pp. 25-26.
13. McIlwain (ed), *Political Works of James I*, p. 52.
14. Holderness, "Introduction: Theatre and Court," p. 132.
15. Peck, *Court Patronage*, p. 40.
16. Smuts, *Court Culture*, p. 77.
17. Smuts, *Court Culture*, p. 78.
18. R. Malcolm Smuts, "Introduction," in *The Stuart Court and Europe: Essays in Politics and Political Culture*, ed. R. Malcolm Smuts (Cambridge: 1996), p. 9.

19. Lawrence Stone, *The Crisis of the Aristocracy 1558-1641* (Oxford: 1965), p. 93.
20. Peck, *Court Patronage*, p. 54.
21. Simon Adams, "Spain or the Netherlands? The Dilemmas of Early Stuart Foreign Policy," in *Before the English Civil War*, ed. H. Tomlinson (London: 1983), p. 94.
22. A.R. Braunmuller, "Robert Carr, Earl of Somerset, As Collector and Patron," in *The Mental World of the Jacobean Court*, ed. L.L. Peck (Cambridge: 1991), p. 230.
23. Strachan, *Sir Thomas Roe*, p. 44.
24. Several letters penned by Roe, included in *The Embassy*, were sent to George Abbott. Roe, *The Embassy of Sir Thomas*, p. 122, p. 308, p. 311.
25. Strachan, *Sir Thomas Roe*, p. 36.
26. Neil Cuddy, "The Revival of the Entourage: the Bedchamber of James I, 1603-1625," in *The English Court: From the Wars of the Roses to the Civil War*, ed. D. Starkey (New York: 1987), p. 173.
27. Roe, *The Embassy of Sir Thomas Roe*, p. 12.
28. Roe, *The Embassy of Sir Thomas Roe*, pp. 20-22.
29. For a good indication of Mughal bureaucratic sophistication, see John F. Richards, *Document Forms for Official Orders of Appointment in the Mughal Empire* (Cambridge: 1986).
30. Roe, *The Embassy of Sir Thomas Roe*, p. 89.
31. Roe, *The Embassy of Sir Thomas Roe*, p. 105.
32. Roe, *The Embassy of Sir Thomas Roe*, p. 161.
33. Roe, *The Embassy of Sir Thomas Roe*, p. 161.
34. Roe, *The Embassy of Sir Thomas Roe*, p. 311.
35. Peck, *Court Patronage*, p. 40.
36. Roe, *The Embassy of Sir Thomas Roe*, p. 249
37. Roe, *The Embassy of Sir Thomas Roe*, p. 151.
38. Roe, *The Embassy of Sir Thomas Roe*, p. 306.
39. Roe, *The Embassy of Sir Thomas Roe*, p. 199, p. 242.
40. Robert Ashton (ed.), *James I By His Contemporaries* (London: 1969), p. 220.
41. McIlwain (ed.), *Political Works of James I*, p. xxxii.
42. This description appears in a letter written to the Lord Bishop of Canterbury on 30 October 1616, Roe, *The Embassy of Sir Thomas Roe*, p. 272.
43. Roe, *The Embassy of Sir Thomas Roe*, p. 78.
44. Roe, *The Embassy of Sir Thomas Roe*, p. 57.
45. A.R. Disney, *Twilight of the Pepper Trade*, p. 10.
46. Prasad, *History of Jahangir*, p. 175.
47. Roe, *The Embassy of Sir Thomas Roe*, p. 75n.
48. Roe, *The Embassy of Sir Thomas Roe*, p. 319.

SIR THOMAS ROE AS COURTIER 129

49. Roe, *The Embassy of Sir Thomas Roe*, p. 102.
50. Roe, *The Embassy of Sir Thomas Roe*, p. 146, p. 177.
51. Roe, *The Embassy of Sir Thomas Roe*, p. 229.
52. Roe, *The Embassy of Sir Thomas Roe*, p. 250.
53. The sole reference from *Tûzuk* comes in January of 1615, "In the roadstead of the port of Sûrat a fight took place between the English, who had taken shelter there, and the Viceroy [leading Portuguese official of Goa]. Most of his ships were burnt by the English fire. Being helpless he had not the power to fight any more, and took to flight." Jahângîr, *Tûzuk-i Jahângîrî*, Vol. I, pp. 274-75.
54. It should be noted that Indian Muslim scholars have often inflated the significance of the relationship between the emperor and Islamic law, especially since the 1947 partition of India and Pakistan. A good example of this thinking can be found in Naqvi's *History of Mughal Government and Administration* (Delhi: 1990). The ramifications of any incongruencies between ruler and law were probably debated more over a theoretical level during the sixteenth and seventeenth centuries. However English historians, particularly V.A. Smith, have looked to the signing of a *mazhar* by Akbar's *'ulamâ* as an "infallibility decree." As Aziz Ahmad points out, this simply gave Akbar the "right of *ijtihâd*...on a legal point [where] there was a difference of opinion." Aziz Ahmad, "The Role of Ulema in Indo-Muslim History," in *Studia Islamica*, Vol. 31 (1970), p. 7. As for Jahângîr's reign, evidence indicates, as S. Alvi comments, "the continued acceptance of the legitimacy of temporal power, stripped of the theocratic trappings, in Sunnî political thought." Sajida Alvi, "Religion and State During the Reign of Mughal Emperor Jahângîr (1605-1627): Nonjuristical Perspectives," in *Studia Islamica*, Vol. 69 (1989), p. 103. Practically speaking, Akbar and Jahângîr were not threatened by overly orthodox groups' insistence on adhering to the letter of the law *vis-à-vis* a ruler's prerogatives.
55. John F. Richards, "The Formulation of Imperial Authority Under Akbar and Jahângîr," in *Kingship and Authority in South Asia*, ed. J.F. Richards (Madison: 1978), p. 263.
56. This is best represented in V.A. Smith's *Akbar The Great Mogul, 1542-1605* (Oxford: 1892), p. 179, p. 214.
57. Khaliq Ahmad Nizami, *Akbar and Religion* (Delhi: 1989), p. 317.
58. 'Allâmî, *Â'în-i Akbarî*, Vol. I, p. 2.
59. 'Allâmî, *Â'în-i Akbarî*, Vol. I, p. 2.
60. Richards, 'The Formation of Imperial Authority," p. 263.
61. 'Allâmî, *Â'în-i Akbarî*, Vol. I, p. 3.
62. Richards, "The Formation of Imperial Authority," pp. 262-63.

63. Richards, "The Formation of Imperial Authority," p. 264.
64. 'Allâmî, *Â'în-i Akbarî*, Vol. I, p. 631.
65. 'Allâmî, *Â'în-i Akbarî*, Vol. I, p. 3.
66. 'Allâmî, *Â'în-i Akbarî*, Vol. I, p. 173.
67. Nizami, *Akbar and Religion*, p. 242.
68. Sarkar, *Mughal Polity*, p. 71.
69. Ziyâ al-Dîn Barânî, *Fatawa-i Jahândârî*, trans. and ed. M. Habib, *The Political Theory of the Delhi Sultanate* (Allahabad: 1960), p. 94.
70. 'Allâmî, *Â'în-i Akbarî*, Vol. I, p. 3.
71. 'Allâmî, *Â'în-i Akbarî*, Vol. I, p. 173.
72. It should be noted Akbar's *mansabdârî* system was essentially modeled on a series of reforms initiated by Sher Shâh Sûrî in the 1550s.
73. Stephen Blake, "The Patrimonial-Bureaucratic Empire of the Mughals," in *Journal of Asian Studies*, Vol. 39 (1979), No. 1, p. 79.
74. M. Athar Ali, *The Apparatus of Empire: Awards of Ranks, Offices, and Titles to the Mughal Nobility (1574-1658)* (Delhi: 1985), p. xi.
75. Blake, "The Patrimonial-Bureaucratic Empire," p. 90.
76. 'Allâmî, *Â'în-i Akbarî*, Vol. I, pp. 267-68.
77. John F. Richards, "Norms of Comportment Among Imperial Mughal Officers," in *Moral Conduct and Authority: The Place of Adab in South Asian Islam*, ed. B.D. Metcalf (Berkeley: 1984), p. 262.
78. Richards, "Norms of Comportment Among Imperial Mughal Officers," p. 264.
79. Jahângîr, *Tûzuk-i Jahângîrî*, Vol. I, p. 51.
80. Sânî, *Mau'izah-i Jahângîrî*, p. 15.
81. Sajida S. Alvi, "*Mazhar-i Shâhjahânî* and the Mughal Province of Sind: A Discourse on Political Ethics," in *Islam and Indian Religions*, eds. A.L. Dallapiccola and S.Z. Lallemant, Vol. 1 (1993), p. 241.
82. Jahângîr, *Tûzuk-i Jahângîrî*, Vol. I, p. 3.
83. Jahângîr, *Tûzuk-i Jahângîrî*, Vol. II, p. 29.
84. Jahângîr, *Tûzuk-i Jahângîrî*, Vol. I, p. 21. Besides restoring the tomb of Mu'în al-Dîn Chistî to the tune of one *lakh* rupees, he also donated to the mosque-building project of Shaikh Pîr and gave Khvâjah Qâsim of the Naqshbandîyyah a startling gift of 12,000 rupees.
85. Originally appeared in Khânazâd Khân Fîrûz Jang, *Inshâ'-yi Khânazâd Khân*; parts of this are transcribed in Momin Mohiuddin, *The Chancellery and Persian Epistolography Under the Mughals* (Calcutta: 1971).
86. S.A.I. Tirmizi, *Ajmer Through Inscriptions* (New Delhi: 1968), p. 37.
87. Jahângîr, *Tûzuk-i Jahângîrî*, Vol. I, pp. 269-70, p. 341.
88. 'Allâmî, *Â'în-i Akbarî*, Vol. I, p. 173.

89. Transcription and translation provided in Nizami, *Akbar and Religion*, p. 255.
90. In 1605 Jahângîr led an expedition against the Rânâ of Mewârî. Jahângîr, *Tûzuk-i Jahângîrî*, Vol. I, p. 18.
91. Jahângîr, *Tûzuk-i Jahângîrî*, Vol. I, p. 60, p. 109, p. 309, Vol. II, p. 17, p. 37. Khvâjah Kâmgâr Husainî is referred to as a *khânazâd* in Khvâjah Kâmgâr Husainî, *Ma'âthir-i Jahângîrî*, ed. Azra Alvi (Bombay: 1978), p. 1.
92. Sânî, *Mau'izah-i Jahângîrî*, p. 72.
93. Sânî, *Mau'izah-i Jahângîrî*, p. 74.
94. Jahângîr, *Tûzuk-i Jahângîrî*, Vol. I, p. 394.
95. M. Bhatia and K. Behari, "The Mughal Court Etiquette and Matters of Protocol," in *Journal of Indian History*, Vol. 56 (1978), p. 112.
96. 'Allâmî, *Â'în-i Akbarî*, Vol. I, pp. 166-68.
97. Jahângîr, *Tûzuk-i Jahângîrî*, Vol. II, p. 54, p. 66.
98. F.W. Buckler, "The Oriental Despot," in *Legitimacy and Symbols*, ed. M.N. Pearson (Ann Arbor: 1985), p. 243.
99. J. Pedersen, 'Nadhr', in *Encyclopedia of Islam*, Vol. VII, p. 847.
100. 2: 270, 76:7, *The Holy Qur-an: Text, Translation and Commentary*, ed. Abdullah Yusuf Ali (Washington: 1946).
101. Roe, *The Embassy of Sir Thomas Roe*, p. 365.
102. Jahângîr, *Tûzuk-i Jahângîrî*, Vol. II, p. 50, p. 115, p. 186.
103. Roe, *The Embassy of Sir Thomas Roe*, p. 477.
104. Roe, *The Embassy of Sir Thomas Roe*, p. 387.

4

SIR THOMAS ROE AS AMBASSADOR

Broadly intended as a general history and fledging ethnography of Mughal culture, *The Embassy*, we must not forget, was also an official narrative of Roe's tenure as England's first ambassador to the Indian subcontinent. One of the principal duties of an ambassador, in any period, is information gathering. While ostensibly serving as a head of state's official representative, a diplomatic envoy was also meant to be his master's eyes and ears in a foreign court. He was expected to observe and record his perceptions of the host state since his own liege would ultimately be demanding detailed descriptions of foreign political climates, economic conditions, and other factors important for formulating state foreign policy. For the historian, foreign ambassadors' written reports can be valuable historiographical tools; analyses of Renaissance European courts invariably rely on memos and letters drafted by envoys from Venice, the diplomatic power *par excellence*. In the case of Sir Thomas Roe, his station, mandate, and overall identity between 1615 and 1619 were defined by diplomacy and much of what he wrote has to be seen from that perspective. While we have already asserted that Roe's commentary was influenced by his amateur and professional literary and courtier career, we also have to ponder to what extent *The Embassy* was moulded by his experience and training as a Jacobean diplomat. His fulmination on Mughal diplomacy, "barbarous customes" leading him to opine that "this place is either made, or of it selfe unfitt for an ambassador," have to be questioned for their intensity, if not outright belligerency. Was the Mughal state truly wanting for sophisticated diplomatic etiquette, or do Roe's descriptions stem from his own deeply affronted diplomatic sensibilities? Is it, once again, possible that features of Roe's description have more to do with early seventeenth-century Jacobean England than with early modern Islamic India?

As has been done in the previous two chapters, we will shift back to early seventeenth-century England and specifically examine Roe's participation in various diplomatic ventures and how they reflected the overall early modern European approach to international etiquette. In doing so, we can learn more about what he was expecting while waiting to disembark from the *Lion* in September 1615. Understanding Roe's convictions on this matter is critical when considering the overall historiographical worth of *The Embassy* since the generally hostile presentation of Jahângîr's court becomes especially acute when Roe is reflecting on the role of diplomacy in the Mughal government. This hostility is especially focused during his initial descriptions of the Mughal empire and tends to set the tone for the entire corpus of *The Embassy*. By understanding how Roe viewed the ambassadorial office and its position in a foreign court, and moreover the level of dedication he attached to these views, we can better appreciate why he castigates the Mughal government under Jahângîr so tenaciously.

The decision of King James I and Sir Thomas Smythe, the director of the English East India Company, to appoint Sir Thomas Roe as the ambassador and main Company representative to the Mughal court of Jahângîr is not entirely surprising. As discussed, Roe had been knighted in 1603 and used his contacts in the Jacobean court to guarantee a number of official postings. His experience as a counselor in the Royal Council for the Virginia Colony had also introduced Roe to the intricacies of running a mercantile 'regulated' company and, likewise, his participation in the Guiana expedition of 1610 had familiarized him with the details and logistics of mounting an economic venture in a non-European environment. However, when considering the monarchy's decision to nominate Roe as the official English ambassador to Mughal India, we have to examine Roe's early experiences with seventeenth-century diplomacy and international etiquette. The contemporary European diplomatic scene was certainly a dynamic, if not hopelessly complicated, one. The Holy Roman Empire was in the critical stage of fragmentation as regions like Bohemia and Slovakia in southcentral Europe and the city-states in Germany were beginning to itch under the centralized Catholic absolutism of the Habsburgs. Holland had just recently concluded a decades-long civil war over this issue of overthrowing Habsburg suzerainty and, with more and more European monarchs and heads of state looking to the nation state model, the medieval legacy of "one empire, one religion," in Europe was rapidly dissipating. Although the Catholic League had been formed by the Papacy and Spain to contain the recent spread of Protestantism, it would be folly to describe the divisions in early seventeenth-century Europe simply as Protestant versus Catholic. One of Spain's biggest threats was Catholic France, indicated by the Duke of Alençon's support of William of Orange and his later 1581 invasion of the Spanish Netherlands during the Dutch revolt. Nonetheless, religious allegiances could still heavily influence a monarch or nation state's foreign policy. Religious considerations, however, were not always dictated by a ruler's personal faith or belief system; pressure on governments to join one international religious alliance or another could come from vocal, often agitated, domestic elements. Mentioned earlier, the newly crowned James I fashioned himself a diplomat-monarch who was keen to usher in a new era of peace after decades of confessional warfare on the continent.

Specifically, England's war with Spain had dominated the last two decades of the sixteenth century and James I's first goal was to cease hostilities. By 1603, after roughly fifty years of intermittent war with Catholic Spain, generations of Englishmen had been raised in a bitter hispanophobe environment and consequently many courtiers and politicians were reticent to run happily into the arms of the Spanish king, Philip III. On the other hand, the government debt amassed by Elizabeth I was a staggering one and England was showing symptoms of the price inflation that would grip all of Europe a decade later: dragging out the war with Spain would be financial suicide.

In his first year of rule, James proffered olive branches to Madrid and, by 19 August 1604, the practical details of the negotiated peace were settled. All that remained was the official ratification of the peace treaty in Spain. A massive retinue was then assembled under the negotiations' architect, and former commanding officer of the English fleet during the 1588 Armada, the Earl of Nottingham. Pomp and pageantry were naturally expected to accompany this landmark development in Anglo-Spanish relations and, consistent with King James I's proclivity for spending, little expense was spared. Ships were commissioned and constructed, carriages and liveries were handcrafted, and London's most talented tailors and milliners were contracted. Thomas Roe, recently knighted and now appointed as the Princess's Gentleman-In-Waiting, was selected as one of the 650 Englishmen to be sent to Spain. A fleet of small vessels escorted by the *Advantage* was sent ahead to Corunna to ferry Nottingham's accouterment of horses, coaches, litters, furniture, and royal presents. Ambassador Nottingham sailed in the *White Bear*, while lords, knights and gentlemen were transported in the *Repulse* and the *Warspite*. Plans were disrupted however when Nottingham discovered that the Spanish had switched the hosting ceremonies from Corunna to Santander; furthermore, the Spaniards had become slightly alarmed at the size of the English retinue and asked Nottingham to downsize his entourage. After these initial delays and changes in logistics, hundreds of nobles and lesser gentry finally landed and marched through the streets of Santander with companies of trumpeters, footmen and pages. Roe was present at the opening ceremony in Valladolid to observe how,

> the King (of Spain), descending from his chair, gave entertainment to his Lordship (Nottingham) with most kind and affable behavior, appointing him to sit down by him and that very near; which especial favour was much observed, and reported as a thing never used to any ambassador before that time. His Highness was pleased to take notice of such nobles and gentlemen as accompanied his Lordship in this his long and painful journey; and thereupon required they should draw near, which they did each after other to their reverence, and as they say *besar los manos*, which was only in bowing low to the ground, without touching either hand, or foot or any other part of his garments.[1]

Apropos of international diplomatic etiquette, the English visitors were allowed to attend a number of Spanish state functions, including the grand procession commemorating the christening of the future Philip IV. Later that week, the English officially presented their gifts to the King and Queen of Spain in the Duke of Lerma's private garden: six horses with embroidered saddles and cloths, two intricately crafted crossbows, four fowling pieces richly garnished and inlaid with gold, and a pair of bloodhounds. On 30 May, the English entourage were in attendance for another procession, the Feast of Corpus Christi; Roe and other Protestants must have viewed the arrangement of bishops and archbishops and their lavish display of iconography, with the Host being borne by four priests under a canopy, with some askance. Later that day Nottingham, with his complement of lesser and greater nobles, was received at the royal court to participate in the ratification ceremony,

> Before the king was brought a little table, whereon lay the Bible and a crucifix upon it. The Archbishop of Toledo read the oath with a reasonably loud voice; at one part of the oath [Nottingham] held the King's hands between his; to which oath the King sware kneeling, and laying his hand upon the Book, and afterwards subscribed to the articles and agreements drawn and concluded by both Kings.[2]

A tournament was staged the next day by the Duke of Lerma where two thousand lancers, light horsemen, and *carabiniers* fought a mock battle for the entertainment of the English visitors and, on the last day of formalities, the King expressed his satisfaction with the smooth proceedings by presenting Nottingham with a diamond ring valued at £3,000.[3] The English entourage, after two more weeks of farewells, complimentary gestures, and gift-giving, finally left Spain on June 20. This three-month ambassadorial mission was no doubt influential for Roe's seedling understanding of international diplomatic conduct. He had been able to examine firsthand the customs and court standards of continental Europe as well as make note of how other European ambassadors comported themselves during their foreign assignments. The intricacy of procedure and precedent would have been at its highest during the English ambassadorial mission to Satandar; although Roe was roughly a decade away from his first ambassadorial appointment, his participation in such a series of complex ceremonies, where any breach in the highly regimented protocol could prove disastrous, must have been formative. Most importantly, for three months Roe was in a position to observe the Earl of Nottingham and how he fulfilled his duties as an extraordinary ambassador representing the King of England. Nottingham's dedication to serving his king and country responsibly, and Philip III's respectful reception of him and his retinue, would have been significant lessons for Roe and his career as a foreign ambassador. Nottingham's bearing during the Anglo-Spanish treaty ratification illustrated to Roe that an ambassador's demeanor is fundamental to a diplomatic mission's success; to compromise or expect less in matters of protocol was unthinkable and generally contrary to the conduct of statecraft.

Eight years later, Roe was sent to Europe as part of a royal entourage escorting Princess Elizabeth to her new husband, the Prince of the Palatinate. This pairing was one stage in James I's ambitious scheme to bring peace to Europe through diplomatic marriages. Tension between the Catholic Habsburgs of Madrid and Vienna and the Protestant region of Bohemia had escalated since the Cleves-Jülich crisis of 1610. The marriage of James's daughter to the Palatine Elector, and his later plan to marry his son Charles I to the Spanish princess, the Infanta Maria, was designed to restore and secure peace through dynastic ties. On 21 April 1613, Elizabeth and her husband, accompanied by their various attendants, left England on the *Prince Royal*; interestingly, Roe was once again under the charge of Earl of Nottingham, who intended this voyage to be his last official act as Lord High Admiral. Although the marriage contract stipulated that the Queen was allowed forty-nine permanent English attendants, the number of persons on the *Prince Royal* and other official vessels neared seven hundred.[4] Several prominent courtiers were included in this mission: Lord Harington and his Lady, Lord Arundel, Lord Isle, and the Duke of Lennox. Frederick, his wife, and her entourage were received at Flushing and after touring through Middelburg, The Hague, Haarlem, Amsterdam, Utrecht, Thenen, and Arnhem, they reached their destination at Heidelburg. Starting in early June, the Germans entertained their visitors with six days of tournaments, pageants, and banquets.[5] In mid-June, the English entourage began to disperse and begin their respective journeys back to England but Roe, who was now suffering from twinges of gout or arthritis, decided to convalesce at the natural springs of Spa and it was here that Roe had his well-chronicled debate with the Apostolic Nuncio of Cologne, Father Wright. Roe soon returned to Frederick's court at Heidelburg whereupon his former charge revealed that she was in a state of near bankruptcy; unwilling to bring it to the attention of her father or husband, she entrusted Roe with pleading her case to Prince Frederick. Roe demonstrated a convincing talent for mediation as he delicately convinced the German prince to accept his new wife's financial burden. Roe's assignment to escort and ease Elizabeth's entry into the Palatine court was called short when news reached Heidelberg that King James was preparing to summon a new Parliament for 1614.[6]

These early diplomatic experiences tell us that, by 1613, Roe had a competent, if not masterful, understanding of the different facets involved in conducting an ambassadorial mission: the requisite supplies and finances, the importance of gift-giving and generosity, and the highly refined comportment with which ambassadors and their functionaries were expected to carry themselves. We also cannot overestimate his serving under one of the premier diplomatic agents of early seventeenth England, the Earl of Nottingham. Roe's proximity to this legendary figure during the 1604 Spanish ratification ceremonies, and then again during the formal procession through Germany in 1613, suggests at least a partial education and training in the art of diplomacy. However, there are other features of Renaissance diplomacy, of a more abstract nature, which need more attention here if we are to understand Roe's later behavior while serving in India.

Diplomacy, as a political art and as an extension of an organized state government, began developing in the Middle Ages under the auspices of the Papacy and powerful Italian city-states like Venice, Florence, and Milan. During the twelfth and thirteenth centuries, ambassadors were often referred to as *ambaxator, orator, nuncius,* or *legtus* and, more often than not, they were temporary envoys dispatched to a specific court to conduct specific negotiations. A critical development in the fourteenth century, according to diplomatic historians like Mattingly and Queller, was the evolution of "a permanent *officium* in which the ambassador, provided with a general mandate, is the titulary during his assignment; and when the existence of such an *officium* is not diminished if it should be temporarily deprived of a titulary, when such a vacancy creates the necessity of nominating a successor."[7] During the course of the fifteenth century, the establishment of permanent ambassadors in various European states became common practice. A new emphasis in the period of "a thousand formalities" was placed upon the ceremonial function of envoys; alongside this was the understanding that the ambassador was now the most solemn type of diplomatic representative.[8] As the contemporary political theorist Maulde La Clavière comments, "whether a prince was present in his own person or in that of his ambassadors did not make any difference."[9] Concurrent with these developments was a growing investigation by jurists of various legal questions, including the judicial implications of the ambassador's position and in particular his rights, immunities, and privileges.[10]

Understanding of an ambassador's duties, both in England and continental Europe, was highly regimented by the seventeenth century. The growth of independent nation states, combined with the improvements in governmental, financial and military organization, resulted in the refinement of diplomatic procedure as well as an increase in the number of permanently resident ambassadors. Like the military, clergy and judiciary, ambassadors acquired the status of professionals with their own rules of conduct, methods, and group identity.[11] Essentially, there were two types of ambassadors. First, the ordinary resident ambassador who served in a foreign country for a period of three years, during which he looked to routine diplomatic matters, and second, the special ambassador of ceremony who was accorded a considerably higher rank since his duties involved attending special negotiations or treaty signings.[12] The office of ambassador, and the duties and obligation it carried with it, was not an unpopular topic among seventeenth-century political theorists. François de Callières, a highly respected ambassador for Louis XIV, wrote several tracts on ambassadorial duties and the art of diplomatic negotiations.[13] Besides requiring technical competence, intellectual refinement, and a detailed knowledge of men and events, ambassadors are required to purport themselves theatrically: "an ambassador resembles in some respect a comedian, exposed upon the theatre to the eyes of the world, to act there the parts of great personages."[14] De Wicquefort, a contemporary Dutch commentator, also used this analogy,

> [the ambassador] ought to have a tincture of the comedian...perhaps in the whole commerce of the world, there is not a more comical personage than the ambassador. There is not a more illustrious theatre than a court; neither is there any comedy where the actors seem less what they are in effect than ambassadors do in their negotiations, and there is none than represents more important personages.[15]

Extrapolating from the earlier work of mediaeval jurists, seventeenth-century political theorists discussed at length the various rights and privileges to be enjoyed by ambassadors in foreign courts. It was generally understood that diplomatic enjoys were not to abjectly molested and were considered immune to local law. Moreover, it was the expected duty of a hosting king to guarantee that his functionaries followed this code of ethics, "a Prince, or Commonwealth, ought never to suffer any of his officers of justice, or any others of his subjects, of whatever degree of quality they be, to violate the Laws of Nations in the person of any foreign minister, who is owned as such in his dominions."[16] Ceremonial niceties were also standardized by this time. Specifically, the issue of precedence, a point Roe would have some difficulty with upon disembarking on the coast of India, was quite clear: "when a minister is arrived in a court, and has notified it to the Prince, he ought to give notice of it to all the foreign ministers who are in the same court, by a gentleman, or by a secretary. They pay him, upon that, the first visit, which is due to the last comer."[17]

With respect to English diplomatic sensibilities, observing proper protocol was so elaborate that a special officer was appointed to "receive and entertaine, Ambassadours, and Princes, during their abode in England; in all honourable manner as is used in France and other places."[18] Typical reception of a foreign dignitary started with the Master of Ceremonies meeting the arriving ship at Dover with royal coaches and wagons to transport the retinue to London. The procession was then welcomed by the Lord Chamberlain and a body of courtiers, who would then escort the ambassador and his staff to comfortable, occasionally luxurious, lodgings.[19] Within a few days, James I would meet the embassy at Whitehall Palace amidst an atmosphere of splendour and grandeur. Taking pains to acknowledge the innumerable gradations of honour, a series of courtiers greeted the ambassador and ushered him into the king's presence. This ceremony was finalized by the exchanging of gifts between the king and the ambassador; these items went beyond simple material value and were construed as symbolic representations of the relationship between two monarchs. Given the competitive nature of seventeenth-century politics, it was not uncommon to use gift-exchange as a means of conveying impressions of wealth and power and, with that, such often assumed gigantic and expensive proportions.[20]

The resident English ambassadors, routinely dispatched to various courts, constituted a small corps of career diplomats. The chief duty of the ambassador was to speak for his king, gauge the views and policies of the court he was accredited to, and to inform his own government about significant developments. However, a diplomatic envoy had to walk a fine line in the art of negotiating with a sovereign prince and, as de Callières warns, excessive subtlety and intrigue could be counterproductive. The great secret of negotiation is "to find out the means of reconciling those common advantages [between two nations] and of making them, if it is possible, to keep even pace together."[21] He was also expected to foster a climate as favorable as possible to his nation and, in doing so, should occasionally offer gifts to state functionaries in key positions. Diplomatic envoys understood that they were operating in a system moulded by patronage and gift-giving; as aspiring courtiers were expected to curry favour through 'bribes,' likewise ambassadors contracted patrons and contacts to advance their agenda. As de Callières advises: "[the ambassador] ought to express on all occasions a great zeal and good will for the interests of the court where he resides, and to impart to the chief minister all the good news for that court that comes to his knowledge, and to congratulate him thereupon, as well as upon the particular advantages that may happen to the said minister and his family."[22] Above all else, the resident ambassador was obliged to maintain and, if possible, expand his own nation and sovereign ruler's prestige. Consequently, an ambassador had to seriously scrutinize both oral and written diplomatic rhetoric to ensure there were no damaging nuances or insults. They were also instructed to preserve any national claims or prerogatives while concurrently limiting those of their competitors and, if a court had five or six foreign representatives, competition for the monarch's favours could become fierce and occasionally violent. With an entire nation's prestige dependent on protocol, disputes over precedents, titles, and seating arrangements became commonplace.[23]

"To Repayre a Ruynd House": Roe's Struggle with Mughal Diplomacy

Roe announced his arrival on 20 September 1615 by dispatching a letter to the governor of Sûrat, Muqarrab Khân. This dispatch declared that Roe was "authorised with full commission under the Great Seale of England and firma of His Maiestie as His Ambassador as well as to congratulate the said mighty King of the Great Mogull as to propound, treate, and conclude of sundry matters of consequence."[24] Undoubtedly, he believed himself to be leading a critical ambassadorial mission on James I's behalf; Roe was adamant on advancing English prestige in India, as was the standard practice of seventeenth-century European diplomacy. Hitherto, the English presence was isolated to a trading factory in Sûrat and a loose collection of trading factors centered in Ajmîr, Âgrâ, Burhânpûr, and Ahmadabâd. With the arrival of this embassy, England, or more specifically the EIC, hoped to expand their presence into a more comprehensive system of trading factories which could access the lucrative commercial traffic of the Arabian and Indian Oceans.

Roe's confidence and self-assuredness as an envoy of a Christian king is clear: "vnderstanding the custome of the Kings officers to scearch euerie thing that came ashoare… I, being an ambassador from a mightie King, did expect to haue all things appertayninge to my selfe and my followers free of priuiledg."[25] The Mughal port officials at Sûrat were nonetheless skeptical of Roe's claim; so many English ship captains and trading factors had acted 'officially' on behalf of James I that "at this name of an ambassador they laughd one upon another; it beeing become ridiculous, so many hauing assumed that title, and not performed the offices."[26] Roe quickly realized his would prove an uphill battle and that proper diplomatic negotiation would be impossible without first establishing the uniqueness of his station and the respect it should accord. While he naturally should have expected a certain level of hospitality and graciousness, Roe's objective to "make streight that which was crooked" became palpably righteous: "If I had beene the first that euer landed vnder that title, I would haue done noe less... The Kings honor was engaged more deeply then I did expect, and I was resolued to eyther rectifye all or lay my life and fortvne both on the ground."[27] This resolve began to dissipate in the face of Mughal bureaucracy and capriciousness and, within three days of his arrival, he was drafting a letter to the Mughal emperor complaining of Muqarrab Khân's "faythlesse" and "barbarous" reception.[28] The crux of Roe's complaint was the Sûratî governor's insistence that no negotiations could proceed without the English ambassador ceremoniously visiting him first. Roe's rationale for refusal was predictably blunt; "I could not thinck he wronged himselfe to visitt me that did represent the person of a King... I was not sent to him, and therefore would not see him."[29] After three weeks of delays, bureaucratic entanglements, and numerous attempts to search Roe's personal luggage, the English ambassador was livid in his summation of Mughal diplomacy:

> For noe profitt can be a good pennyworth at soe mvch dishonor; the person of euery man landing loccked up and searched like a theefe; sometymes two dayes before leaue can be had for any man to passe the riuer; a poore bottle of wyne sent to the sick deteyned; and euery trifle ransacked and taken away, with unsufferable insolencyes.[30]

Roe's immediate reaction to Mughal standards of diplomacy, "barbarous" and "want of Civilitye," can be explained by his previous ambassadorial assignments in Europe. It is obvious that these assignments shaped and reinforced his understanding of the rules of diplomatic conduct as he continuously cites European norms in his complaints against various affronts. In one memorable speech to a crowd of local port officials, he claimed: "I would engage my honovr (which I esteemed as my life) that no follower of myne had the worth of a *pice* of trade or marchandice: and that in Europe and most parts of Asia all ambassadors and theyr traynes were so far priueledged as not to be subiect to common and barbarous vsage."[31] His belief in the office of ambassadorship was obviously based on an *apriori* model; as he described in a letter to Âsaf Khân, "the honovr and qualety of an ambassador is not ruled by the cvstoms of England, but the consent of all the world."[32] Other examples ("it was the cvstome of Europe…", "as in Europe") suggest that he was determined to judge Mughal diplomatic etiquette in relation to his own European training. It is intriguing that Roe had already been warned several months earlier of the danger in assuming that international diplomatic customs were homogeneous. In a letter dated 10 October 1615, Captain Kerridge wrote: "the cvstom of these princes is not to receaue embassadours with such dewe consideration and honourable respect as is accostomed in Christendom." If we accept that Roe was already aware of a discrepancy between European and Mughal approaches to international etiquette prior to his arrival, his decision to repair the "ruynd house" of diplomacy was not a sudden response to substandard international etiquette. Rather, the stridency and highhanded manner with which he approaches these issues seems to suggest that Roe arrived with a predetermined goal of introducing "proper" diplomacy to the Mughal empire.

Roe's perception of Mughal attitudes towards sovereign nations and their representatives differs slightly from the earlier literary and court descriptions of *The Embassy*. Roe expends little energy in "transforming" or "translating" Mughal diplomatic practices but rejects them outright. Beginning with when he first stepped off the *Lion* until his arrival in Ajmîr three months later, Roe refused to see the Mughal culture as diplomatically sophisticated. However, within his diatribe, we find a change, or evolution, of sorts. The views expressed in the first two months are founded on European diplomatic value systems, but these change when he witnesses the arrival, and eventual success, of the Persian ambassador Muhammad Rizâ Beg in October of 1616. Hereafter, Roe begins to appreciate the symbolic importance attached to valuable gifts and makes the appropriate recommendations to the EIC Board of Directors. Lastly, six months before his departure, Roe slowly begins to grasp the Mughal approach to ambassadorships and why his designation as a diplomat/ trade envoy was so problematic.

The collision between Roe's ambassadorial style and the indigenous customs of the Mughals goes beyond simple linguistic or cultural miscommunication. One significant problem for Roe's mission was the lack of any formal precedence established by the EIC. Previously, ship captains like Hawkins and Best had arrived bearing royal letters from James I and in all likelihood comported themselves as ambassadors.[33] Roe was keen to rectify this misunderstanding of the Mughals and, as he explained to Muqarrab Khân, "for the prescedents of former men, they were noe rules to me that was a full Ambassador, and they, though sent by the king, yet were but Agents to prepare my way and to negotiate in the behalfe of the Honorable Company."[34] The arrival of an imperial entourage, sharing the same nationality as previous ones under Hawkins and Best, was probably confusing, and more than a little suspicious, to the Mughal state functionaries. Furthermore, Roe's affiliation with a trading company, while concurrently representing a sovereign king, would have baffled Mughal sensibilities. Fraternizing with "mean" merchants and traders badly impinged on Roe's claims to be a noble "man of qualetye"; his dual mandate of procuring trade privileges as well as representing a sovereign head of state could only hamper his success. Nonetheless, Roe failed to see the importance of this distinction and continually berated the Mughal lack of respect due to the ambassador of a Christian king.

The largest tangible stumbling block for Roe was the inability or unwillingness of the EIC to furnish him with the high quality goods needed to impress the royal court. Roe was aware of the importance of gift-giving in international relations, but he and the Board of Directors badly underestimated the profound symbolism attached to this ceremonial function by the Mughal rulers. After showing Muqarrab Khân a motley collection of swords, looking glasses, leather goods, some paintings and a velvet-upholstered horse-drawn coach, the governor tersely commented: "it was little and poore."[35] By this point, three weeks into his tenure, Roe was not reacting well to the Mughal government and he resolved either to establish a binding trade agreement or, failing that, encourage the suspension of English activity in the Indian subcontinent. This pessimism appears to have influenced his decision to bring less gifts than more to the emperor in Ajmîr since the English "residence here [is] standing on such fickle tearmes."[36] After two months in Sûrat, Roe had had enough time and opportunity to observe the standard of living among the nobles and elite of Mughal society and he was now painfully aware of how insufficiently he was prepared:

> Here are nothing esteemed but of the best sorts: good cloth and fine, and rich pictures, they comming out of Italy ouer land and from Ormus; soe that they lavgh at vs for svch as wee bring...Soe that for my welcome, if it depend on presents, I haue smale encouragement, and shalbe ashamed to present in the Kyngs name (being really his embassador) things soe meane, yea, woorse then former messengers haue had; the Mogull doubtlesse making iudgment of what His Maiestie is by what he sends...[37]

When Roe finally arrived at Ajmîr and made his presentation, the king seemed reasonably impressed but later made inquiries to the Jesuits in attendance whether the "King of England were a great Kyng, that sent presents of so small valewe, and that he looked for some iewells."[38] An interesting conversation took place shortly afterwards in which Jahângîr replied to Roe's repeated demands for an exclusive trading agreement by caustically asking, "what hath [James I] sent mee?" In a surprisingly poetic attempt to defend himself, Roe supposedly responded: "That my Master knew hee was lord of the best Part of Asia, the richest Prince of the east, that to, send his Maiestie rich Presentes were to Cast Pearles into the sea."[39] The emperor's question as to what *James I* had sent is important since it reflects the Mughal belief that diplomatic relations are the domain of kings and ambassadors, not trading factors and ship captains. Moreover, the cynicism of this rhetorical question reflects a certain level of resentment on Jahângîr's part. Whether or not Jahângîr realized or cared that the EIC were responsible for these goods is not important; in the Indo-Islamic environment, *shâhân bih shâhân dihand* ("only kings give to kings") and the implied message from James I was clear: the Mughal emperor did not justify or deserve lavish attention.

As Roe increasingly interacted with the court, he began to realize the importance of gift-giving in Mughal polity, both domestically and internationally. While he never fully grasped the symbolism underscoring the presentation of gifts, whereby a noble or ambassador expressed his oath, or *nazr*, to the emperor, Roe could discern that it was a requisite ritual in any royal audience. Two days after the aforementioned conversation with the emperor later, he witnessed 'Abd Allâh Khân's visit to Prince Khurram and made a meticulous list of what the Mughal noble had brought to express his loyalty to the Mughal *khândân*.[40] While Roe had been impressed by the quality of gifts presented by 'Abd Allâh Khân, he was apparently overwhelmed by what the newly-arrived Persian ambassador, Muhammad Rizâ Beg, offered two days later: twenty-seven Persian and Arabian horses, seven camels loaded with silk, several intricate velvet wall hangings and looking glasses from Venice, two chests of Persian handicrafts, forty muskets, five clocks, a load of gold-embroidered cloth, a number of silk carpets, a small collection of precious stones, several casks of distilled water and Persian wine (probably from Shîrâz), and an impressive array of jeweled swords and daggers. He also jealously noted the sumptuousness of the Persian entourage and how Rizâ Beg's turban was "wreathed [with] a chayne of pearles, rubies, and turqueses, and three pipes of gould." Roe was curious to compare his own reception with that of the Persian's and in doing so found "[Rizâ Beg] had in nothing more grace..in ranck far inferiour to that alowed mee."[41] This skepticism turns to mockery two nights later in a description of the court's reception of the Persian envoy; Roe commented how "[Muhammad Rizâ Beg] appeared rather a Iester or Iugler then a Person of grauety, running vp and downe...," and we are curiously reminded of the analogy between ambassadors and comedians made by the European political theorists de Callières and de Wicquefort.[42] The Persian representative was nonetheless ultimately successful in soliciting funds for 'Abbâs I to wage war against the Ottomans; moreover while *Tûzuk-i Jahângiri* carefully recounts Rizâ Beg's visit and includes the entire text of the Safavid *shâh's* letter, not one mention is made of Roe's entire four-year mission in India.[43] The Englishman's contempt for Rizâ Beg's behavior was apparently short lived since he soon turned to the time-old aphorism "when in Rome..." by writing a letter of recommendation to the EIC, reiterating the importance of gifts in the Mughal court.[44] October 1616 could be construed as a turning point for Roe's ambassadorial experience in India. One year had already passed and he was no closer to achieving his missions objective. While

Roe was quick to discredit his Persian counterpart, Muhammad Rizâ Beg's success with the emperor was humbling and must have made Roe seriously take stock of himself and his situation. Is it possible that Roe had realized that ethnocentric attitudes, the meager quality of English gifts, and the Mughal refusal to combine imperial diplomacy with trade matters were all proving to be hindrances in soliciting the exclusive English trading *farmân*?

In November 1616, Roe wrote a detailed report of his progress in the Mughal court to the EIC Board of Directors. Interestingly, Roe's aforementioned righteousness is visibly subdued and we find a clear and frank presentation of the diplomatic gaffes to be avoided. First and foremost, gifts being sent by a king should reflect his stature and wealth: "if they had not beene named as from a monarch, it had beene lesse despiceable." Second, in drafting imperial letters, the addressee should always preface the sender of the letter. And third, discussion of commerce or trade by a monarch was unbecoming and offensive: "[Jahângîr] despeth to heare of that."[45] This realization is evident in an interesting conversation the ambassador had with Âsaf Khân shortly before his departure from India. Not unsympathetically, the minister summoned Roe to his chambers and gave him some valuable advice regarding his two-fold capacity as commercial agent and political emissary,

> This Counsell Asaph Chan first gaue, telling me we were fooles and had brought vp a Custome to our owne hurt: the King expected nothing of merchantes but to buy, and at entrance (as fashion) a toy, and when anie petition, the like: that when we haue in the name of the King it should be seldomer, and then benefitting his honour. He demanded who practiced this Course but yourselues, neither Duitch, Persians, nor Armenian merchantes; neither did the King expect it.[46]

In a letter to James I, written a day after Âsaf Khân's admonition, Roe acknowledges the difficulty of his mandate but unfortunately this realization only came a few months before his return to England,

> I dare not dissemble with your Maiestie their pride and dull ignorance takes all things done of duty, and this yeare I was enforced to stande out for the honor of your free guifts, which were sceazed vncivilly. I haue sought to meyntayne vpright your Maiesties greatenes and dignitie, and withall to effect the ends of the Merchant; but these two sometymes cross one another.[47]

There can be little doubt that the Mughals were reluctant to unilaterally commit themselves to the English. With the Portuguese displaying obvious symptoms of institutional decay and the Dutch now making overtures, a binding treaty with the EIC was simply unnecessary. Apart from the larger strategic picture, the English lack of success can also be partially explained by Roe's unyielding approach to diplomacy. By the seventeenth century, the European model of diplomacy had elevated the status of an ambassador considerably; with the evolution of the permanent ambassadorial *officum* concept in this age of nation-state alliances and treaties, diplomatic envoys were considered one of the highest officials in Renaissance governments. A hosting nation was exceedingly cautious in their handling of ambassadors for it was widely understood that they were, in every respect, a personification of foreign sovereignty. The office of ambassador, as will be discussed shortly, differed significantly in the Perso- and Indo-Islamic context. While they were occasionally leading nobles and important personages who could not be lightly treated, envoys were not synonymous with sovereignty like their European counterparts. Another key difference, especially in the Mughal court, was that arriving ambassadors were expected to pay homage and swear oaths in the same manner as the Mughal nobility. From arrival until departure, the envoy, if anything, lost his status as a foreign emissary and became of one of the Mughal elite rank-and-file. Roe himself underwent this ceremony one year after his arrival when given a "picture of him [Jahângîr] sett in gould hanging at a wire gould Chaine...it beeing the Custome, when soever hee bestowes any thing, the receiuer kneeles downe and putts his head to the ground (which hath been exacted of the Embassadores of Persia)."[48] Moreover, Roe realized that accepting this new relationship would probably be conducive to his objectives; as he remarked of Muhammad Rizâ Beg, "I am allowed rancke aboue the Persian but hee outstripps mee in rewards. I know one that might creepe and sue would effect more busines than I." But Roe would never allow himself to do anything "unwoorthy [to] the honovr of a Christian king" and this would prove one of his largest obstacles. Acknowledging this discrepancy regarding the status of ambassadors in the east and west, Roe's appraisal that "[the Mughals] vnder Coulor of Ceremony did vse villany" seems to be more of an issue of agitated personal sensibilities than an accurate assessment of Mughal diplomatic standards.[49]

Diplomacy in the Indo-Islamic Context

Diplomatic dialogue with neighboring regions, rival or otherwise, is a core feature in any political state; with disputes over succession, militant regionalism, ethnic conflict, and religious pluralism characterizing most of the medieval Islamic period, diplomacy eventually assumed a prominent role in the Islamic context. Beginning with the Umayyad and 'Abbâsid Caliphates, when rulers like Mu'âwiyya (r. 661-80) and Mansûr (r. 754-75) had established offices like the *dîvân al-rasâ'il* (state department of correspondence) and the *dîvân al-rasâ'il wa'l sirr* (state department of correspondence and confidential records), diplomacy came to figure predominantly in Islamic state bureaucracy.[50] Moreover, during the subsequent medieval period in Iran, Central Asia, and India, diplomatic correspondence was widely recognized as part of a flourishing Persian literary tradition; letters and state missives were, in addition to bureaucratic documents, also examples of creative and elegant prose-writing.[51] We know, thanks to the work of scholars like H.R. Roemer[52], that the *'ilm-inshâ'* ("science of letter-writing") reached its zenith during the Tîmûrid period in Iran and Central Asia and considerable diplomatic activity was occurring among the various contemporary Islamic states (the Ottomans of Anatolia, the Mamlûks of the Levant, the Âq-Qoyûnlû and Qarâ-Qoyûnlû of Iraq and Iran, the Delhî Sultans, and the Bahmanids of India).[53]

By the mid-sixteenth century, the "age of gunpowder empires" was in full swing and the *dâr al-islâm* was roughly divided among the three great dynasties of the day: the Ottomans, the Safavids, and the Mughals. Keen to limit the centrifugal effects bound to plague any large, tribal-based empire, the rulers of these states worked hard to establish formidable bureaucracies which could handle the necessary duties of administration, public works, and taxation. This Islamic world was a politically and religiously heterodox one and, predictably, these three states were set on a course of intermittent competition, if not outright conflict. With imperial egos to be assuaged, religious toleration to be promised, borders to be disputed, and alliances to be forged and later broken, the Ottoman, Safavid and Mughal *dîvâns* were constantly engaged. This diplomatic dynamism was added to by the recent arrival of the Portuguese, Spanish, English and Dutch trade elements in the Indian and Arabian Oceans. As potential allies against other competing Muslim states as well as prosperous trading partners, the Europeans were soon included in the diplomatic scope of the various Islamic empires.

We know that the medieval Indian subcontinent was not excluded from the political and literary renaissance taking place in Iran and Central Asia. Due to the Mongol invasions, and then those of Tîmûr's a hundred and fifty years later, the thirteenth and fourteenth century witnessed a constant stream of religious scholars *('ulamâ')*, governmental ministers *(vuzarâ')*, poets *(shu'arâ')*, writers *(kâtibs)*, and scribes *(munshîs)* fleeing from the devastated cities of Shîrâz, Nîshapûr, Herât, and Kâbul to the relatively peaceful haven of northern India. When Bâbur established the Mughal empire in 1526, the Persian and Central Asian heritage had significantly influenced the sophisticated political diplomatic tradition being established by the Tughluq, Lodi, and Bahmanid dynasties. One of the classic didactic texts on *inshâ'* and the drafting of imperial correspondence *(tarassul)*, *Manâzir al-inshâ'*, was written by Khvâjah 'Imad al-Dîn Mahmûd Gâvân Sadr-i Jahân, who had emigrated from Âq-Qoyûnlû Iran to India and served as the Bahmanid chief *vazîr*.[54] Another pre-Mughal Indian contribution to the diplomatic arts was the Delhî Sultanate court *litterateur* Amîr Khusrau, whose *Rasâ'il al-'ijâz* is considered one of the finest of the early *inshâ'* works.[55] However, Bâbur also brought with him the literary and political culture of Bukhârâ and Samarqand developed earlier under Tîmûr and his successors. Sophisticated governmental infrastructure, as well as active schools of literature and poetry, had peaked in the reign of Sultân Husain Bâiqarâ of Herât (r. 1469-1506); his principal minister, Mîr 'Alî Shîr, is thought to be one of the foremost cultural and literary figures of early sixteenth-century Iran and Central Asia.[56] It is no coincidence that present day Indian archives and libraries have numerous copies of Central Asian *inshâ'* works from this period: 'Abd Allâh Marvârîd's *Sharaf nâmah*, *Nâma nâmî* by Khvândamîr, and the *Makhzan al-inshâ'* by Husain Vâ'iz Kâshifî are but a few.[57] This initial influx of Central Asian heritage, combined with Akbar's later mass-scale incorporation of *emigré* Persian bureaucrats, scholars, poets, and painters into the Mughal court, concretized Islamic India's ties with the rest of the Islamic world. Diplomatic activity between India and other empires to the north and northwest would always be framed and defined by this mutual cultural awareness and appreciation. Moreover, this acculturation homogenized the art of diplomacy (*îlchîgirî, sîfârat, risâlat*) to the extent that each of the three Islamic empires subscribed to a near-identical international etiquette, both in theory and in practice.

To understand more about the theoretical approaches of Perso-Islamic diplomacy, we should of course look to the medieval political theoretician Nizâm al-Mulk and his *opus magnum*, *Siyâsat nâma*. He dedicates an entire chapter to discussing the importance of ambassadors and their role in Islamic polity. First and foremost, the envoy spoke for a foreign king's sovereignty and Nizâm al-Mulk cautions "whatever treatment is given to an ambassador, whether good or bad, reflects on the respect for the king who sent him."[58] The duties of the ambassador are predictable: delivering of messages, negotiating of treaties, etc., and his qualifications are equally innocuous: he should be courageous in speaking, well travelled, knowledgeable, and have a pleasant countenance.[59] But an interesting Machiavellian tone is introduced by al-Mulk when he suggests that an ambassador should also use his visit to scrutinize the size, organization, and state of readiness of an empire's army, examine the defensive capabilities of forts and cities, and make himself familiar with the location and condition of major routes. This information should be later documented and submitted to his ruler and the state *dîvân* for perusal.[60] Using ambassadors for reconnaissance purposes was certainly not unique to the Islamic context but al-Mulk's recommendation here does tell us something regarding some of the underlying rationale of diplomacy in medieval Islam. Al-Mulk was acting as a state minister for the Saljûq dynasty and, like almost all other Islamic empires, the Saljûqs were land based and depended heavily on territorial expansion to fill the imperial coffers.

Taxation, usually arbitrary and repressive, served as a dangerous means to subsist on solely, and rulers periodically turned to *ghâzî* warfare as a lucrative source of revenue. The military backbone of any medieval Islamic state was essentially tribal and nomadic; a perennial domestic threat, these politically unstable frontier *amîrs* were often focused towards the periphery. Raids and small-scale invasions were fast, inexpensive to organize, and could yield a high return in precious goods, horses, and slaves. This strategy proved to be timeless as the later Ottomans, Safavids, and Mughals used their respective *beylerbeg*, Qizilbâsh, and Afghân *amîrs* to stage numerous invasions into south central Europe, the Christian Caucasus, and the predominantly Hindu areas of India. Waging war against Muslim states posed no serious theoretical problems either: the *sunnî* Ottomans could proclaim *jihâd* against the Safavid heresy to the east and vice versa, while the Mughals had the *shî`ah* states of Bîjâpûr and Golkundâ to contend with. The point being belaboured here is that expansion of empire through conquest was a core feature in Islamic polity and, predictably, this had certain influences on the art of international diplomacy. As Dr. Rizvi states of Nizâm al-Mulk's theory of diplomacy: "the ability of the negotiator, however, is limited by the nature of the matters of negotiations well as the equation established by the relative strength of the parties and their real interests."[61]

The strongest mitigating factor in determining diplomatic relations was the proximity and potential threat of a foreign empire. Aware of the overly military ethos of the Islamic state and the need for continued expansion, rulers were predictably most concerned with their Muslim counterparts. Tension was always at its highest at the inception of an empire or upon the accession of a new ruler. A freshly-crowned *sultân* or *shâh* was often fond of announcing a quick war in the hopes of consolidating internal support among the nobility. In 1504, Ottoman emissaries arrived at Isma'îl I's winter court in Isfahân to congratulate the young shâh on his enthronement, but Isma'îl's recent *blitzkrieg* success in 'Irâq-i 'ajam and his future programme for the *shî'ah*-dominated regions of eastern Anatolia probably has more to do with Sultân Bayâzîd II's overture.[62] Likewise, diplomatic tensions between the Mughal and Safavid empires grew considerably after Tahmâsp's crushing victory over the Uzbeks at Jâm in September 1528; with a temporary power vacuum in nearby Tûrân and the perennially uncontrollable Qizilbâsh on the march, Bâbur was quick to arrange an immediate exchange of envoys to determine the young *Shâh's* intentions.[63] The overly military nature of Islamic diplomacy is further seen with the arrival of the European trading powers of Portugal, England, and Holland. The Mughals and Safavids had little interest in negotiating trade matters but were primarily interested in the Europeans as a source of military assistance and technology. For example, the English were keen to corner a percentage of the valuable Persian silk market but soon realized that this was impossible without first offering military assistance to Shâh 'Abbâs I in expelling the Portuguese from their island-stronghold of Hormuz in 1622. Relations would be conducted under the guise of religious discourse but, very often, this served as the pretext for some form of military diplomatic arrangement. Shâh 'Abbâs II hailed a new era in *shî'ah* camaraderie with several missions to the 'Âdilshâhs and Qutbshâhs of the Deccan, but these were only part of a larger strategic programme of containing the growing might of the Mughal empire under Shâh Jahân.[64] Likewise, 'Abbâs I used the Carmelite monks in Isfahân as a link with Philip III in his plans to orchestrate a grand alliance against the Ottoman Turks.[65] The military capability of potential enemies and allies was the *prima mater* for Islamic diplomats and it served as the framework for political, religious, and cultural dialogues.

Dispatching an ambassadorial mission to initiate or augment diplomatic relations between two political states was an intricately defined procedure. The first step for the Islamic ruler, selecting an ambassador (*safîr, îlchî*), could be problematic for a number of reasons. If the ruler's objective was to negotiate a treaty or to discuss an overly sensitive issue, a special or extraordinary ambassador would have to be selected from among the elite nobility. Ordinary ambassadors, on the other hand, were usually sent as a gesture of a ruler's commitment to continuing preexisting relations. Given the competitive, occasionally cut-throat, nature of medieval Islamic courts, leading nobles were reluctant to volunteer for either special or ordinary ambassadorships. Prolonged absences from the political arena could result in the rise of enemy factions and/or the noble's displacement from the court; moreover, an ambassadorial assignment, especially a remote one, was often construed as a form of imperial punishment for some past misdeed. Functionaries of the *dîvân* were usually appointed to lead extraordinary ambassadorships such as, in the Safavid case, the *Ishîk Âqâsî Bâshî*, or Master of Ceremonies. Islamic rulers also liked tapping the religious administrations for special ambassadors; Khvâjah Jândâr led a mission from Bâbur to Iran in 1527, and likewise, Qâzî Shaikh 'Alî was sent by Humâyûn in 1549.[66] The Tûrânî Uzbeks, well known for their *sunnî* orthodoxy and erudite religious scholars, often send men of piety like the famous *khvâjahs* of Jûibâr to the Mughal and Safavid courts. The Mughal emperors preferred to send *sayyids* as ambassadors to Iran since their claims to be descendents of the *ahl al-bait*, or family of the Prophet, were thought to be pleasing to the *shî'î* Safavids.[67] Ordinary ambassadors were usually up and coming courtiers who lacked the political will and/or family connections to earn a prominent position in a ruler's court. Two of the requisite skills of an ambassador were *charb zubânî* (ability to please, entertain, and flatter) and, more importantly, *mizâj dânî* (ability to gauge another's mood or inclination).[68] Besides the ambassador, principal officials sent with a diplomatic mission included the *vâqi'a nigâr* (official reporter) and the *tahvîl dâr* (keeper of the gifts).[69] Prior to departure, an ambassador's status was usually registered by a *mansab* increase of 500 or a 1000; his rank was also included in the accompanying royal letter so as to inform the receiving sovereign of the envoy's high station.[70] If an ambassadorial mission was successful, the envoy was rewarded with a *mansab* increase. For example, when Khân-i 'Âlam returned from his six-year ambassadorial sojourn in Iran in 1619, Jahângîr "loaded him with all kinds of favours and kindnesses, and added to his rank and dignity."[71]

Dispatching a diplomatic mission could never be done without drafting a letter from the envoy's master and, in the Perso- and Indo-Islamic culture, diplomatic correspondence (*tarassul*) had become a literary genre in of itself. Such letters were usually drafted by a leading *munshî* of the court which would then be read and sealed by the ruler himself; on occasion, letters were written by the *vazîr*, as Abû al-Fazl and I'timâd al-daulat Hâtim Beg both did repeatedly for Akbar and 'Abbâs I respectively.[72] The rules and regulations for drafting letters, such as which honorifics to employ, what Qur'ânic and poetic verses to quote, and even the type of paper and ink to use, were mindbogglingly vast and meticulous. Scribes had a large number of didactic *inshâ'* works to consult for reference but some of the more prominent ones included Muhammad Hindûshâh Nakhjuvânî's *Dastûr al-kâtib fî'l ta'yyin marâtib* (c. 1365), Khvâjah 'Imad al-Dîn Mahmûd Gâvân Sadr-i Jahân's *Manâzir al-inshâ'* (c. early 15 century), and Husain Vâ'iz Kâshifî's *Makhzan al-inshâ'* (c. 1501).[73] Letters are traditionally begun with an *invocatio*, or *tahmîdiya*. Occasionally written in a different coloured ink (red or gold), *invocatios* are Arabic words of praise to God such as *huwa Allâh subhânahu* ("He is God, glorious is He") or *al-mulk lî Allâh* ("Sovereignty belongs to God").[74] *Invocatios* are immediately followed by the *elevatio*, or *iftitâh*, a distinct line of honorifics in Arabic that ended with the name of the addressee. It appears that the distinctive location of the *elevatio* (above and to the right of the main text) was designed to alert the reader immediately as to who the recipient was. The text of the letter then begins with a standard introductory phrase, such as *bi-hazrat* ("to his exaltedness") or *bi-janâb* ("to his excellency"). This is then followed by the *inscriptio*, or *khitâb*, a series of titles (*alqâb*), epithets (*nu'ût*), and benedictory formulas (*du'â, salâm*) designed to exalt the royal recipient.[75] The length of this *inscriptio* can vary widely depending on the *munshî*, the status of relations between the two corresponding parties, and the general style being used by the chancellery in question. The *inscriptio* of royal letters very often contain abundant Qur'ânic phrases, verses, and rhetorical analogies. Knowledge of both religious and profane verses was considered a key skill for *munshîs*; a scribe used this general introductory section of the letter (*anenga*) to adorn the letter with examples of "[his] knowledge of the religious sciences...proverbial sayings of the Arabs, and the wisewords of the Persians."[76] It is not uncommon for these portions of the letter to extend before the main text (*matn*) is introduced.

When the *inscriptio* is concluded, a short space appears in the text; it is here that the reader is expected to insert the above mentioned *elevatio*. Following this space, and thus immediately positioned after the addressee's name, is a standard blessing (*du'â*). Typical short Arabic blessings for kings are: *khalladu Allâh mamlakatahu* ("may God make his rule everlasting"), *ja'ala Allâh al-ayyâm* ("may God extend his days"), and *abada Allâh saltanatahu* ("may God perpetuate his rule").[77] The opening protocol of imperial *tarassul* is concluded with the *taqdîm-i khadamat* (greetings) and *sharh-i ishtîyâq* (expressions of eagerness); this section, the *salutatio*, is dedicated to communicating felicitations and guarantees of mutual concord (*mahabbat, ittihâd*) and friendly relations (*vidâd, mûvadat*).[78] The main part of the letter (*narratio*) is usually introduced with the expression *ammâ ba'd* ("now then"), *ba'ada hâdhâ* ("after this"), or *makshîf-i khâtir-i 'alâ bâd kih* ("it should be revealed to your lofty mind that..."). It should be noted that these expressions correspond to the *promulgatios* (*bidânand kih...*) we find in imperial decrees; understandably, the use of *promulgatios* and *dispositios* would have offended royal sensibilities and are rarely found in imperial *tarassul*.[79] Throughout the main text, the scribe would cater to Arabic expressions, quotations from the Qur'ân and *sunnah*, and, more often than not, interrupt the flow of the letter with lines of Persian and Arabic verse. It is in the *narratio* that the sovereign expresses the purpose of the letter which, in many cases will be indicated by the *intitulatio* (*maktûb-i tahniyyat*, etc.). Nakhjuvânî spends close to 400 pages discussing every possible topic (*dhikr-i ahvâl*) a letter might discuss: opening the routes for pilgrimage, deaths in the family, seeking a matrimonial alliance, and requesting protection for traders and caravans.[80] The concluding portion of the letter, the *eschatacollum*, usually contains a *corrobatio* and a reference to the seal (*muhr*), the date of the letter, and a *sanctio* (an invocation to God and/or the Prophet Muhammad) to validate the document.

Along with the letter, the ambassador was expected to ferry a large assortment of gifts and it is during the reign of Jahângîr that we find the quality and number of gifts, received and sent, reaching extraordinary levels. The demeanour of an ambassador, the size of his entourage, and the quality of gifts, were all measures by which the host sovereign judged an empire. Sincere in fostering good relations with his 'brother,' Shâh 'Abbâs of Iran, Jahângîr sent Khân 'Âlam to Isfahân in 1611, and the chief Safavid source of the early seventeenth century, Iskandar Beg Munshî's *Târîkh-i 'âlam-i ârâ-yi 'Abbâsî*, comments on the Mughal ambassador's arrival,

...but all were agreed from the beginning of this divine dynasty no ambassador ever came from India or Rum with such splendid and lavish equipments; and it is doubtful whether, even in the days of the great kings of the past, such an embassy ever came from a foreign land...from the day Khan Alam set foot on Persian soil, he had with him 1000 royal servants, his own private servants and 200 falconers and hunters. He also had with him mighty elephants with golden ornaments and turrets of innumerable kinds, and Indian animals such as lions, tigers, leopards, monkeys, deer, cows, etc...[81]

This particular embassy also had the added cultural element of being accompanied by Bishân Dâs, one of Jahângîr's most celebrated court artists, who eventually returned to India with many elaborate Persian miniatures and portraits.[82] Jahângîr's welcoming of ambassadorial entourages was equally sumptuous. As soon as he heard the news of an impending arrival, he ordered the suitable arrangements which involved the *mehmândâr*, an official host, arranging proper accommodations and seeing to the ambassador's wishes. During an ambassador's residency in Mughal India, he was treated as a royal guest and a considerable portion, if not all, of his expenses were subsumed by the king.[83] There are many references to the arrival of Persian and Uzbek diplomatic envoys in *Tûzuk* and, for the most part, they are lavishly received with cash, jewels, and *mansabs*.[84] Incorporation of visiting dignitaries was not isolated to Muslim relations since we know that Jahângîr gave William Hawkins of England a *zât* and *savâr* of 400 in 1611.[85] In fact, one letter to Shâh 'Abbâs in 1620 relates how Jahângîr was so impressed with Zain al-Beg's tenure in India that, if the Persian ambassador ever chose to return, the emperor was willing to travel to Kashmîr and receive the envoy himself.[86] Although Jahângîr's treatment of Persian ambassadors was tempered by his wish to retain control of Qandahâr, his attitude to other Muslim envoys was similarly grandiose,

...the ambassador of 'Izzat K[han], the ruler of Ôrganj, by name of Muhammad Zâhid, came to the Court...I distinguished him with the eye of kindness, and on the spur of the moment gave the ambassador 10,000 darbs (Rs. 5,000) as a present, and ordered the officials of the *buyûtât* to prepare and send things as he might ask for.[87]

The Uzbeks were aware of the Mughals' proclivity for hunting and often sent the official *mîr-i shikâr*, or Master of the Hunt, to accompany their ambassadors to India. Upon hearing of an embassy's imminent arrival, the emperor would issue a *hukm* (general order) to his provincial governors, ordering them to meet the foreign ambassadors and meet their every need while travelling towards the court. When a foreign envoy was approaching the royal camp, the *mehmândâr* was sent out to meet the ambassadorial train and escort it to the *darbâr*. The Mughal would then, via the *vazîr* or the *mehmândâr*, issue a *farmân-i istiqbâl* (*farmân* of reception) to the ambassador. A date for the formal reception of the ambassador was fixed in advance and, on that day, the envoy would arrive with his entire train, the royal letter, and a few choice gifts to present to the emperor. The formal segment of an ambassador's arrival was conducted in the public audience hall (*dîvân-i 'amm*) in full view of the court nobility and functionaries of the *dîvân*. Here he was expected to offer *sijda* (prostration), hand over a few choice gifts, and to convey the royal letter from his master. More sensitive details of diplomacy were discussed later in the *darbâr-i khâss* or the emperor's private baths (*ghusâl khâna*).[88] The minimum duration of an extraordinary ambassador's stay was three to six months and an early dismissal was thought to be indicative of good relations. The Mughals, however, were unique to their Ottoman and Safavid counterparts for their tendency to keep visiting ambassadors in their court longer than was necessary. François Bernier, the famous mid-seventeenth-century French traveller, noted accurately how "the Great

Mogol is in the habit of detaining all ambassadors as long as can be reasonably done, from an idea that it is becoming his grandeur and power, to receive the homage of foreigners, and to number them among the attendants of the court"[89]

The most intriguing, and possibly unique, feature of Mughal diplomacy is this incorporation of visiting ambassadors into the rank and file of nobility. Alluded to earlier, ambassadors staying any length of time were expected to express an oath of loyalty to the emperor; an envoy, in effect, served two masters while in a foreign court. However decently diplomatic envoys were stewarded, an ambassador was expected to observe those same regulations regarding *kornish* and *taslîm* that Abû al-Fazl had listed for the Mughal nobility in *Â'în-i Akbarî*. In some instances, demarcating a visiting ambassador from the rest of the Mughal nobility is difficult. For instance, Tahmâsp I's envoy to the court of Bâbur, Sulaimân Âqâ, fought alongside the Mughal emperor at the battle Kânwâ.[90] Likewise, the *Akbar nâma* describes how Walad Beg Takkalû and thirty Safavid *qûrchî* soldiers accompanied and fought for Humâyûn's army during the Badakhshân campaign of 1546.[91] In addition to the gifts being presented on behalf of his ruler, an ambassador was also expected to offer a small number of personal presents to formalize the oath of loyalty. For example, Jahângîr described how Zambîl Beg, ambassador of 'Abbâs I, performed "salutation" and then "presented 12 'Abbâsî (coin) as *nazar*."[92] Mughal understandings of sovereign-nobility relations, i.e. expressions of loyalty through the giving of the material vow, or *nazr*, were apparently extrapolated to diplomacy. While European observers defined such gift giving as a means of currying favour, the Mughals perceived an ambassador's *nazr* as, not only an acknowledgment of the emperor's power and dominion, but essentially a vow of obedience. This paralleling of envoys with high-ranking nobility is further seen in various *mansab*-like transactions of the period such as Zambîl Beg being further presented with control of a village valued at Rs. 16,000.[93] However, improper behavior or insufficient *nazr* only hampered an ambassador's success—when a Turkish emissary arrived in 1608, Jahângîr deemed his entourage insufficient and coolly dismissed him.[94]

In summation, the Mughals possessed an intricate, if not entirely consistent, appreciation for diplomatic matters. As Jahângîr declares, "the maintenance of the compacts and treatises of great princes is the cause of the order of Creation and repose of mankind."[95] Mughal diplomacy under Jahângîr was mostly characterized by the exchange of elaborate entourages with Shâh 'Abbâs I and this was certainly in line with the tenets of medieval Islamic diplomatic theory—maintain relations with those neighboring states which present the largest military threat. This certainly proved the case considering 'Abbâs's attempted seizure of Qandahâr in 1606 and his eventual successful invasion in 1622. Other key features of Indo-Islamic diplomacy included the exchange of royal letters, the appointment of special ambassadorial officials and administrators, and adhering to a specialized protocol. Especially worth noting is the need to reinterpret gift-giving as a material transaction; Mughal sources suggest gifts were symbolic of an ambassador's profession of loyalty to his hosting overlord. Lastly, topics of diplomatic discourse invariably included issues of sovereignty, territory, conquests, and religious matters; commercial issues were of no value given the Mughal indifference for overseas trade. Considering these characteristics, it is no surprise that Thomas Roe felt out of his element. Convinced that he was being foiled at every turn, Roe concluded the Mughals not only had little proper respect for international norms of etiquette, but their existing standards were surreptitious and founded on a voracity for gifts. Nonetheless, scholarship, particularly of the colonial era, has traditionally emphasized the significance of Roe's mission. He has been accredited with introducing "proper diplomacy" to the Mughal context, thus laying "the first step in a march of conquest which has only of late years reached its limits."[96] By the same token, he is applauded for his ability to overcome the underdeveloped criterion of the Mughal state and its stagnant sense of economics. As William Foster comments, "the victory rests with the Englishman, whose cool and resolute fence proved more than a match for the Oriental cunning of his adversary."[97] Traditional historians are fond of recounting Roe's near-militant reaction to the luggage-searching episode during his first month in Sûrat, but such port procedure, i.e. searching, itemizing, and taxing of all incoming goods, was part of a much larger Mughal administrative infrastructure.[98]

While European standards of international etiquette were similar in some respects (special ambassadorial appointments, transmission of royal letters, lavish entourages with equally lavish accommodations), there are some critical discrepancies. First, England did not and could not fit into the Mughal diplomatic scope; unfamiliarity, the great distance between the two states, and, most importantly, the EIC's refusal to act as a military institution (unlike the Portuguese) explain the Mughals' indifference to James I and the English nation. Although it should be noted that Chakrabarty has recently pointed out that Roe's inability to procure an exclusive trading agreement from the Mughal emperor might be rooted in Jahângîr's reluctance to supersede Prince Khurram's sovereignty as *sûbadâr* ("governor") of Gujarât, where the principal English trading station of Sûrat was located.[99] However, both Jahângîr and Âsaf Khân seemed genuinely puzzled by Roe's two-fold capacity as imperial representative and trade negotiator. Mughal definitions of diplomacy could not fathom a king's representative being sent to secure trading *farmân*s. Third, Roe's tendency to render the value of *nazr* as "daylye bribing" was a dramatic and naive simplification of a well-entrenched Mughal value system; by not acknowledging the importance of *nazr* to the relationship between ambassadors and emperors, Roe fumbled an extremely important step in Indo-Islamic diplomatic procedure.

NOTES

1. For an excellent contemporary description of Nottingham's mission to Spain, see Robert Treswell, *A Relation of...the Journey of the...Earl of Nottingham...*, London, 1605, reprinted in *Harleian Miscellany* (London: 1745), pp. 405-28.
2. Strachan, *Sir Thomas Roe*, p. 10.
3. Strachan, *Sir Thomas Roe*, p. 10.
4. Carola Oman, *Elizabeth of Bohemia* (London: 1938), p. 99.
5. Strachan, *Sir Thomas Roe* , p. 38.
6. Strachan, *Sir Thomas Roe*, pp. 45-46.
7. Garrett Mattingly, *Renaissance Diplomacy* (New York: 1955), p. 64. Another good study is Donald E. Queller, *The Office of Ambassador in the Middle Ages* (Princeton: 1967).
8. Queller, *The Office of Ambassador*, p. 99.
9. Quoted in Queller, *The Office of Ambassador*, p. 99.
10. H.M.A. Keens-Soper and Karl. W. Schweizer, "Diplomatic Theory in the Ancien Régime," in *The Art of Diplomacy*, eds. H.M.A. Keens-Soper and Karl W. Schweizer (New York: 1983), p. 21.
11. H.M.A. Keens-Soper and Karl. W. Schweizer, "Diplomatic Theory in the Ancien Régime," p. 23.
12. G.P.V. Akrigg, *Jacobean Pageant or the Court of King James I* (Cambridge: 1962), p. 56.
13. While writing *Du bon et du mauvais usage dans les manières de s'éxprimer* and *De la science du monde et des connaissances utiles à la conduite de la vie*, his most important tract was *Manière de négocier avec les souverains*, published in 1714. It was translated into English by A.F. White shortly afterwards. See François de Callières, *On the Manner of Negotiating with Princes*, ed. Stephen Kertesz (Notre Dame: 1963).
14. François de Callières, *On the Manner of Negotiating with Princes*, p. 23.
15. Abraham de Wicquefort, *L'Ambassadeur et ses fonctions* (The Hague: 1682), p. 294.
16. De Callières, *On the Manner of Negotiating with Princes*, p. 80.
17. De Callières, *On the Manner of Negotiating with Princes*, p. 99.
18. Akrigg, *Jacobean Pageant*, p. 57.
19. Akrigg, *Jacobean Pageant*, p. 57.
20. Akrigg, *Jacobean Pageant*, p. 58.

21. De Callières, *On the Manner of Negotiating with Princes*, p. 110.
22. De Callières, *On the Manner of Negotiating with Princes*, p. 104.
23. Akrigg, *Jacobean Pageant*, pp. 63-67.
24. Roe, *The Embassy of Sir Thomas Roe*, p. 28.
25. Roe, *The Embassy of Sir Thomas Roe*, p. 29.
26. Roe, *The Embassy of Sir Thomas Roe*, p. 30.
27. Roe, *The Embassy of Sir Thomas Roe*, p. 30.
28. Roe, *The Embassy of Sir Thomas Roe*, p. 37.
29. Roe, *The Embassy of Sir Thomas Roe*, p. 37.
30. Roe, *The Embassy of Sir Thomas Roe*, p. 49.
31. Roe, *The Embassy of Sir Thomas Roe*, p. 32.
32. Roe, *The Embassy of Sir Thomas Roe*, p. 140.
33. Holden Furber, *Rival Empires*, p. 40. Roe comments on this, "I landed at Suratt, where I was esteemed an Imposture like my predecessors; two befoer having taken the title of ambassador. Master Hawkins and Master Edwards, but so that they haue almost made yt ridiculous to come vnder that qualetye..." Roe, *The Embassy of Sir Thomas Roe*, p. 78.
34. Roe, *The Embassy of Sir Thomas Roe*, p. 38.
35. Roe, *The Embassy of Sir Thomas Roe*, p. 49.
36. Roe, *The Embassy of Sir Thomas Roe*, p. 55.
37. Roe, *The Embassy of Sir Thomas Roe*, p. 77.
38. Roe, *The Embassy of Sir Thomas Roe*, p. 99.
39. Roe, *The Embassy of Sir Thomas Roe*, p. 251.
40. "Abdala-chan came to visitt the Prince, so brauely attended as I haue not seene the like. To the gate his drums and musique a horsback, about 20, made noyse enough, fifty Peons with white flagges carried before him, and 200 souldiers well mounted in Coates of Cloth of Gould, veluett, and rich silkes, which entered with him in ranck; Next his Person 40 targiteers in like liueryes. He made humble reuerence, and presented a black Arabian horse with furniture studded with flowers of gould and enameld and sett with small stones. The Prince according to Custome returnd a Turbant, a Coate, and a Gyrdle." Roe, *The Embassy of Sir Thomas Roe*, pp. 255-56.
41. Roe, *The Embassy of Sir Thomas Roe*, p. 259.
42. Roe, *The Embassy of Sir Thomas Roe*, p. 262.
43. Jahângîr, *Tûzuk-i Jahângîrî*, Vol. I, p. 374.
44. This letter covers many aspects of the situation in the Mughal Empire and the Indian Ocean; the references to gifts, however, come on pages 305 to 306. Roe, *The Embassy of Sir Thomas Roe*.
45. Roe, *The Embassy of Sir Thomas Roe*, p. 306.
46. Roe, *The Embassy of Sir Thomas Roe*, p. 459.
47. Roe, *The Embassy of Sir Thomas Roe*, p. 465.

48. Roe, *The Embassy of Sir Thomas Roe*, p. 214.
49. Roe, *The Embassy of Sir Thomas Roe*, p. 35.
50. Fath-Allâh Mujtabâ', "Correspondence: ii. In Islamic Persia," In *Encyclopaedia Iranica*, ed. Ehsan Yarshater, Vol. VI, p. 290.
51. See Colin Paul Mitchell, "Safavid Imperial *Tarassul* and the Persian *Inshâ'* Tradition," in *Studia Iranica*, Vol. 26, No. 2 (1997), pp. 173-209.
52. H.R. Roemer significantly expanded scholarly understanding and interest in *inshâ'* works by translating and publishing the *Sharaf nama*, a collection of letters and state missives of one of Sultân Husain Bâiqarâ's junior functionaries working under the great secretary and *litterateur*, Mîr 'Alî Shîr. See H.R. Roemer, *Staatsschreiben der Timüridenzeit: des Sharaf Nâmâ des 'Abdullâh Marwârîd im kritischer Auswertung* (Weisbaden: 1952).
53. A number of *inshâ'* works, essentially collections of copied state missives, date from the fifteenth century. Notables include Khvândamîr, *Nâma nâmî*, 'Abd Allâh Marvârîd, *Sharaf nama*, Nizâm al-Dîn 'Abd al-Vâsi' Nizâmî, *Manshâ al-inshâ'*, Husain Vâ'iz Kâshifi, *Makhzan al-inshâ'* and Khvâjah 'Imad al-Dîn Mahmûd Gâvân Sadr-i Jahân, *Riyâz al-inshâ'*.
54. Besides *Manâzir al-inshâ'*, Khvâjah 'Imad al-Dîn Mahmûd Gâvân Sadr-i Jahân also produced *Riyâz al-inshâ'*, which contains a number of letters illuminating the diplomatic relations between the Bahmanids and the Âq-qoyûnlû and Qarâ-Qoyûnlû tribes of Iran. For more information on the contribution of this Khvâjah to Bahmanid bureaucracy, see Jean Aubin, "Les relations diplomatiques entre les Aq-qoyunlu et les Bahmanides," in *Iran and Islam* (Edinburgh: 1971) and H.K. Sherwani, "The Bahmanids," in *History of Medieval Deccan*, Vol. I, eds. H.K. Sherwani and P.M. Joshi (Hyderabad: 1973), pp. 183-93.
55. Roemer, *Staatsschreiben der Timüridenzeit*, p. 14.
56. Maria E. Subtelny, "Mîr 'Alî Shîr Navâ'î," in *EI*, Vol. VII, pp. 90-93.
57. For Khvândamîr's *Nâma nâmî*, see III No. 2, Mulla Firuz Library, Bombay, No. 2752, Rampur Raza Library, No. 774, Salar Jang Museum and Library, Hyderabad, and P891.556 K556I, Lucknow University Library. Copies of Marvârîd's *Sharaf nâmah*, or *Inshâ'-yi Marvârîd*, are located at No. 573 (Inshâ'), Andhra Pradesh Government Oriental Manuscripts Library, Hyderabad, 50/152 Habib Ganj Collection, Maulana Azad Library, Aligarh Muslim University, III No. 8 Mulla Firuz Library, Bombay, No. 113, Fort William College Collection, National Archives of India, Delhi, No. Ia 15 Curzon Collection, Royal Asiatic Society of Bengal Library, Calcutta, No. 782 Salar Jang Museum and Library, Hyderabad and

No. 2749, Rampur Raza Library. Look for Kâshifî's *Makhzan al-inshâ'* at No. 866, Khudabakhsh Library, Patna and No. 2747-2748, Rampur Raza Library
58. Nizâm al-Mulk, *Traité de gouvernement (Siyaset-Name)*, trans. and ed. C. Schefer (Paris: 1984), p. 164.
59. S. Rizwan Ali Rizvi, *Nizam al-Mulk Tusi: His Contribution to Statecraft, Political Theory and the Art of Government* (Lahore: 1978), p. 149.
60. Al-Mulk, *Traité de gouvernement*, p. 165.
61. Rizvi, *Nizam al-Mulk Tusi*, p. 155.
62. Khvândamîr, *Habîb al-siyar*, Vol. III, No. 4 (Bombay: 1857), p. 41, Bîjân, *Târîkh-i Shâh Isma'îl*, British Museum Or. 3248, fol. 112b.
63. Bâbur, *Bâbur nâma*, pp. 630-32.
64. Two 1657 letters to Qutbshâh 'Abd Allâh of Golkundâ and 'Alî Adilshâh II of Bîjâpûr from Shâh 'Abbâs II frankly encourage an attack on the Mughals. Ff. 6b-8a and 29b-31a of Mîrzâ Muhammad Tâhir Qazvînî, *Munsha'ât-i Tâhir Vahîd*, No. 50/182, Habib Ganj Collection, Maulana Azad Library, Aligarh Muslim University. See also J.N. Sarkar "A Little Known Chapter in Indo-Iranian Diplomacy in the Mid-Seventeenth Century," in *Indo-Iranica*, Vol. 25 (1972), pp. 51-56.
65. Steensgaard, *The Asian Trade Revolution*, p. 268.
66. Bâbur, *Bâbur nâma*, p. 566.
67. Riazul Islam, *Indo-Persian Relations: A Study of the Political and Diplomatic Relations Between the Mughal Empire and Iran* (Tehran: 1957), p. 227.
68. Islam, *Indo-Persian Relations*, p. 228.
69. Islam, *Indo-Persian Relations*, p. 228.
70. Islam, *Indo-Persian Relations*, p. 226.
71. Jahângîr, *Tûzuk-i Jahângîrî*, Vol. II, p. 115.
72. Many of Akbar's letters can be found in Abû al-Fazl 'Allâmî, *Maktûbât-i Abû al-Fazl*, while Hâtim Beg's letters have been included in 'Abd al-Husain al-Nasîr al-Tûsî's *Munsha'ât al-Tûsî*.
73. Elsewhere, I have argued that, in fact, there was a type of didactic *inshâ'* work which operated on the principle of offering massive indexes of possible verses and honorifics to select from and *Makhzan al-inshâ'* can definitely be considered one of these. Mitchell, "Safavid Imperial *Tarassul* and the Persian *Inshâ'* Tradition," p. 181.
74. L. Fekete, *Einführung in die persische Paläographie* (Budapest: 1977), pp. 26-27.
75. Khvâjah 'Imad al-Dîn Mahmûd Gâvân Sadr-i Jahân, *Manâzir al-inshâ'* (Istanbul: 1800), pp. 130-31.

76. Ahmad ibn 'Alî Nizâmî 'Arûzî, *Chahâr Maqâlah*, ed. Muhammad 'Abd al-Wahhabî Qazvînî (n.p.: 1909), p. 13.
77. Muhammad ibn Hindûshûh Nakhjuvânî, *Dastûr al-kâtib fi'l ta'yyin marâtib* (Moscow: 1964), Vol. I, pt. 1, p. 132.
78. Nakhjuvânî provides a number of possible formats for the *salutatio*. Nakhjuvânî *Dastûr al-kâtib*, Vol. I, pt. 1, pp. 140-48.
79. Occasionally the contents of letters were also announced as decrees to the *dîvân*. In these cases, *promulgatios* and *dispositios* were used. See Document 96, Fekete, *Einführung in die persische Paläographie*, p. 530.
80. See the index of Nakhjuvânî *Dastûr al-kâtib*.
81. As translated by Abdur Rahim, *Mughal Relations With Persia and Central Asia* (Aligarh: 1936), p. 28.
82. Islam, *Indo-Persian Relations*, p. 228.
83. Islam, *Indo-Persian Relations*, p. 230.
84. Jahângîr, *Tûzuk-i Jahângîrî*, Vol. I, p. p. 133, p. 193, p. 299, pp. 337-338, p. 374, Vol. II, p. 94, p. 115, p. 186, p. 195, p. 211.
85. M. Athar Ali, *Apparatus of Empire*, p. 49.
86. Calendar No. J.85, Riazul Islam, *A Calendar of Documents on Indo-Persian Relations*, Vol. I (Tehran: 1979), p. 10.
87. Jahângîr, *Tûzuk-i Jahângîrî*, Vol. II, p. 165.
88. Islam, *Indo-Persian Relations*, p. 231.
89. François Bernier, *Travels in the Mughal Empire*, trans. A. Constable and ed. V.A. Smith (London: 1916), p. 155.
90. Bâbur, *Bâbur nâma*, p. 540, p. 566.
91. 'Allâmî, *Akbar nâma*, Vol. I, p. 249, 252, 259.
92. Jahângîr, *Tûzuk-i Jahângîrî*, Vol. II, p. 186.
93. Jahângîr, *Tûzuk-i Jahângîrî*, Vol. II, p. 211.
94. Naimur R. Farooqi, *Mughal-Ottoman Relations: A Study of Political and Diplomatic Relations Between Mughal India and the Ottoman Empire, 1556-1748* (Ann Arbor: 1986), p. 44.
95. Jahângîr, *Tûzuk-i Jahângîrî*, Vol. II, p. 242.
96. William Foster, "Preface," in Roe, *The Embassy of Sir Thomas Roe* (Hakluyt Edition), Vol. I, p. 2.
97. William Foster, "Introduction," p. xxviii.
98. John F. Richards, "Mughal State Finance and the Pre-Modern World Economy," in *Comparative Studies in Society and History*, Vol. 23 (1981), p. 307.
99. Phanindranath Chakrabarty, *Anglo-Mughal Commercial Relations* (Calcutta: 1983), p. 92.

5
SIR THOMAS ROE AS POLITICIAN AND HISTORIAN

The constitutional history of Jacobean England edged to the forefront of historical studies in the 1920s when Wallace Notestein hinted that the causes of the Civil War (1640-49) could find their roots in the development of an aggressive parliamentary tradition under James I.[1] Since then, the debate has intensified regarding the extent to which we can consider the reign of "the philosopher king" a beginning point for constitutional democracy and the decline of absolute monarchy.[2] The idea of Jacobean MPs envisioning a constitutional monarchy, where the king would essentially be supplanted by parliament, is tenuous at best, but it would not be inaccurate to describe early seventeenth-century English politics as a period of parliamentary self-realization. The king's proclivity for debating features of English monarchical theory, something his predecessors had wisely avoided, sparked a new evaluative consciousness in the House of Commons. Coinciding with the aforementioned passion for the Roman tradition, this phase saw MPs and lawyers beginning to independently research the history of representative assemblies and their relationship with the English monarchy under Roman law.

Another unique aspect to the Jacobean reign was the growing suspicion among Englishmen that absolute monarchy under James I was conducive to a revival of Catholicism in the Church of England. Elizabeth I had astutely navigated her way through this political minefield by shielding her personal beliefs while at the same time steadfastly refusing to bow to pressure from Protestant or Catholic interest groups. Keen to limit the power of the prelates and ecclesiastics, she jealously preserved her position as the head of the Church while distancing religious doctrine sufficiently enough from both Calvinist and Catholic tenets to make the Church a thoroughly English institution. James I, on the other hand, upset this precarious balance due to his public Calvinist inclinations and his willingness to meet with leaders of the 'Puritan' committee at Hampton Court only one year after his accession. While he ultimately did decide that the Church of England was a settled matter, James's eagerness to debate theology and church structure was a new and dangerous development to an already tense environment. The new king's fondness for waxing poetic on the virtues of divine monarchy was also problematic. Parliamentary sessions under Elizabeth I, the few times they had been convened, were strictly controlled and monitored; the prospect of further restrictions and/or dissolutions predictably did not sit well with the House of Commons. Under the Tudors, absolute and infallible monarchy had not been scrutinized for the simple reason that neither Henry VIII nor Elizabeth I ever allowed for it to become a topic of debate. However during the course of James I's reign, MPs and commoners alike began to suspect the appearance of continental, specifically Catholic, absolutism at Westminster Palace. His conciliatory foreign policy towards Spain and France, along with the perceived threat of undue influence from courtiers like the pro-Spanish Howards and the Catholic Duke of Buckingham, seemed symptomatic of such trends in monarchical theory. John Hoskyn's comparison of James I's court to the "Sicilian Vespers" during the most heated stage of the Parliament of 1614, whereupon the king abruptly dissolved the proceedings, was no accident.[3]

In addition to his courtly appointments, Roe's grasp of such political trends is also attested to by his brief tenure as one of the MPs for Tanworth borough during the Parliament of 1614.[4] By 1614, the parliamentary environment was palpably tense; the two previous parliaments (1604, 1610) were characterized by obstructive courtier strategies and proved ultimately unproductive as the Crown and House of Commons locked horns over issues of royal prerogative and finance. By the spring of 1614, the royal debt (£680,000) could not be ignored and James was forced call another Parliament and, on 5 April, 472 members of both the Houses of Commons and Lords had arrived at Westminster to be sworn in by the Lord Steward, the Earl of Nottingham.[5] Although rumors of "undertaking" (essentially fixing the nomination and election of MPs to support a pro-Crown caucus) were already circulating, neither James nor the House of Commons predicted this session's unequivocal failure and its later dubious title, "The Addled Parliament of 1614." However, to fully appreciate the events of 1614 and what Roe gleaned from them, it would be helpful to look deeper into the parliamentary tradition between 1603 and 1614 and why James I's relationship with the House of Commons was so problematic. The Parliaments of 1604, 1610, and 1614 conformed to a similar pattern: the House of Commons using the incentive of parliamentary subsidies, which the king badly needed, to elicit the redress of grievances like purveyance and wardship. These parliaments, however, proved reflective of some larger issues, namely the unpopularity of James I's court-oriented absolute monarchy and the theoretical implications of the king's claims to be above the law of the land.

The underpinnings of Jacobean political thought were James I's respect and admiration for the Divine Right of Kings. Discussed briefly before, this approach contended how kings might come to power through a variety of means (election, conquest) but a monarch's authority was still derived from God alone.⁶ During the 1610 Parliament, James's opening remarks were decidedly provocative, "The State of the Monarchie is the supremest thing upon earth: for Kings are not onely God's Lieutenants upon earth and sit upon God's throne, but even by God himselfe they are called Gods."⁷ As Christianson observes, James believed that "just as God chose to channel his grace through the church, so kings chose to exercise their power through courts of law and parliaments; like God, they could not go back on their word."⁸ In matters of law, James I was equally righteous: "From this imitation of God and Christ, in whose Throne wee sit, in the government of all Commonwealths, and especially Monarchies, hath bene from the beginning setled and established. Kings are properly Judges and Judgement properly belongs to them from God: for Kings sit in the Throne of God, and thence all Judgement is derived."⁹ These declarations were not inconsistent with early seventeenth-century English political thought. People agreed that the king was God's anointed, His vicar on earth, and was responsible for administering divine justice to man. Sir Henry Finch, in his *Law, or a Discourse Thereof*, describes how "the king is the head of the commonwealth, immediate under God. And therefore carrying God's stamp and mark among men, and being as one may say, a God upon a earth, as God is a king in heaven..."¹⁰ During the 1610 Parliament, when MPs raised the question of whether the monarchy was answerable to common law, John Cowell replied that the king of England was "above the Law by his absolute power" and "to simply binde the prince to or by these laws were repugnant to the nature and constitution of an absolute monarchy."¹¹ Englishmen were probably not surprised with James's elucidation of Divine Right; this concept of how the king derived authority from God dates back to the Middle Ages and became a given understanding during the Tudor era. However, James I's constant need to reaffirm his infallibility in written testimonies and speeches brought the issue to the forefront.

With the rise of Renaissance Humanism, many English thinkers began to entertain the idea of a king's authority being limited by English law and the constitution. As Judson has remarked, "to believe in both the divine right of kingly authority and at the same time in its limited nature was perfectly natural and consistent for many excellent seventeenth-century minds."[12]

A component of this debate was the relationship between royal prerogative and the rights of the English subject. It was commonly understood that the king was due his prerogatives as long as they did not interfere with the welfare of the people. Furthermore, thanks to the integration and growth of the state under the Tudors, institutions and administrative government began to entrench themselves in the political landscape and, at the turn of the sixteenth century, the state, represented by Parliament and the Judiciary, had become intricately connected with the monarchy. Participants in the political arena accepted parliament without question and agreed, to some extent, on its role in English polity.[13] Supporters of the Crown during the Jacobean era (Bacon, Ellesmere, Wentworth), as well as proponents of parliamentary prerogative (Coke, Sandys, Phelips), concurred that parliament was an instrument by which the king and his subjects, lords and commoners, could assemble and debate relevant issues. It was the highest council and court of the king as well as the state, and it was through this institution that Englishmen's rights were preserved.[14]

Despite these common understandings, James I's first Parliament in 1604 was fraught with difficulties and, prophetic of future sessions, crown and parliament met to satisfy their own agendas. In the case of 1604, James was keen to effect a union between Scotland and England while the House of Commons intended to take this opportunity to raise and address grievances of abuse and corruption.[15] The House of Commons called for a curbing of both the wardship and purveyance institutions. When a tenant-in-chief died and left an heir under the age of eighteen, one of the king's prerogatives allowed him to appoint a guardian. Yet this practice was hotly contested because the Crown, hoping to relieve its financial burden, would sell these profitable wardships to aspiring courtiers and nobles who would then ignore their wards' education and upbringing to the point that when the ward came of age, he found his "woods decayed, old houses, stock wasted, land ploughed to the bare."[16] This concern turned to outrage when it was discovered that the Master of the Court of Wards, the widely detested Lord Cecil, had been working in conjunction with the Lord Treasurer to raise cash for the Crown.[17] The other item on the parliamentarian agenda was purveyance. The Crown could force merchants to sell at a discount to supply the various royal households and, with James I's lavish spending on his three households, purveyance was soon one of the most resented prerogatives.[18] The English people and the House of Commons considered wardship and purveyance serious grievances and wanted them attended to immediately, but the session came to a standstill when James refused any infringements on his monarchical right to access these institutions.[19] It would probably be more accurate to suggest that the underlying reason for James I's 1604 dismissal of the House of Commons was their refusal to accept the king's beloved project of uniting Scotland and England. The unpopularity of this proposal goes beyond simple xenophobia. As we know, James had brought a sizable contingent of Scottish courtiers with him (including the much villified Duke of Lennox) who were upsetting the institutional arrangements in the royal court; as a result, many disgruntled Elizabethan courtiers, who served in both Houses, used their influence to drum up opposition to the king's project of unification.[20] Still very much a king in a foreign land, James was tangibly upset by this parliamentary rebuff and retreated further into the now Scottish-dominated Bedchamber.

The 1610 Parliament was simply a continuation of the issues discussed six years earlier. However, one key difference was the debate over impositions, additional customs over and above tonnage and poundage levied at the ports for the purpose of protecting native trade. This regulating power had always been regarded a right of the Crown, but discontent over a decline in foreign trade and the provocative language used by the king in his revised *Book of Rates* (1608) brought the dispute to the attention of the House of Commons.[21] James reacted harshly by sending a message through the speaker, "to command the House not to dispute of the king's power and prerogative in imposing upon merchandises exported or imported."[22] An alarmed Parliament responded by stating their ancient privilege of freedom of speech was "an ancient, general, and undoubted right of Parliament" and that they were free "to debate...all matters which do properly concern the subject and his right or state."[23] In fact, John Chamberlain was so worried about the ramifications of James's strident absolutism, he wrote how the king

> made another speech to both the Houses, but so little to their satisfaction that I hear it bred generally much discomfort, to see our monarchical power and regal prerogative strained so high and made transcendent every day, that if the practice should follow the positions, we are not like to leave to our successors that freedom we received from our forefathers, nor make account of anything we have long that they list that govern.[24]

Unwittingly, James had introduced the precarious matter of the ancient constitution vis-à-vis parliament's right to debate matters of state. The king intensified the situation by chiding the House of Commons further, "you should not go to the root and dispute my prerogative and call in question that power which I have in possession, confirmed by law, derived from my progenitors and which my judges have denounced."[25] Parliament equated the taking of impositions with the taking of property and such an act violated a subject's rights and the law of the land. Sufficiently alarmed that the ancient constitution was in danger, members of parliament, many of whom were lawyers by training, began to research historical records in an attempt to provide interpretations of the English constitution which avoided the derivation of authority from monarchs alone.[26] Although the House of Commons was eventually assuaged after James agreed to declare it illegal to levy future impositions without the consent of Parliament, the 1610 session represented a critical stage in constitutional thought for England. The other significance of this parliament was James's growing disenchantment with the House of Commons and a deep-rooted unwillingness to summon future sessions. After the 1610 proceedings, James claimed he had suffered "more disgraces, censures and agnominies than ever Prince did endure" and that "no house save the house of Hell" could have treated him as the Commons had done.[27]

Needless to say, the chances of an auspicious beginning for the 1614 Parliament were slim. Opposition in the Parliament centered around Sir Edwin Sandys, Sir Dudley Digges, Nicholas Fuller, John Hoskyns, and Christopher Brooke, the last two being close friends of Roe's from his days at Oxford.[28] From the outset, the crux of the debate was whether or not further bills should be introduced addressing the question of impositions, and the first month was spent haggling over the order of business and which issue should be tackled first. Supporters of the crown, keen to repair James's dire financial situation, hoped to table bills of supply calling for parliamentary contributions to the crown debt but certain members of parliament insisted that the royal prerogative to levy impositions be settled first.[29] Pro-crown MPs, specifically Sir Henry Wotton and Sir Ralph Winwood, declared that historical precedents did not deny a hereditary king's right to impose. Predictably, these speeches elicited strong reactions from the opposition, most notably Thomas Roe himself, who argued that all kings had originally received their crowns by election and with the consent of their subjects.[30] Debate became more heated with Bishop Neile of Lincoln's personal attack on the House of Commons during an opening speech to the House of Lords. Greatly incensed, the Lower House insisted that King James punish the Bishop of Lincoln and moved to suspend the session until the matter was settled. A deadlock ensued until Neile made a public apology but, by this point, the House of Commons had been stirred into serious agitation.[31] A series of bitter statements were issued concerning Neile's behavior, including one from Thomas Roe who proposed that the Commons should enter an order to disable Neile "ether to be aboute the kinge or to be a bishop or to be amonest reasonable men, but to runne awaye and bewayle his estate in the woodes amongest wilde beastes."[32]

The House continued its berating of various Lords until James issued an ultimatum that either the members approve a bill of supply or parliament would be dissolved. The MPs were convinced that the king was suffering "ill councell" from foreigners, and John Hoskyns delivered a speech referring to the "swarm" of Scots around the king and how a wise prince would send the foreigners home as King Canute had done with his Danish followers some centuries earlier.[33] Sir Christopher Neville added to the growing hysteria by calling the court personages of James's court "spaniels to the King but wolves to the people."[34] Outraged, James closed the parliament and had Hoskyns and several others arrested and sent to the London tower. While the visible grounds for discontent were based on the issue of granting parliamentary subsidies in exchange for redress of grievances, the 1614 Parliament also attempted to address the larger theoretical question of whether a king is answerable to common law and the wishes of his subjects. The most outspoken parliamentarian critics were not motivated by the threat of divine monarchy itself but by the direction it seemed to be taking under James I. To these men, Jacobean divine kingship meant arbitrary rule from a man who was thought to be under the sway of self-serving courtiers. The fact that James I had already begun isolating himself in the court and indulging in elaborate and costly courtly functions like masque plays only reinforced popular resentment against the court.

During the 1614 Parliament, Roe was appointed to a number of committees to investigate the various issues being brought up in the two Houses. While there are no written records of Roe's suggestions, his comments and recommendations in the House suggest that he had a cautious, rational approach to these committees and what they were to recommend. Despite supporting the preservation of parliamentary prerogative and the ancient constitution, Roe was fearful of an unruly Lower House igniting the king's propensity for arbitrarily dismissing parliaments. As he sadly remarked after the 1614 debacle, "it was a dissolution not of this but all parliaments."[35] While historians like Hexter and Zagorin have suggested that parliaments such as the one in 1614 were evidence of an aggressive representative assembly attempting to expand their relative power, the stance of most MPs, including Roe, suggests otherwise. The House of Commons' agitation during the Addled Parliament was not evidence of an offensive strategy of expanding parliamentary prerogative but, rather, a defensive reaction to James I's belief that parliament was unnecessary to the smooth running of government. To some extent, their fears were well founded—it would be another seven years before the king would call another parliament. During the reign of Elizabeth, there had been significant gaps without parliament; the key difference here, however, was that MPs could not trust James to rule in an independent and unbiased fashion. He was too easily influenced by the likes of Lord Cecil and the Duke of Buckingham.

With respect to Roe, we know that he believed in the principle of elected representative assemblies, as his parliamentary remarks against Wotton, Winwood, and Neile seem to suggest. This, combined with the close friendships he shared with fire brand MPs like Christopher Brooke and John Hoskyns, point to his substantial reservations regarding absolute monarchical rule, especially when coloured by a strong courtier element. This antagonism towards both rigid absolute rule and courtier machinations was often expressed in Jacobean England via plays, pamphleteers, poetry, and, interestingly, historiography. Early seventeenth-century gentry did not study politics or statecraft as an independent discipline; rather, understanding how a monarchy and state were supposed to function was done from a historical perspective. In Renaissance Europe, history was inextricably connected to political judgment and served as the framework for analyzing any state or empire and, in vein with the Humanist tradition, scholars and court *litterateurs* looked to the classical histories of Greece and Rome in the spirit of *similitudo temporum*. For early seventeenth-century Englishmen, the historian of choice was the Roman Tacitus; his *Annals* and *The Histories* tended to serve as valuable case studies "for a general typology of political regimes."[36] In the case of *The Embassy*, Roe was obviously fond of Tacitus and continually turns to the sayings and maxims of the Roman historian to illustrate a description or commentary in his narrative. By investigating more about the Tacitean tradition in the Jacobean context, we can hopefully better appreciate the popular relationship between history and politics in seventeenth-century England and how this might have later influenced Roe's perception of a despotic monarchy like the Mughal empire.

Roman history was without a doubt the most important era of historical study in sixteenth and seventeenth-century England. Besides the driving influence of Renaissance classicism, contemporary English historians and antiquarians were drawn to the history of Rome to specifically learn more about how the emperors administered government and law in the island province of Britannica. Translations of classical historians of Greece (Herodotus, Thucydides, Xenophon, Polybius) and Rome (Sallust, Livy, Tacitus, Marcellinius) were tremendously popular and in constant reprinting in the early seventeenth century.[37] However, the emphasis of Roman historians, internal state conflict and constitutional changes, was more appealing for the nation state era than the Greek histories which tended to concentrate on military events.[38] Starting in 1574 with the Renaissance Tacitean scholar *par excellence* Justus Lipius and his translation and commentary of *The Annals,* Tacitus began attracting a significant following. After further translations, compendiums, and commentaries by Carolas Paschallas (1581), Scripione Ammirato (1594), Cauriana (1600), Piccolomini (1609), Pagliari del Bosco (1612), Frachetta (1613), Alamos de Barrientos (1614), Arias Montano (1614), Frezza (1616), Puccio (1621), and Gölnitz (1636), it would be safe to say that a "Tacitean" tradition had firmly established itself in early modern Europe.[39] England closely followed these continental scholarly fashions and, in 1591, the Warden of Merton College of Oxford, Henry Savile, produced an English translation of *The Annals* and *The Agricola,* which was later followed by Richard Greneway's translation of *Germania* in 1598. Salmon has recently demonstrated how English scholarly interest in Tacitus revolved around men like Savile, Greneway, and Henry Cuffe who had been part of a court network supporting the ambitious and ultimately rebellious Earl of Essex.[40]

With the change of English monarchs in 1603, a political tradition oriented around the Tacitean themes of intrigue and the corrupting influence of power had developed among the court historians and writers. Connecting Sir Thomas Roe was such streams of thought is not difficult. His education at the Inns of the Court came at a time when a "reinforced Taciteanism" had become popular thanks to the translation efforts of Savile and Greneway.[41] Moreover, one of the principal Senecan and Tacitean scholars of the Jacobean era was a courtier named Charles Cornwallis who had served alongside Roe as Prince Henry's household treasurer from 1609 until his death in 1612. In fact, the network of courtiers and scholars surrounding Prince Henry had a "common interest" in Seneca and Tacitus which allowed them to see their own age "as the analogue of first-century Rome."[42] Prince Henry himself remarked in 1610 that "Tacitus [was] a writer of admirable sagacity."[43] As translations and commentaries were diffused through English and European society, a demand for simplified, or abridged, translations grew. Essentially "vulgarizing" Tacitus, works like Frachetta's 1613 *Il seminario dei governi* or the 1608 reprint of the French scholar Paschallus's *Gnomae seu axiomata politico ex Tacito* were compilations of axiomatic gems designed to offer an easy-to-consult reference source for fledgling Tacitean scholars. A cursory examination of quotes made in *The Embassy* suggests that Roe was very much a product of this "Tacitean axiomata" tradition circulating in early modern Europe.

The basic premise of Tacitus's writing is that violent change is an inherent feature in any empire—states rise to power through violence and they collapse through violence. Moreover, empires cannot maintain equilibrium and are in a constant state of flux towards one of two directions: accession and decline. Obsessed with an empire's internal features and their contradictions, Tacitus concentrates on the events of Tiberius's court and how such political forums prove to be natural breeding grounds for vice and voraciousness. The duty of the historian is "to ensure that virtues are not left unrecorded, and that evil words and deeds are made subject to the tears inspired by posterity's denunciation."[44] We learn of the intrigues, suspicions, and cunning of Tiberius and his mother Livia against

Germanicus, the virtuous prince who can do no wrong; the ruler's propensity for viciousness is soon accentuated by the allure of absolute rule. For Tacitus, an empire cannot reach its greatest extent without the eventual imposition of autocratic rule yet, by imposing an autocracy, an emperor endorses and encourages the dissemination of intrigue and vice which leads to a state's eventual collapse. Considering the closed-door political maneuvering and the expansive network of conflicting courtier groups during the early years of James I's reign, it is no surprise to find Tacitus so in vogue. Thanks to theatrical productions like Jonson's *Sejanus*, these more unsavory characteristics of Taciteanism was diffused to a greater public audience. Perception of the court was being changed through the influence of such classical models which stressed political subterfuge and a moral corruption tinged with ostentatious displays of wealth and cultural refinement.[45] The moralizing tone of Tacitus against absolute, autocratic rule was also predictably popular among the parliamentarian-minded of Jacobean England. For them, James I's Divine Right of kings was edging suspiciously close to a style of autocracy which had ultimately led to the collapse of the greatest civilization in the western world. *The Annals* were "a story of constitutional instability and subversion" and "showed how a decline in social cohesion and virtue, together with the conspiratorial actions of ambitious men, might subvert ancient constitutional forms, giving rise to despotism."[46] Sir Thomas Roe's analysis of the Mughal empire through *The Annals* and *The Histories* suggests a political mind which agreed wholeheartedly with the Tacitean model of polity—avoiding absolute rule through republicanism. If this was Roe's personal political orientation, coming face to face with an autocracy such as the Mughal empire was sure to be problematic. By looking at some of the Tacitean references in *The Embassy*, and other political commentary, we can see the extent to which Roe's rendition of the

Mughals was influenced by the aforementioned issues and concerns of Jacobean political life.

"Pride, pleasure, riches": Roe's Characterization of Mughal Polity

Previously, we discussed the extent to which Sir Thomas Roe catered to the popular earlier perceptions of Asian despotism in his description of the Mughal nobility (chap. 3). Likewise, in his first meeting and description of the Jahângîr and the *darbâr* of Ajmîr we find the ambassador subscribing to an overly romantic imagery. Roe was obviously awed by the "richest prince in Asia" but he sensed a certain ostentatiousness in this display of wealth "as if it seemed to strive to show all, like a ladie that with her plate sett on a cupboard her embrodered slippers."[47] Most importantly, we find Roe reveling in the more sundry aspects of an Oriental court where the "woemen watch within [the court], and guard [Jahângîr] with manly offences" and the nightly entertainment consists of "presents, elephants, horses and many whores."[48] In a letter to Prince Charles I, Roe makes little effort to dampen this exotic imagery:

> noe man enters [Jahângîr's] house but eunucks; his weomen are neuer seene; his nobilitye are like covnters, placed high and low at his pleasvre: his seruants base and barbarovs: and all his life as regular as a clock that stricks at sett howers. For hee comes to bee seene at a wyndow at svnne rising to all his idolaters; at noone to the fight of the elephants and wild beasts; at euening hee remoues to a theatre vnder canopyes, wher in a gallery hee sitts to receiue sutes, to see and to bee seene.[49]

Likewise, the English ambassador was a little horrified at Jahângîr's tendency to oversee public executions and dryly quoted a Senecan axiom: *illi mereures: sed quit tu ut adesses ?* ("Doubtless they have merited their punishment but should you be present?").⁵⁰ These initial observations were fairly superficial and probably heavily coloured by the popular legends and myths of Asia circulating Europe. More importantly, we can sense Roe's Tacitean inclination to see such a court, or any court for that matter, as a forum for displays of wealth, moral corruption, and licentious behavior. During this period of familiarization, Roe himself refused to acknowledge any cultural or political sophistication, "a description of the land cvstomes and manners, with other accidents, are fitter for wynter nights. They are eyther ordinary or mingled with mvch barbarisme."⁵¹

However as time passed and the English ambassador became more familiar with the important personalities and the developments of the court, his analysis of the political climate became sharper. By October 1617, Roe was convinced of a power struggle between Princes Khurram and Khusrau and in one particular passage, he commented how "the issue if uery dangerovs; principally for vs, for among them it matters not who wynns." He finalized his prediction of doom and despair "as Tacitus did of the Empire of Roome when it was contended for by Otho and Vitellius,"

> The world...was well-nigh turned upside down when the struggle for empire was between worthy competitors, yet the Empire continued to exist after the victories of Caius Julius and Caesar Augustus; the republic would have continued to exist under Pompey and Brutus. And is it for Otho and for Vitellius that we are now to repair to the temples? Prayers for either would be impious, vows for either a blasphemy, when from their conflict you can only learn that the conqueror must be the worse of the two.⁵²

Once again, we have to wonder whether Roe's presentation of this courtier factional strife was not a product of his own Tacitean leanings. For Tacitus and his Jacobean advocates, imperial politics cannot be anything but conspiratorial; a despotic monarchy like Jahângîr's would naturally be synonymous with instability and subversion. As Roe goes into more detail about the various machinations of Khurram, Nûr Jahân, Âsaf Khân and I'timâd al-daulat, we find a corresponding increase in the number of quoted Tacitean axioms. Roe agreed wholeheartedly with Tacitus's conviction that power breeds immorality and cruelty and warns that "although [Khurram] is not yet in armes, nor so like to tyrannise, yet it is to bee feared, *Rebus secundis eatiam egregios duces insolescere* ("In the day of success even great leaders grow insolent.")."[53] As Tacitus wanted to show how absolutism and autocracy disseminated the politically corrosive elements of intrigue and rivalry in Tiberian Rome, Roe likewise wanted to reveal

> the beginnings and groweth of this empire; what fortvnes and what impediments it hath ouercame; what frendships it hath needed and affected; the ambitions and diuisions in the present state, that like impostumes lye now hidd, but threaten to breake out into the rending and rvine of the whole by bloody warr; the practises, subtiltyes, and carriages of factions and court secretts, falsly called wisdome.[54]

The obsession to uncover these "practises" and "subtiltyes" is not surprising for it was the responsibility of any good Tacitean-trained scholar and historian to reveal and expose the *arcana imperii* (secrets of state) and *arcana domus Augustae* (secrets of the court). This was a crucial point for Henry Savile while annotating his 1591 translation of *The Annals*: the *arcana imperii* "are the secret truths of appearances in affairs of state. For the mass of people is guided more by ceremonies or show than matter in substance."[55] The Tacitean model of polity, however, also stipulates that although absolutism will inevitably lead to an empire's collapse, autocratic rule is still necessary for an empire to reach its greatest potential. Jahângîr's brutal subjugation of an autonomous Rajpût territory in January 1617, while en route to the Deccanî front was simply summed up by Roe: *Haud facile libertus et domini miscentur* ("Liberty and lords go not well together.").[56] And when the emperor subsequently ordered the burning of the main city and the appointment of a new governor and accompanying military contingent, Roe was once again reminded of a Tacitean axiom: *nam neque quies gentium sine armis, neque arma sine stipendiis, neque stipendia sine tributis, haberi queant* ("For neither can the tranquility of nations be obtained without armies, nor armies without pay, nor pay without taxes.").[57]

As Salmon has discussed, Jacobean Taciteanism, principally due to the work of Thomas Gainsford and his publication of *Observations of State and Military Affairs for the most part collected out of Cornelius Tacitus* in 1612, had absorbed a strong Senecan philosophical angle. A "confluence" resulted between the streams of Senecan and Tacitean ideas whereby "Tacitus politicized Senecan philosophy and gave it a cynical bent, while Seneca strengthened the lessons that private prudence and withdrawal were the best policies."[58] As Roe became closer to Jahângîr, the ambassador soon believed him to be the epitome of a Senecan king living in Tacitean times—"for, if the King did gouerne, his nature is just, easy, and good... but hee, good man, doates, and heares only by one eare..."[59] The motif of just rulers being undone by unjust courtiers is a familiar Senecan one and we are reminded of Gainsford's comments, "a good prince governed by evil ministers is as dangerous as if he were evil himself." Moreover, Gainsford contended that there is no difference between Christian and pagan rulers in their failure to dispense justice; Christian princes will "take no more lessons than will serve their own turns."[60] Roe himself applies these cynical humanitarian principles in his rendition of the Mughal emperor but with an interesting twist. After the emperor's kindly reception of a Hindu holy beggar (*sadhu*), Roe felt 'fvll of admiration of such a virtue in a heathen prince" and commented that "wee, hauing the true vyne, bring forth crabbs, and a bastard stock grapes: that either our Christian princes had this deuotion or that this zeale were gvided by a true light of the gospell."[61]

The seemingly lawless nature of the Mughal empire was, however, a point of some concern for Roe, himself a product of the Inns of the Court where most Jacobean lawyers had received their education and training. In his never ending tirade against the Mughal proclivity for seizing and searching ambassadorial trains, Roe occasionally remarks on the Mughal disdain for the "Lawes of Nations." While securing the arrangements for his future journey to Ajmîr during the fall of 1615, Roe recounts a conversation with the governor of Sûrat,

> I tould him...that I was a stranger and Could not be suddenly prouided for so great a Iourny. Hee tould me I should haue his assistance. I thanked him, and replyed I did expect no more then what the Lawes of Nations cast vpon me, securitye and safe Conduct in his Gouerment.[62]

Moreover, while negotiating a special *farmân* for the port of Sûrat, Roe broaches this concept of "lawes" through a series of articles proposed to Khurram in August of 1618. The majority of the proposed points are economic in nature. but Roe's postscript provides an interesting insight,

> That in all causes of complaynet of controuersie the Governors and *Cazies* of the place should doe them [the English] speedy justice and protect them from all Injuries or oppressions whatsoeuer...that which I demand is bare justice and which no man can deny that hath a hart cleare and enclined to right, and no more then the Lawes of Nations doth freely giue to all strangers that arriue, without any contract; and in no case so much as the great kyng doth promise and command.[63]

The significance of these examples becomes clearer if we were to understand common Jacobean perceptions of law and its role in society. The crises of the 1610 and 1614 Parliaments, i.e. the monarchy's alleged encroachment on the rights of the House of Commons, witnessed the evolution of the "Common-law mind" which was essentially the belief in the existence of an "immemorial ancient constitution." In their attempts to procure precedents regarding the sanctity of representative assemblies, Jacobean lawyers made conscious attempts "to push the origins of the law so far back in time that they lay, in effect, beyond infinity."[64] In theory, historians and lawyers alike contended that "all laws in generall are originally equally ancient" and any differences between various national customs and legal systems thus resulted from variations and limitations on a natural law originally imposed by God.[65] Consequently, Roe's contention "they haue no written Law. The King by his owne word ruleth...he giueth sentence for crimes Capitall and Ciuill...and the Countrey so euill builded," interprets Jahângîr's inflated absolutism as contributing to the absence of a legal system which would have provided the necessary protection of subjects' rights. This equation, whereby natural law disappears in the wake of strident absolutism, is summarized excellently in Roe's letter to the Archbishop of Canterbury,

> Lawes they haue none written. The Kyngs judgment byndes, Who sitts and giues sentence with much patience, once weakly, both in Capitall and Criminall causes; wher sometymes he sees the execution done by His Eliphants, with two much delight in blood. His Gouernors of Prouinces rule by his *Firmanes*, which is a breefe lettre authorising them. They take life and goodes at pleasure.[66]

The Embassy, in some parts, is essentially a subtle Tacitean commentary of how overly rigid definitions of absolute monarchy impinge on the rights of his subjects. In a letter to Sir Ralph Winwood, James I's, compares his interpretation of Mughal polity with that of Europe,

> I could write your Honor may remarckable accidents in this Gouerment and Kingdome. All the Policye and wicked craft of the Diuill is not practised alone in Europe; here is enough to bee learned, or to be despisd.⁶⁷

The most telling feature of this particular commentary, however, is that it was sent directly to the English Secretary of State. The idea of issuing a polemic on unyielding royal authority directly to James I would have been untenable; however, by using the king's principal and closest advisor as a recipient and potential intermediary, Roe could contribute, albeit in a limited fashion, to this critical Jacobean debate. There are some discernibly consistent themes in Roe's summation of political Mughal India which seem to have been largely shaped by his own experiences in Jacobean England. An advocate of monarchy tempered by representative assemblies, Roe spared little energy in defending the despotic nature of Mughal rule. While his condemnation of Mughal courtly practices fits into the popular anti-court rhetoric of early Jacobean England, there exists a strong scholarly element which seems chiefly the result of his exposure to early modern Taciteanism. This 'school' of thought, which stressed the inevitability of subterfuge and tyranny in any political state, appears consistently, if not blatantly, throughout Roe's written perceptions. Besides broadcasting an aggressive anti-court sentiment, Roe's use of Tacitean and Senecan axiomata also serves in illustrating the inherent danger in allowing a monarch to rule without any checks and balances. Roe's finely turned legal sensibilities equated such tyranny with the disappearance of the "Lawes of Nations" and the subjugation of the Mughal populace. To suggest that the Mughal empire was anything but despotic would be foolhardy. However, one begins to question the intensity, if not the validity, of Roe's remarks after realizing the extent to which he was influenced by the political and scholarly trends of early seventeenth-century England.

Jahângîr's Obligations as Mughal Emperor

Roe's depiction of the Mughal monarchy is discernably one-dimensional. The breadth of Jahângîr's power overwhelmed the English ambassador and, as a result, the journal is consistent in its presentation of a stereotypical despotic Oriental monarchy but does little to comment on the subtle underpinnings of Indo-Islamic rule. As we have remarked in chap. 3, Perso-Islamic monarchical theory, to which the Mughals were loyal subscribers, iterated the need for a just and stable society. While the breadth of a ruler's power allowed extraordinary taxation and arbitrary rule, a king or sultân was subsequently obliged to ensure regular and smooth collection of revenue by, in turn, guaranteeing an orderly and productive society. Moreover, a ruler was expected to personally involve himself in his government and its maintenance of the empire; as Abû al-Fazl's remarked, "for monarchs the worship consists in the proper discharge of their duties to their subjects."[68] Only by being personally involved in day-to-day state business could the emperor guarantee the social and political stability he promised to the masses.[69] The Mughal empire was unique to its medieval Islamic counterparts due to the presence of an overall Hindu majority. If anything, an Indo-Muslim ruler's success was gauged by his ability to tread the fine line between being an orthodox *sunnî khalîfah,* while at the same time mollifying a potentially aggressive, non-Muslim subject population. *Sharî`ah* law stipulates that a subject population is divided between the *muslimûn* (Muslims) and the *kâfirûn* (non-Muslims). Non-Muslims, or *zimmîs,* were considered second-class citizens but still enjoyed civil protection and the right to continue their religious beliefs.

Despite pressure from orthdox *sunnî* elements to adhere to the letter of the law, i.e. Hindus being *kâfirûn* and not *ahl al-kitâb* (Christian or Jewish) and thus unable to enjoy *zimmîs* status, Akbar believed that

> Justice and Beneficiance must be exercised alike for all subjects (*jamî 'ri'âyâ*). The king is the shadow of God and the gift of Divine mercy is common to have believers and non-believers. A king must curtail the hand of oppressions (*zulm*) upon the weak because the prophet says 'the cry of the victim of injustice even if he be a *kâfir* is never rejected by God.[70]

Akbar and Abû al-Fazl wisely solved the dilemma by painting and propogandizing the image of the Mughal emperor as a supreme dispenser of justice. While a comprehensive system of judicial officials (*quzâ'*) existed for the minority Muslim populace, it was commonly understood that the emperor could try both criminal and civil cases for Muslim and non-Muslim alike. Furthermore, he heard all appeals and his personal sanction was necessary for sentences of capital punishment. As Ibn Hasan has remarked, "the Mughal policy was *not* to leave wide powers of punishment in the hands of the executive or judicial officers, and the regulations definitely required the sanction of the king for all capital punishments."[71] The most visible manifestation of the emperor's role in judicial affairs was the evolution of the *jharoka-i darshan,* which had been a Hindu institution innovated by Akbar to facilitate public appearances, and further illustrates the personal, patriarchal nature of Mughal rule. Adapting a previously Hindu facility such as this was one of the many examples of Muslim Indianization common to the sixteenth and seventeenth centuries. At the rural level, Hindus were governed by Hindu religious law and the judgements of Hindu Pandits; Badâ'ûnî once remarked that Akbar insisted that the cases of Hindus be decided by Hindu judges and not *qâzîs*.[72] In espousing the principles of justice and equality for all, thus promoting stability and social order, Akbar appeased the Hindu majority while concurrently preserving Mughal sovereignty.[73] It is difficult to accept that an astute politician like Akbar was solely motivated by the humanitarian principles of *sulh-i kul*. It is more likely that such judicial policies were meant to reassure the Rajpût nobility now serving in the Mughal court. The Mughal approach to law and order, nonetheless, accurately reflected Nizâm al-Mulk's axiom, "a polity can endure without disbelief but it cannot last without justice."[74]

When Jahângîr ascended the throne in 1605, he inherited his father's definition of the Mughal emperor as a just ruler and worked hard to ensure the proper dispensation of justice. As a newly entroned king, he wrote: "the first order that I gave was for the fastening up of the Chain of Justice, so that if those engaged in the administration of justice should delay or practise hypocrisy in the matter of seeking justice, the oppressed might come to this chain and shake it so that its noise might attract attention."[75] This was complemented by a proclamation of twelve ordinances, varying from the banning of river toll fees to prohibitions against facial disfigurement.[76] In fact, 'Usmân, a *sûfî* poet from Ghâzîpûr, lauded Jahângîr's chain of justice in his poem *Chitravali*.[77] When Jahângîr periodically shifted the royal court, one of his first orders was to have a temporary judiciary built in the new city, as he did in Ajmîr and Ahmadabâd. Here, he tended to his weekly routine of hearing criminal and civil cases meticulously, as both William Hawkins and de Laet had noted in their travel accounts.[78] Jahângîr took his responsibility as protector of the people so seriously that, after hearing how the governor of Panjâb, Sa`îd Khân Chaghtâ'î, was ruthlessly extracting revenue in his locality, the emperor sent "a message to him that my justice would not put up with oppression from anyone, and that in the scales of equity neither smallness nor greatness was regarded. If after this any cruelty or harshness should be observed on the part of his people, he would receive punishment without favour."[79] Nobles and high-ranking officers were not above the law in the emperor's eyes. When the nephew of Khân ʿĀlam, Hushang, was found guilty of murder, Jahângîr lamented, "God forbid that in such affairs I should consider princes, and far less I should consider *amîr*s. I hope that the grace of God may support me in this."[80] With these words, the emperor had Hushang executed. There is documentation beyond *Tûzuk-i Jahângîrî* further illustrating Jahângîr's vigilance in guaranteeing the rights of minority groups. In a *farmân* from 1608, he ordered the governors, officials and *jâgîrdârs* of *sûba* (province) Gujarât to safeguard the temples and *dharamsalas* of the Jain community. The Gujarâtî officials were also directed to ensure that houses of the disciples were left undisturbed and that no taxes were levied on pilgrims visiting the tirtha of Shatrunjaya.[81] However, we have to make an important distinction between Jahângîr's conviction to promote justice as a Muslim and his obligations as the ruler of an empire. Thanks to S. Alvi's research, we know that the Mughals distanced orthodox Muslim jurisprudence from run-of-the-mill civil law, evident in their creation of two separate institutions, the *Mahkamah-i ʿAdâlat* and the *Mahkamah-i Sharîʿah*.[82]

An absence of Mughal legal sensibilities is only a part of Roe's collage of tyranny, absolutism, and general chaos. The root of this lawlessness, according to *The Embassy*, lies with the Mughals' adherence to strident despotic rule. In Roe's eyes, there was no intermediary government infrastructure that could efficiently transmit imperial commands or act as a system of checks and balances. Cushioned by a lavish court culture, as well as being mislead by the self-serving whispers of Nûr Jahân and Khurram, Jahângîr's style of rule is presented as essentially a court-based political phenomena. *The Embassy*'s emphasis on despotism, however, disallowed any detailed discussion on Mughal government. An examination of this administration, however, suggests a sophistication that Roe either failed to notice or refused to acknowledge. We know, of course, that the emperor was the epicenter of this government: all central ministers and provincial governors were appointed by him; he determined when and how much *mansabdârîs* were appointed, and, finally, he reserved the right to revoke any political office or landholding (*jâgîrdârî*) when it suited him. Beneath the emperor was a layer of central ministerial positions which were designed to streamline the emperor's imperial commands. The chief officer, the *vakîl* or *vazîr-i mamâlik*, was the emperor's right-hand man who, in turn, was responsible for the smooth running of the *dîvân-i tan* (overlooking *jâgîr* assignments), *dîvân-i khâssa* (maintaining personal land of the king), and *dîvân-i buyûtât* (royal workshops of handicrafts, precious items, etc.). The minister overseeing the revenues realized in the emperor's personal domain (*khâssa*) as well as determining assessment figures (*djamâ'*) for *jâgîrdârs* and the paying of all expenses was the *dîvân-i a'lâ*. The next central minister was the *mîr bakhshî* who was in charge of grants of *mansabs*, upkeep of the army, and intelligence reports. The last central officer was the *sadr al-sudûr* who looked after the judiciary and the processing of charity grants. These ministers served in the central court, wherever it may have been temporarily located, and worked diligently to transmit the emperor's commands and to enforce centralized rule. These central functionaries, in turn, were supported by a network of provincial subordinates throughout the empire. Each province (*sûba*) was controlled by a governor (*sâhib-i sûba, sipâh sîlâr*) selected by the emperor himself. The governor, in turn, was severely restricted by a series of imperially-appointed agents, including the *faujdâr* (military commander), *qâzî* (religious judge), and *chaudharî* (revenue collector). As we mentioned in chap. 3, the bulk of the Mughal nobility were paid in cash as *mansabdârs*; however, a sizable number of officers were also appointed as *jâgîrdârs*, or landholders. Nobles were given these *jâgîr*-lands to generate revenue and taxation, a portion of which would be paid into the imperial coffers. However, as earlier Indian Muslim history had demonstrated, allowing nobles to cultivate a sizable local power base was always perilous and later Mughals like Akbar and Jahângîr were quick to ensure a rapid turnover of *jâgîrdârs* through dismissals and transfers.

We can conclude that Jahângîr conformed to the model of empire established by his father, Akbar. The perception of the monarch being shrouded in Divine light, in addition to his roles as judge and head administrator, continued into the first three decades of the seventeenth century and beyond. Moreover, the argument that the emperor represented a patriarchal figure who maintained a close relationship with his nobility class seems to apply to Jahângîr's approach to maintaining *mansabdârs*. The patriarchal element of Mughal rule, where the emperor looked upon his ruling elite as a family household, stemmed from Turco-Mongol traditions of the fourteenth century. Most important, however, the emperor ruled with daily, personal affirmations of loyalty from his subjects. These various features of monarchical status and power do not find any representation in *The Embassy*. Even if Roe was interested in presenting Mughal kingship from an indigenous perspective, he would have been forced to try and understand a wide-ranging number of variables, Turkish and Mongol culture and history, *sunnî* and *shî'î* definitions of authority, the *Sharî'ah*, and, most importantly, the administrative legacy left by Akbar at the turn of the sixteenth century.

Nonetheless, various historians of the nineteenth and twentieth centuries, in using Roe as a viable account, have failed to observe the vast discrepancy between seventeenth-century English models of government and the Mughal equivalents. The most glaring example is the accessibility of the monarch to his people. While Roe interprets the centrality of Jahângîr's position in the Mughal court as that of a stereotypical Oriental despot, or as a lead actor in a play, Indo-Muslim accounts prove this exposure was symbolic of the Mughal personal, patriarchal approach to administering an empire. Furthermore, Roe's description of court sedition does not reflect the deeply imbued understandings of loyalty and subservience held by the noble elite. Another incongruency, although far less obvious, is the perception of political authority and its position in the state. The language of Mughal authority and its acceptance, is a language of personal allegiance and loyalty between a bestower and a recipient of favours and gifts. Moreover, this dialogue of authority cannot be sustained without repeated personal encounters. This is somewhat different from Jacobean understandings of authority. In King James I's case, his authority is of a *contractual* nature, with specific terms and obligations understood between the two parties—the king and his subjects.[83] This contractual approach establishes a status quo, where both parties have a static, unyielding understanding of their relationship. Jahângîr's authority, however, is based on the premise of *consensus*, where the noble expresses loyalty and accepts his master's rule. The concept of arranging agreement among various tribal and clan heads for governing purposes dates back to the Chingîzîd period and was a tradition jealously preserved throughout later Central Asian dynasties, including the Tîmûrids.[84] Consequently, while the consensual nature of this relationship is decidedly one-sided in the favour of the emperor, there exists a dynamism and personal involvement in Tîmûrid courts like that of the Mughals which has no counterpart in England.

NOTES

1. Wallace Notestein, *The Winning of the Initiative by the House of Commons* (New Haven: 1924).
2. The charge has been led by Conrad Russell with such works as "Parliamentary History in Perspective," in *History*, Vol. 61 (1976), pp. 1-27, *Parliament and English Politics, 1621-29* (Oxford: 1979), *The Origins of the English Civil War* (London: 1973), and *The Causes of the English Civil War* (Oxford: 1990). Other revisionist works include David Underdown, *Pride's Purge* (Oxford: 1971), Kevin Sharpe's edited works *Faction and Parliament* (London: 1982), *Culture and Politics in Early Stuart England* (London: 1994) and his lengthy monograph, *The Personal Rule of Charles I* (London: 1993).
3. The "Sicilian Vespers" referred to an episode in 13th century Italian history in which Phillip III of Aragon organized a wide-scale massacre of French knights and nobles serving Charles of Anjou on the island of Sicily. It had long since been perceived as a tale of intrigue and murder in medieval lore.
4. Strachan, *Sir Thomas Roe*, p. 47.
5. Thomas L. Moir, *The Addled Parliament of 1614* (Oxford: 1958), p. 10.
6. Sommerville, "James I and the Divine Right of Kings," p. 63.
7. McIlwain (ed.), *Political Works of James I*, p. 307.
8. Paul Christianson, "Royal and Parliamentary Voices on the Ancient Constitution, c. 1604-1621," in *The Mental World of the Jacobean Court*, ed. L.L. Peck (Cambridge: 1991), p. 77.
9. Paul Christianson, "Royal and Parliamentary Voices," p. 85.
10. Margaret A. Judson, *The Crisis of Constitution, An Essay in Constitutional and Political Thought 1603-1645* (New Brunswick: 1949), p. 17.
11. John Cowell, *The Interpreter*, Cambridge: 1607, sig. 2QRr, 3A3v.
12. Judson, *The Crisis of Constitution*, p. 20.
13. Judson, *The Crisis of Constitution*, p. 68.
14. Judson, *The Crisis of Constitution*, p. 69.
15. Wallace Notestein, *The House of Commons, 1604-1610* (New Haven: 1971), p. 64.
16. Notestein, *The House of Commons*, pp. 86-87.
17. Notestein, *The House of Commons*, p. 88.
18. Alan G.R. Smith, "Crown, Parliament and Finance: the Great Contract of 1610," in *The English Commonwealth, 1547-1640*, ed. P. Clark, A.G.R. Smith, and N. Tyacke (Leicester: 1979), pp. 114-115.
19. Notestein, *The House of Commons*, p. 95.

20. See my comments above in chap. 3.
21. J.R. Tanner, *English Constitutional Conflicts of the Seventeenth Century* (Westport: 1983), p. 43.
22. Tanner, *English Constitutional Conflicts of the Seventeenth Century*, p. 44.
23. Loades, *Politics and the Nation*, p. 337.
24. Notestein, *The House of Commons*, p. 325.
25. Christianson, "Royal and Parliamentary Voices," p. 78.
26. Christianson, "Royal and Parliamentary Voices," p. 95.
27. Sommerville, "James I and the Divine Right of Kings," p. 67.
28. Moir, *The Addled Parliament of 1614*, p. 59.
29. Tanner, *English Constitutional Conflicts*, p. 47.
30. Moir, *The Addled Parliament of 1614*, p. 115.
31. Loades, *Politics and the Nation*, p. 347.
32. *Commons Debates, 1621*, Vol. VII (New Haven: 1971), p. 649-650.
33. Moir, *The Addled Parliament of 1614*, p. 138.
34. Strachan, *Sir Thomas Roe*, p. 53.
35. McIlwain (ed.), *Political Works of James I*, p. 506.
36. Francois Furet, *In the Workshop of History* (Chicago: 1984), p. 142.
37. R.R. Bolgar, *The Classical Heritage and Its Beneficiaries* (Cambridge: 1954), p. 328.
38. Arnaldo Momigliano, "Tradition and the Classical Historian," in *Essays in Ancient and Modern Historiography*, ed. A. Momigliano (Oxford: 1977), p. 165.
39. Ainaido Momigilanio "The First Political Commentary of Tacitus," in *Essays in Ancient and Modern Historiography*, ed. A. Momigliano (Oxford: 1977), pp. 206-11.
40. J.H.M. Salmon, "Seneca and Tacitus in Jacobean England," in *The Mental World of the Jacobean Court*, ed. L.L. Peck (Cambridge: 1991), p. 172.
41. Malcolm Smuts, "Court-Centred Politics and the Uses of Roman Historians, c. 1590-1630," in *Culture and Politics in Early Stuart England*, eds. K. Sharpe and P. Lake (London: 1994), p. 30.
42. Salmon, "Seneca and Tacitus in Jacobean England," p. 178.
43. Smuts, "Court-Centred Politics and the Uses of Roman Historians," p. 34.
44. Cornelius Tacitus, *The Annals of Imperial Rome*, trans. M. Grant (London: 1959), p. 14.
45. Smuts, "Court-Centred Politics and the Uses of Roman Historians," p. 30.
46. Smuts, "Court-Centred Politics and the Uses of Roman Historians," p. 41.
47. Roe, *The Embassy of Sir Thomas Roe*, p. 129.

48. Roe, *The Embassy of Sir Thomas Roe*, p. 85, p. 132.
49. Roe, *The Embassy of Sir Thomas Roe*, p. 270.
50. Roe, *The Embassy of Sir Thomas Roe*, p. 87.
51. Roe, *The Embassy of Sir Thomas Roe*, p. 104.
52. Given in the original Latin by Roe: *Prope euersum orbem etiam cum de principatu inter bonos certaretur: vtrasque impias preces, vtraque detestanda vota inter duos quorum bello solum id scrircs deteriorem fore qui vicissitt*. Part of this passage was omitted by Roe, hence obscuring the sense of the entire quote as given above. Cornelius Tacitus, *The Annals and the Histories*, Vol. I, trans. A. J. Church and W.J. Brodribb (Chicago: 1952), p. 50.
53. Roe, *The Embassy of Sir Thomas Roe*, p. 257. The quote comes from Tacitus, *The Annals*, Vol. II, p. 7.
54. Roe, *The Embassy of Sir Thomas Roe*, p. 272.
55. Quoted in Smuts, "Court-Centred Politics and the Uses of Roman Historians," p. 28.
56. Roe, *The Embassy of Sir Thomas Roe*, p. 339.
57. Roe, *The Embassy of Sir Thomas Roe*, p. 339. The original quote comes from Tacitus, *The Histories*, Vol. IV, p. 74.
58. Salmon, "Seneca and Tacitus in Jacobean England," p. 188.
59. Roe, *The Embassy of Sir Thomas Roe*, p. 338.
60. Quoted in Salmon, "Seneca and Tacitus in Jacobean England," p. 182.
61. Roe, *The Embassy of Sir Thomas Roe*, p. 328.
62. Roe, *The Embassy of Sir Thomas Roe*, p. 48.
63. *Articles Proposed to the Prince Sultan Coronne, Lord of Amadauaz and Sûratt, By the Ambassador, Vpon the Breach With the Portugalls, August 15, 1618* in Roe, *The Embassy of Sir Thomas Roe*, p. 477.
64. Woolf, *The Idea of History*, p. 25.
65. Richard Tuck, "The 'Ancient Law of Freedom': John Selden and the Civil War," in *Reactions to the English Civil War*, ed. J.S. Morill (London: 1982), p. 143.
66. Roe, *The Embassy of Sir Thomas Roe*, p. 104.
67. This letter was written on 30 November 1616, Roe, *The Embassy of Sir Thomas Roe*, p. 319.
68. 'Allâmî, *Â"în-i akbarî*, Vol. I, p. 163.
69. Hasan, *The Central Structure of the Mughal Empire*, p. 85.
70. 'Allâmî, *Akbar nâma*, Vol. III, p. 257.
71. Hasan, *The Central Structure of the Mughal Empire*, p. 320.
72. Badâ'ûnî, *Muntakhab al-tavârîkh*, Vol. II (Calcutta: 1898-1925), p. 356.
73. Sarkar, *Mughal Polity*, p. 192.
74. Sarkar, *Mughal Polity*, p. 473.

75. Jahângîr, *Tûzuk-i Jahângîrî*, Vol. I, p. 7.
76. Jahângîr, *Tûzuk-i Jahângîrî*, Vol. I, pp. 7-10.
77. Alvi, "Religion and State," p. 106.
78. Hasan, *The Central Structure of the Mughal Empire*, p. 318.
79. Jahângîr, *Tûzuk-i Jahângîrî*, Vol. I, p. 13.
80. Jahângîr, *Tûzuk-i Jahângîrî*, Vol. II, p. 211.
81. S.A.I. Tirmizi, *Mughal Documents (1526-1627)* (New Delhi: 1989), p. 82.
82. Alvi, "Religion and State," p. 106.
83. Hardy, "The Authority of Muslim Kings," p. 47.
84. See Martin Dickson, "Uzbek Dynastic Theory in the Sixteenth Century," in *Trudy XXV-ogo Mezhdunarodnogo Kongressa Vostokovedov* (Moscow: 1960), Vol. 3, pp. 208-216.

6

TRACING THE HISTORIOGRAPHY OF *THE EMBASSY OF SIR THOMAS ROE*

At this juncture, the reader might ask him/herself why the subject matter of the five previous chapters deserved such intensive discussion. Why should one primary account, albeit an important one, receive such scholarly scrutiny, especially considering it is but one of many contemporary sources shedding light on seventeenth-century Mughal India. It is in this chapter, an examination of how later historiography was influenced by what appeared in *The Embassy*, that we might be able to justify such an extensive analysis. Previous chapters have highlighted Roe's education and training in Jacobean court culture and the way elements of his environment became diffused throughout his later written commentary of the Mughal empire between 1615 and 1619. What we have found, so far, has been interesting. *The Embassy* undoubtedly borrows from a corpus of mediaeval Oriental imagery that depicted the East as a land of despotism and riches. The portrayal of a monarchy tinged with "barbarisme" which also hails to have the greatest treasures in Asia would not have been surprising for Roe's future readers. However, at the same time we find a subtle integration of some of the issues, concerns, and traditions circulating England in the early seventeenth century. Those who follow the 'Said-ian' school might point at Roe's contribution to that early modern European "collection of dreams, images, and vocabulary" as early evidence of the West's agenda to "control, manipulate, even to incorporate, what is manifestly differennt."[1] Doubtless, Said is right to believe that, in the early modern period, perceptions of the East tended towards a common vocabulary and conformity. However, European exposure to such areas was so limited that any intentions to describe or record the Asian would have been more motivated by a desire to learn more about a mysterious, potentially titillating, 'Other.' This is not to say that *The Embassy of Sir Thomas Roe* did not eventually serve political interests in the "Western style for dominating, restructuring, and having authority over the Orient."[2] There was indeed a growth of Western scholarship which, in its heyday, flagrantly manipulated the historiography of Mughal India to accentuate the importance of the British arrival and the success of their administration. As this chapter will hopefully reveal, Roe's written comments would later become a key component in this later discourse of rationalization. It is this historiographical repositioning that I wish to call attention to and how it has influenced modern scholarship up to as recently as this decade.

During the course of the seventeenth and eighteenth centuries, the EIC reoriented their holistic trade practices of the Indian Ocean and East Asia to an intense focus on the Indian subcontinent. The potentially lucrative proceeds from cotton, muslin, saltpeter, and indigo from the north Indian interior, combined with Holland's success in controlling most of the East Indies trade, convinced the EIC Board of Directors to concentrate their efforts on Indian trade. With the waning of Mughal centralized power in the latter years of Aurangzîb's reign (r. 1658-1707) and the rise of two aggressive non-Muslim powers, the Marathas and the Sikhs, EIC officials began to contemplate usurping military and administrative control of their immediate areas of trade. After the Battle of Plassey (1757), a series of developments (the grant of the *Dîvâni* in 1765, allowing the Company to collect land revenue and administer justice on behalf of the Mughal emperor; the

Permanent Settlement of Bengal in 1793; the defeat of the Marathas in 1818) slowly facilitated the Company's ability to control parts of the Indian subcontinent. As the construction of fortified factories and settlements intensified, especially in the area of Bengâl, there was a concurrent growth of problematic issues and concerns in understanding and administering the economic facets of Indian life. Local officers were directed to make inquiries into land revenue systems and modes of provincial and central administration; eighteenth and early nineteenth-century governors like Clive and Cornwallis were leery of drastic reorganization and were content to work with the preexisting models.[3] As a result, the eighteenth century witnessed the Company's patronizing of scholars to research, translate, and interpret indigenous documents in an effort to facilitate the transition to direct administration.[4] As Cornwallis told the Company directors in 1772, "we have endeavoured to adapt our Regulations to the Manners and Understandings of the People, and the Exigencies of the Country, adhering as closely as we are able to their ancient uses and Institutions."[5] However, the resulting proliferation of Indian histories and gazetteers was intricately connected with two influential factors: a) contemporary English trends of intellectual and academic thought; and b) understanding India's history, both Mughal and pre-Mughal, in relation to the looming economic and political presence of the British. The predominant intellectual trends of this period, be it Utilitarian or Romantic, had profound effects on Indian historical writing. Moreover, various traits of this initial wave of academic work has only recently begun to be questioned under the guise of "colonialism discourse."[6] Proponents of subaltern studies argue against the natural evolution of a bourgeois nationalist sentiment and suggest that changes taking place in India have more to do with "confrontation" and "crisis" at the popular level.[7]

Described as contributing "greatly to the establishment of his countrymen's position," Roe and his modest accomplishments figured significantly in rationalizing the lengthy, yet ultimately successful, evolution of British rule in India.[8] Politically, Roe was used by historians as a means of solidifying England's historical claim to India during a competitive, occasionally violent, era of overseas empire building. Academically, the marginal success of Roe's ambassadorial mission bolstered certain nineteenth-century convictions that history moves in a progressive and linear fashion; as a result, India's history is seen as thousands of years of painful evolution, culminating with Roe's arrival and the subsequent entrenchment of the English. The critical point here is that it is impossible to understand Roe's historiographical domination of early seventeenth-century Mughal India without examining the intellectual and cultural environment of the nineteenth and twentieth centuries.

Colonial British Historical Writing on India

Until the late eighteenth century, there was little or no academic infrastructure to tackle the gargantuan task of translating the necessary indigenous documents of South Asia. However, the Enlightenment and its emphasis on the natural science and empiricism sparked an interest in dissecting, analyzing, and classifying the various features of Indian society. As Thomas Metcalf argues, the non-European world was decisively set up as the 'Other' during this period and, partially due to works like Montescquieu's *Persian letters* and the invocation of the "noble savage," "the philosophies of the Enlightenment drained non-European societies of all content."[9] In the 1760s, Alexander Dow initiated scholarly interest in India by publishing his three volume *History of Hindostan* which was largely based on recently translated Perisian sources by untrained European travelers. Dow's *History* was typical of other Enlightenment histories which tended to gloss over critical examination of primary sources and rely on tales and anecdotes of a more exotic nature.[10] This probably fit well with the Enlightenment obsession with "Oriental despotism" and the understanding that the British ascendancy was preventing any further downward spiral by a hedonistic, lawless Indian society.[11] Dow's view of Mughal rule was predictably coloured by his belief that Islam was "peculiarly calculated for despotism." The fledgling state of indology was further anchored in 1784 by the creation of the Royal Asiatic Society of Bengal whose mandate was to offer a center of learning where scholars could work on and exchange views regarding indigenous texts. The Society's founder, William Jones, established a historiographical trend which interpreted India's history as a series of epochs which shifted between magnificent Hindu classicism, feudal Muslim despotism, and enlightened rule under the British empire.[12]

The Enlightenment movement was soon introduced to by a wave of envangelism which saw theologians and divinity scholars like John Wesley and Thomas Scott struggling to reintroduce core Christian values to the unchurched and spiritually destitute. Not surprisingly, evangelism was popular among the more-religious mind of the British administrators working in India, and a number of treatises were produced explaining the importance of introducing 'civilized faith' to the ignorant mass of Indians, Muslim and Hindu alike. The earliest and most characteristic of the Evangelical works, Charles Grant's *Observations on the state of society among the Asiatic subjects of Great Britain,* considered the British nation morally obliged to apply principles of Christianity and western education.[13] British Evangelicals, through schools, missionary movements, and overt proselytism, strove to rejuvenate a morally deprived and stagnant India by introducing "the pure and benign principles of [British] religion."[14] To the mind of the Evangelical, there was nothing commendable about Indian societies and their pasts which, prior to the arrival of the English, were tantamount to ignorance and suffering.[15] The later Utilitarians, whose mandate was founded on the need to introduce English concepts of government and law, assumed an equally ethnocentric stance. Their insistence that education be modeled on the British system and a general contempt for unfamiliar cultural features made the Utilitarians see eye to eye with the Evangelical movement on many points. It was out of this vein that the most influential work of the nineteenth century on India was produced—James Mill's *The History of British India.*

Ascribing to the booming capitalist economy of an industrialized England, Mill presented India's history believing that "progress is the natural law of society."[16] Mill clearly disagreed with William Jones' earlier Hinduphile arguments, declaring that ancient India was racked with "immortality and suffering" and that the Mughal dynasty was a relatively prosperous age with some close points of comparison to the feudal era of mediaeval Europe.[17] However, self-enlightenment for the Indians was impossible without the economically and politically evolved British.[18] The solution for rejuvenation was simple: a code of laws which allowed the "release of individual energy" under a larger umbrella of modest governing.[19] The debate regarding EIC administrative capability reached an apex in the late 1850s in the wake of the widespread 'Indian Mutiny.' Certain historians like John William Kaye responded to critics at home by arguing how the administrative principles and policies of the Company indicated a marked improvement over those of the Mughals.[20] Kaye and other Utilitarians' conviction that history was an evolutionary process also went hand in hand with some recent fashionable debates regarding racial theory. Specifically, there had been earlier scholarly assertions that Indians were in fact the progenitors of the Indo-European Aryan race. Such revisionist arguments certainly offended colonial British sensibilities and rallied a number of Utilitarian scholars to explain why the English had evolved to be the obviously 'superior' race. A plethora of ethnographies and philological studies during the nineteenth century, like Robert Caldwell's *Comparative Grammar of the Dravidian or South Indian Family of Languages*, described how Indian racial integrity had been breached and seriously diluted by successive invasions and large-scale immigrations into the subcontinent, while Europe's initial Aryan racial composition had survived relatively untainted. The combination of such racial theories with Utilitarian historiography provided "a scientific account of the diverging paths followed by India and England" while also explaining England's 'progress' in relation to India's 'decline.'[21]

Interpretive values aside, Mill's Utilitarian school assumes an important paradigmatic quality in its use of historical sources and general approaches to historiography. After the Company's late eighteenth-century wholesale sponsorship of document translation, a growing number of Persian sources were now available to aspiring British historians of Mughal India. However, Mill and others were skeptical of the value of Mughal court historians; Mill found many of them unreliable due to inaccuracies, ignorance, and carelessness.[22] Henry Elliot, both a protege of Mill and a staunch advocate of Utilitarianism, significantly expanded the availability of translated documents in his multi-volumed *The History of India As Told By Its Own Historians*. Nonetheless, one wonders at his claims of historical objectivity when he states how "the full light of European truth and discernment begins to shed its beams upon the obscurity of the past, and [relieves] us from the necessity of appealing to the Native Chroniclers of the time, who are, for the most part, dull, prejudiced, ignorant, and superficial."[23] If indigenous accounts were unreliable, than administrative documents (*parvânchas, farmâns, soyûrghâls*) were equally "lifeless" and a historian was subsequently required "to *imagine* the disposition of the people when he reads its ancient statues and ordinances."[24] Mills's suggestion to "imagine" invites dangerous subjective elements and one is reminded of White's recent warning, "once it is admitted that all histories are in some sense interpretations, it becomes necessary to determine the extent to which historians' explanations of past events can qualify as objective, rigorously scientific, accounts of reality."[25]

As the decades passed, the British became increasingly dogmatic with respect to their achievement in India. Historians of the late nineteenth century (Hunter, Hume, Wedderburn, Cotton) stressed that "political power was the great shaping force of civilization, and the great lever by which the vast majority were raised to a higher mental and moral plane."[26] Furthermore, these philosophic historians refuted the contention that British dominion came as a result of a sudden miracle and relied on Mill's earlier assertions that the British Raj was a logical conclusion to the long-working forces of history.[27] In one historian's words, the British success in India "was no sudden achievement but an indomitable endurance during a century and a half of frustration and defeat."[28] In particular they contended that Islamic rule in India marked an improvement for the polytheistic, caste-ridden Hindu society since the rapid military and political expansions of Mahmûd of Ghâznî, Muhammad Ghûrî, and Bâbur allowed a desperately needed revitalization for India. No matter how militarily successful or administratively ambitious, Muslim rule in India, however, could never reach its fullest potential. For historians like Alfred Lyall, Islam was inherently contraposed to democratic rule and responsible government; while the Mughals were considered keen patrons of architecture and poetry, they were ultimately tyrants whose strict notions of absolutism would prove to be their undoing. There can be no mistake that the British historical agenda was clear: India would continue to be in "complete disorganization" without benevolent, foreign intervention.[29] Within the midst of such assurance, there was however a certain confusion and uneasiness. The British tended to view Indians as people like themselves, that is a nation which had the potential of being culturally and politically Anglified; at the same time, there was a distinct Oriental perception of Indians which insisted that they exhibited "enuring qualities of difference."[30] Three critical features of these early historiographical trends are important here. First, there was a pervading sense of linear progress, or evolution, where historians looked admiringly upon the early EIC and its capacity to circumvent difficulties while planting the seeds of a future empire. The second characteristic, almost a subsidiary of the first, was a general depiction of the Mughal empire as a politically stunted and socially depraved state entity. Third, while translated indigenous sources could be valuable for practical, administrative information, their contribution to sociopolitical history was deemed limited and biased.

Appeasing Colonial Interests: *The Embassy of Sir Thomas Roe* in Early Modern Indian Historiography

In the introduction, I referred to the domed interior of the Victoria Memorial Hall and how a panel of Roe's arrival was juxtaposed with other panels depicting great events in British Raj history. The image of England's first ambassador to India confidently exiting a sumptuous carriage amidst welcoming Mughal courtiers and officers was no doubt seen as a momentous occasion by Lord Clive and the Memorial's architect.[31] In nineteenth-century historiography, interpreting history in terms of influential personalities and their deeds was not uncommon. The era of European expansion, and specifically those leading the expansion, was a topic of some significance for those attempting to explain the success of colonial imperialism.

Were men like Christopher Columbus and Alvarez Cabral not ultimately responsible for the introduction of 'civilization' to the remainder of the world? Those figures in history who ventured into unfamiliar and dangerous territory sparked a romanticism in their later biographers and chroniclers. Explorers like Samuel Champlain "watched over the new settlement [in New France] with the tender solicitude of a parent carefully protecting his offspring from danger, and ready to sacrifice his life to save it from disaster"[32] while Sir Walter Raleigh's "themes of thought" would constitute "the future destinies of America."[33] As Stockes reminds us, the function of such historians' work "was to inform and exhort by presenting the national character in its highest examples, and [by doing so] he was to demonstrate how individual character moulded history."[34]

As one of the first Englishmen of note to personally negotiate with the Mughals, Roe was marked as a perfect candidate for this historiographical style. In Lane-Poole's estimation, he was "a true Elizabethan, with the gallant bravery, the passionate devotion to king and country, the great-hearted fanaticism of his age."[35] Foster parallels this tone, "English prestige...was raised to a high pitch by Roe's gallant bearing and indomitable will"[36] and *The Cambridge History of India* lauds his "stout resistance to indignities."[37] Victorian scholars were obviously not reluctant to imbue Thomas Roe with all the biographical features ("indomitable", "gallant", "passionate") that national heroes and heroines alike share. His accomplishments in Mughal India were seen in an equally favourable light, suggesting that his arrival and later tenure in the Mughal court came at a critical time for the English "when [Roe] came to India, the English were very nearly on the point of being driven out of even their slight hold at Surat...the Mughal authorities were accustomed to treat the English as beggars to be spurned. All this changed before he left."[38] For Foster, Roe's mission "was the first step in a march of conqeust" and "the scarlet liveries which escorted the ambassador through Rajputana were prophetic of a time when a descendant of King James would rule over an Indian empire vaster and infinitely more prosperous than ever owned the sway of a Mogul."[39] Some historians go beyond the importance of Roe to British history in India by suggesting that the ambassador's arrival was a significant event in the history of the Mughal empire itself, despite the fact that no contemporary Mughal histories make any mention of this ambassadorial mission.[40]

In the eyes of colonial-era scholars, Roe obviously secured the anchor by which British imperialism was able to grow and consolidate. Such views, however, badly misrepresent the relationship between the English national government and the EIC. To see English activity in South Asia as nationally or imperially motivated is ambitious at best. As Holden Furber succinctly points out, the historiographical trend of describing early EIC missions as 'imperial' or 'colonial' is suspect. Records from the early seventeenth century make no use of the terms "British empire" or "English" in connection with India. Documentation only refers to India's commercial potential while the English monarchy, fearful of disturbing the recent peace with Spain (1604), actually made endeavours to distance itself from the occasionally aggressive policies of the EIC against the Protuguese *Estado da India*.[41] The EIC during the years 1614-18 was essentially represented by a small circle of English mercantile distributing large amounts of capital and had little to do with 'national' interests.[42] As Steensgaard remarks, there was "almost a total lack of appeal to national glory in the Company's paper and in the relevant pamphlet literature."[43] In addition, English factories in India were not only minimal in number but represented a very minute percentage of factories spanning the western Indian Ocean, Persia, Ceylon, southeast Asia, and the Orient. In 1615, the East India Company was evidently unsure of its mandate as Sir

Thomas Smythe and the Board of Directors continued to send agents and expeditions to new areas of trade. While they were certainly keen to gain a foothold in the lucrative textile trade of India, EIC officials saw Roe's mission as a small step towards establishing themselves in the larger network of ongoing Asian trade from Musqat to China.[44] The implications of Roe's ambassadorial 'success' become even further diminished when one appreciates how bitterly EIC agents of this period were complaining about the relative strength of native trade elements and the competing European powers of the *Estado da India* and the VOC John Millward warned in April of 1616 how the "Guzzarats" (Gujarâtis) were "dangerous and malicious" traders while Samuel Boyle wrote of desperate competition with the Dutch in December 1615.[45]

Roe's negotiations with the Mughal court were without a doubt frustrating affairs. His mandate of securing England an exclusive trading position in the Mughal empire was an ambitious one; Âsaf Khan and other Mughal court officers were astutely aware that the EIC was only one of many potential trading partners and were in no hurry to commit themselves. This unwillingness to entirely reject Portuguese and Dutch overtures only increased Roe's overall frustration with Mughal etiquette and diplomacy. However, the journal's increasingly polemic tone connected neatly with the later colonial agenda of castigating Islamic rule in India. A first-hand description of India being ruled by an absolute despot with barely any control over an intrigue-saturated court would not have been overlooked by Victorian-era historians. While Muslim rulers could be admired for their military exploits and architectural projects, their inevitable descent into arbitrary absolutism and divisive court politics only reinforced later colonial convictions that Muslim rule was institutionally flawed. Relying on Roe's account, nineteenth-century historians saw Jahângîr as a rather precarious head of state whose court was "saturated with intrigue, treachery, and corruption."[46] Sir Thomas Roe's penchant for supplementing his account with Tacitean themes of ruthless ambition and debauch courtier conduct was eagerly received by later British historians: "despite his drunkenness, his occasional lapses into cruelty, his weak-minded submission to the influence of his wife and of his favourite son, the portrait of Jahângîr is not favourable...the Conqueror of the World was the slave of a woman."[47]

The Embassy's publication and mass distribution in 1899 by the Hakluyt Society came at a time when native sources were being valued as "a mass of gossiping *Bukkurs* and gasconading *tawareekhs*."[48] Skepticism of Mughal sources, best represented in Elliot's preface to his compilation of Indian Muslim historians, contributed to the persistent dependence on European, especially English, accounts. V.A. Smith totes *The Embassy* as a "faithful record of the manner in which business was done"[49] while Elphinstone argues that "[Roe's] accounts able us to judge the state of India under Jahangir."[50] While European travelling accounts were used for occasional insights into various Oriental courts over the centuries, Roe's comprehensive and detailed manner had quickly solidified its position in early seventeenth-century Mughal historiography. In fact, the quasi-artistic element in Roe's writing was so enthusiastically lauded that Foster wrote,

> ...his position afforded him excellent opportunities for observation; while a natural gift for *literary expression* imparted a vividness to his description which is often lacking in the writings of other travellers of the period. The result is a *picture of India* of the early seventeenth century which is of exceptional value and interest. (italics mine)[51]

What then can we say about Foster's comments of *The Embassy* as "a picture of India" which reflected Sir Thomas Roe's "vivid literary expression" and why, in turn, such observations should be so important to understanding earlier British historiography? I believe this particular quote by Foster reflects well some of the larger issues of nineteenth and early twentieth-century historiography.

As we discussed in chap. 1, the separation of history from literature is no easy task. Historians of earlier times did not present 'historical facts' in a larger, bland chronological framework but preferred to weave historical figures with ongoing developments in an attempt to provide readers with historical accounts which had discernible beginnings, climaxes, and *dénouements*. Not surprisingly, Foster and other historians also supported a tradition which saw history as being dictated by the behavior and decisions of those in power. The court and/or other central ruling institutions were naturally the primary focus for such 'positivist' studies and we subsequently find a particular emphasis on the different relationships among the ruling elite. For colonial-era British historians and their obsession with indicting absolutism, relationships in the Mughal court were fundamentally about seeking, usurping, and preserving power. This constant and contentious struggle for dominance translated easily into the literary genre of inherent character conflict, plot climaxes and *dénouements*; with the addition of key attributes, historical figures could then be cast as protagonists or antagonists in the resulting historical drama. Here, one might be reminded of my earlier arguments that many of Roe's written perceptions were, in fact, framed by literary references and certain dramatic motifs common to Elizabethan and Jacobean England. As I had endeavoured to prove, Roe's penchant for dramatic metaphors and similes was rooted in the literary and historical style of the day; to facilitate his contemporaries' comprehension of a disparate political culture, fairly common Jacobean *mythoi* and motifs were used. What we have, then, is a confluence between a colonial-era of history prone to "emploting" historical events and a primary historical source which regularly made use of literary and dramatic plots, themes, and characters.

Contemporary Mughal Studies and Sir Thomas Roe

The waning of the colonial era ushered in a new generation of Indian scholars working on Mughal studies. Little was done to challenge the historiographical paradigms established by earlier British scholars and, as Peter Hardy has suggested, men like Sir Jadunath Sarkar, Ishwari Prasad, and S.R. Sharma were "immigrants into an already well-settled colony" of historical research.[52] While Pakistani and Indian Muslim historians have attempted to reorient understanding of Mughal systems of government and governance, with works like Ibn Hasan's *The Central Structure of the Mughal Empire* and N.K. Nizami's *Akbar and Religion* for example, there were few or no attempts to question some of the more 'exotic' narratives established earlier by British scholarship. As a result, histories written from the Indian or Pakistani perspective did little to question or disturb Roe's central position in Mughal historiography. Beni Prasad continued the English edification of Roe with adjectives such as "natural shrewdness" and "dextrous" while *The Embassy* was presented as providing a "vivid picture of the court and faithful character of all the prominent members of the royal family."[53] S.R. Sharma and Beni Prasad perpetuated the near-exclusive use of *The Embassy* in their analysis of Jahângîr, although an exception should be noted for Prasad who cautions his reader on many of Roe's inaccuracies.[54] Recently, Pramod Sangar argued that Roe "was able to raise the prestige of his country to a considerable extent by exposing and fighting against the corrupt officials of the Mughal empire." And, true to earlier colonial positivist angles, Roe's embassy was touted a being a "landmark" in the history of Indo-British relations.[55] Sangar seems guilty of a particular willingness to replicate earlier British historiography and quotes William Foster's 1907 summation that it was largely due to the character of

Thomas Roe that Englishmen in India found "free trade, a peaceable residence, and very good esteem with that king and people."[46] It should be noted that Phanindranath Chakrabarty's *Anglo-Mughal Commercial Relations* presents a balanced narrative of Roe's negotiations with the Mughal court which avoids the dramatic overtones and historical caricatures so commonly found in other scholarly works.

For the most part, studies written since Independence replicate, without discernment, Roe's dramatic flair in their interpretations of Jahângîr court. Anil Kumar describes the royalty as "main figures" in a "political drama"[57] while Bamber Gascoigne makes note of Roe's analogy of Jahângîr's court to that of a public theater in London without any qualification.[58] E.B. Findly has catered to the tragedy motif wholly—"the business of the [junta] was such that no matter what the personal style of the players, the faction in power was sure to be seen as cunning and avaricious as having duped an innocent, if lame, emperor into their hands."[59] Findly's estimation of Jahângîr is eerily similar to those views expressed by British scholars of the nineteenth century: "envisioning the uniqueness of his own appearance in the world, Jahangir became self-centered and self-indulgent. He developed grand and inflated views of himself..."[60] She also uses this characterization to impinge on the Mughal sense of diplomacy, "it was a kindred diplomatic policy that dreamt of placing his empire, with him as its symbol, at the center of all other nations of the earth." However, Findly makes no reference to Indo-Islamic definitions of international relations in these categorical statements and, instead, explains how "it would have taken a substantial personality to allow such a mockery to unfold over so many years, but perhaps by [Jahângîr] later life he was such a man: hopelessly entangled in fantasies about his political role."[61] While some scholars have endeavoured to liberate Jahângîr of such unflattering terms as "inept," "innocent," and "submissive," strong threads of Roe's original perceptions, later augmented by colonial historians, have continued to appear in modern historical works. Abdur Rashid's article on Jahângîr in *The History and Culture of the Indian People*, a history generally favourable to Hindu interpretations, serves as an exception to this trend; however, Rashid's conclusion that "neither Nûr Jahân nor the other cliques really dominated over [Jahângîr] so far as the principles of foreign and domestic policy were concerned" might have been influenced by Jahângîr well-known judicial policies and his fair treatment of non-Muslim minorities.[62]

The most tenacious thread, evidently, is the perception of a well-established hegemonic quartet of family figures dominating Jahângîr "so completely that he delegated all his powers and functions to them and accepted their decisions without reservations."[63] Most, if not all, of twentieth-century works on Mughal history make some allusion to this 'junta' and its destabilizing effects on the empire. Discussed earlier, Persian sources like Kâmgâr Husainî's *Ma'asir-i-Jahângîrî* and Mu'tamad Khân's *Iqbâl nâma Jahângîrî* are silent regarding any co-ordinated behavior between Nûr Jahân, Khurram, Âsaf Khân, and I'timâd al-daulat. Furthermore, native histories which do allude to Nûr Jahân's rise to power appeared under the patronage of Shâh Jahân, thus allowing the chroniclers to rationalize his earlier revolt in 1622 as a legitimate rebellion against a power-hungry royal escort. This 'junta' theory, nonetheless, has continued as an accepted component of Jahângîr's reign during the years 1611 to 1620 and, while Nurul Hasan has done much to undermine the documentation of this argument, little has been said regarding how this theory became so fashionable. Understanding of history, as any scholar will concede, is a fluid phenomenon; one generation of historical scholarship readily accepts one particular interpretation while a later generation will sponsor another. In this case, a review of historical studies published between 1817 and 1993 suggests that the 'junta' argument is a relatively recent construct. A comparison of publications before and after Prasad's *The History of Jahangir* (1922) reveals a discernible difference in how scholars perceived the royal family of this period.

In 1922 an unprecedented theory crystallized which, despite its being based mainly on one source, has significantly moulded contemporary scholarship's evaluation of the early seventeenth-century Mughal court. The suddenness of the 'junta' argument is attested to by its non-existence in earlier reputable works. In 1817, Mill commented on the Mughal scenario as follows,

> through the influence of the favourite Sultana, the vizarit was bestowed upon her father; her two brothers were raised to the first rank of Omrahs, by the titles of Ustad Khan and Asaf Jah; but their modesty and virtues reconciled all men to their sudden evaluation; and though the emperor, naturally voluptuous, was now withdrawn from business by the charms of his wife, the affairs of the empire were conducted with vigilance, prudence, and success; and the administration of [Jahângîr] was long remembered in India, as a period of justice and prosperity.[64]

While Mill makes note of the relative power of Nûr Jahân's relations and Jahângîr's rule as an era of "justice and prosperity," there is no suggestion of usurpation or collaboration between the family members. Likewise, Elphinstone discussed the ascendancy of Nûr Jahân with no speculation of factional organization; J.D. Rees' *The Muslim Epoch* (1894) had little to say regarding any collusion and focused his discussion of political scheming to the Queen Begam. In 1903, Lane-Poole concluded that Nûr Jahân was "aided by her subtle brother, Asaf Khan" but did not mention a relationship with Khurram or I'timâd al-daulat.[65] V.A. Smith came closest to alluding to a factional element, "Jahangir, half fuddled with strong drink and opium, had not the strength of will to resist the wiles of his designing queen, her equally unscrupulous brother, Âsaf Khân, and the subtlety of Prince Khurram."[66] However, once again, we find no use of terms like 'junta' or 'faction' in this or any other interpretation of Smith's.

After 1922, Nûr Jahân's relationship with Khurram, Âsaf Khân, and I'timâd al-daulat was transformed from one of informality to an organized and deliberate usurping of power. Beni Prasad's *History of Jahangir* made the speculative leap that Nûr Jahân and her cohorts personally ruled the empire from 1611 until 1620, and the speed with which this theory was incorporated by Mughal historians was impressive. S.R. Sharma reproduced whole passages of Prasad's original argumentation in his 1954 *The Crescent in India*[67] and *The Cambridge History of India* comments how "within a month of his arrival at the court of Ajmer, Roe discovered the power exercised by [Nûr Jahân] and her clique."[68] S.M. Ikram, a prominent Pakistani historian after the 1947 Partition, wrote, "Nur Jahan, Asaf Khan, and Prince Khurram had co-operated in controlling the affairs of the country"[69] while both Gascoigne and Findly consistently implemented "junta", "quartet of power", "faction", "cohorts", and "players" in their descriptions of court movement during this period. J.F. Richards described the arrangement between these family members as an "alliance" which "exerted enormous influence over Jahangir."[70] Kumar's interpretation of the state of affairs illustrates well the extent to which the "junta" theory has been accepted and expanded since 1922: "not even a blade could move on the chessboard in Mughal politics in the period of [Nûr Jahân's] way without the wish of this clique presided over by Nur Jahan with a doting Jahangir to rubber stamp its decision."[71] Prasad was the first to sufficiently document his findings on the relationship between the Queen and the others. He introduced his theory by recounting the oft-mentioned recreational tendencies of Jahângîr and, in doing so, Prasad set the tone where "Jahangir leaned more and more to ease and sloth and Nur

Jahan grew more and more experienced and inured to Power."[72] Nûr Jahân's power is apparently attested to by the far-from-perfect histories of Mu'tamad Khân and Khvâjah Kâmgâr Husainî, while the individual growth in power by Khurram, Âsaf Khân, and I'timâd al-daulat is established by numerous *mansab* boons from the emperor. These individual bases of power are then connected to the Queen to suggest that "for the next ten years, this clique of four supremely capable persons practically ruled the empire."[73] Prasad also discussed the 'two-faction' system, with Khusrau and Mahâbat Khân on one side and the 'junta' on the other, and how this struggle for power overwhelmed the Mughal court from 1611 to 1620. Khusrau's defeat at the hands of Khurram *et alia* in 1616 caused "deep consternation in the palace and the court and country" yet was "naturally deemed a great victory for the junta."[74] These statements, and others like them, were documented by *The Embassy,* and Prasad specifically cited Roe's observations during the years 1616 to conclude that "all through this period, the hopes and aspirations, the intrigues and conspiracies, of the rival parties kept the court in constant agitation."[75]

Gascoigne's chapter on Jahângîr in *The Great Mughals* heavily subscribed to Prasad's arguments, suggesting that "the quartet of advisers whose voices could so easily sway the emperor consisted of Nur Jahan and her father and brother together with Prince Khurram."[76] Findly's *Nur Jahan*, published in 1993, is an amalgamation of new and old theories and, like Prasad and Gascogne, she contends that

> Roe discerned at once the nature and relations of all the *characters* arrayed before him and believed full well that in the peculiarities of their *familial alliances* lay his fate. Powerless before what he called the 'treacherous faction,' Roe found that there was another equally as powerless as he: the emperor. While Jahangir was his only refuge and source of justice, he

was, nevertheless, also at the mercy of the faction's whims. (italics mine)[77]

Findly"s use of the term "character" and "familial alliances" to describe the system of courtier relationship is interesting. Throughout her chapter, "The Rise of the Junta," there is an undercurrent of drama, where one son is pitted against another due to the machinations of all-knowing Queen ("Nur Jahan"s control of [information gathering and policymaking] could be found in all parts of the government"); meanwhile the king, having "bowed to the effects of alcohol and opium," was "powerless" to put a stop to the ongoing "fratricidal fighting."[78] Any dramatic elements, Findly contends, are explainable by Jahangir"s aesthetic approach to ruling his empire,

> What satisfied Jahangir was what gave him pleasure, and what gave him the most pleasure were things he could see. He was guided not by principles of right or wrong or standards of good behavior, but by an effective and material order, which could be known, admired, and manipulated by him as viewer...*All this, Roe noted, was part of the theater-like quality of Jahangir's court.* (italics mine)[79]

While this work has endeavoured to argue that Roe's metaphors and synecdoches might have been part of a larger attempt to "familiarize" the Mughal reality, historians like Findly accept the Englishman's account as an objective representation and, in doing so, prolong and preserve Roe's 380-year old observation of the Mughal court having "soe much affinitye with a Theatre." Findly qualifies her exclusive reliance on European accounts by stating, "I have made extensive use of quotations from original texts in order to ground opinions, events, and people and to make clear as possible what was known and thought, and when and by whom."[80]

Overlooking the danger of inaccuracy and misrepresentation, Findly totes European observations as "the earliest documentation for scandalous portions of today's oral traditions."[81] Much like Prasad, Findly describes the relative power of the various family members in an individual context; the missing piece, the piece which transforms the four personages into a "quartet of power," is provided by *The Embassy*.

The Embassy of Sir Thomas Roe has enjoyed healthy representation in almost every history of India written since the early nineteenth century. The political and administrative climate of India in the nineteenth century contributed to a genuine interest in learning more of India's past. However concurrent with this exploration of India's heritage, there were various trends in historical scholarship that directly affected how the Mughals era was perceived. Three fundamental characteristics of colonial scholarship's treatment of India's early modern period were: a) presenting the Mughal dynasty as an interim stage of progressive development between the primitive Indian kingdoms and the present British Raj; b) highlighting unsavory Mughal features in an effort to rationalize the administrative policies of the English in India; and c) a skepticism for Persian sources of the Indo-Islamic period.

Various qualities of *The Embassy of Sir Thomas Roe* matched these trends in British historical writing on India. First, Roe was the first English ambassador to visit Indian soil, thus establishing a linear connection between early seventeenth-century English activity and the later claims being made in the nineteenth century. Second, the polemic tone of Roe's writing was advantageous to the British historical mandate of presenting the Mughal rulers and the court as politically and morally stagnant. Lastly, *The Embassy's* status as an English, 'objective' account superseded the use of "biased" and "ignorant" indigenous sources of the period.

NOTES

1. Edward W. Said, *Orientalism* (New York: 1978), p. 69, p. 12.
2. Said, *Orientalism*, p. 3.
3. Eric Stokes, *The English Utilitarians and India* (Oxford: 1959), pp. 1-13.
4. J.S. Grewal, *Muslim Rule in India: The Assessments of British Historians* (Delhi: 1970), p. 23.
5. Cited in Bernard Cohn, "The Command of Language and the Language of Command," in *Subaltern Studies IV; Writings on South Asian History*, ed. R. Guha (Delhi: 1985), p. 289.
6. Javed Majeed, *Ungoverned Imaginings: James Mill's* The History of British India *and Orientalism* (Oxford: 1992), p. 8.
7. G.C. Spivak, "Subaltern Studies; Deconstructing Historiography", in *Subaltern Studies IV: Writings on South Asian History*, ed. R. Guha (Delhi: 1985), pp. 330-31.
8. William Foster, "The East India Company, 1600-1740," in *The Cambridge History of India: British India 1497-1858*, Vol. 5, ed. H.H. Dodwell (New Delhi: 1958), p. 80.
9. Thomas Metcalf, *The New Cambridge History of India (III.4): Ideologies of the Raj* (Cambridge: 1994), p.5.
10. Grewal, *Muslim Rule in India*, pp. 6-11.
11. Metcalf, *Ideologies of the Raj*, p. 7.
12. Metcalf, *Ideologies of the Raj*, p. 15.
13. C.H. Philips, "James Mill, Mountstuart Elphinstone, and the History of India," in *Historians of India, Pakistan, and Ceylon*, ed. C.H. Philips (London: 1961), p. 218.
14. Grewal, *Muslim Rule in India*, p. 65.
15. J.S. Grewal, "Characteristics of Early British Writing on Medieval India," in *Historians of Medieval India*, ed. M. Hasan (New Delhi: 1968), p. 228.
16. James Mill, *The History of British India*, Vol. 1 (New Delhi: 1972 [reprint]), p. 5.
17. Mill, *The History of British India*, Vol. 1, pp. 252-55.
18. Grewal, *Muslim Rule in India*, p. 172.
19. Metcalf, *Ideologies of the Raj*, p. 30.
20. Nihar Nandan Singh, *British Historiography on British Rule in India* (New Delhi: 1986), p. 91.
21. Metcalf, *Ideologies of the Raj*, p. 84.
22. Mill, *The History of British India*, Vol. 2, pp. 219-221.
23. Henry Elliot, "Preface," in *The History of India As Told By Its Own Historians*, Vol. 1, eds. H.M. Elliot and J.D. Dowson (London: 1867), p. xvi.
24. Mill, *The History of British India*, Vol. 2, p. 147.

25. White, "Interpretation in History," p. 51.
26. E.T. Stokes, "The Administrators and Historical Writing on India," in *Historians of India, Pakistan, and Ceylon,* ed. C.H. Philips (London: 1961), p. 401.
27. Stokes, "The Administrators and Historical Writing on India," p. 403.
28. W.W. Hunter, *History of British India* (New York: 1966 [reprint]), p. 11.
29. Alfred Lyall, *The Rise and Expansion of the British Dominion in India* (New York: 1968 [reprint]), p. 62.
30. Metcalf, *Ideologies of the Raj,* p. x.
31. If this panel is meant to celebrate Roe's arrival at the Mughal court in Ajmîr (it is unlabelled), the artist conveniently overlooked the fact that the English ambassador was greviously suffering from dysentery and had to be carried into the city on a litter!
32. N.E. Dionne, *Champlain* (Toronto: 1905), p. 270.
33. E. Edwards, *The Life of Sir Walter Raleigh* (London: 1868), p. xxxviii.
34. Stokes, "The Administrators and Historical Writing on India," p. 385.
35. Stanley Lane-Pool, *Mediœval India Under Mohammadan Rule* (New York: 1906), p. 307.
36. Foster, "Introduction," p. xliv.
37. Haig and Burns, *The Cambridge History of India,* p. 162.
38. Lane-Poole, *Medieva India,* p. 308.
39. Foster, "Preface," p. 2.
40. J.D. Rees, *The Muslim Epoch* (New Delhi: 1978 [reprint]), p. 129.
41. Holden Furber, "The Theme of Imperialism and Colonialism in Modern Historical Writing on India," in *Historians of India, Pakistan, and Ceylon,* ed. C.H. Philips (London: 1961), pp. 332-34.
42. Philip Lawson, *The East India Company: A History* (London: 1993), p. 4.
43. Steensgaard, *The Asian Trade Revolution,* p. 123.
44. Steensgaard, *The Asian Trade Revolution,* p. 103.
45. *Letters Received by the East India Company* Vol. 3, p. 262, Vol. 5, p. 92.
46. Vincent A. Smith, *The Oxford History of India* (Oxford: 1923), p. 369.
47. Foster, "Introduction," p. xvi.
48. T.E. Colebrooke, *Life of the Honourable Mountstuart Elphinstone,* Vol. 2 (London: 1884), p. 137.
49. Smith, *The Oxford History of India,* p. 369.
50. Mountstuart Elphinstone, *History of India,* Vol. 2 (New Delhi: 1988 [reprint]), p. 181.

51. Foster, "Preface," p. 2.
52. Peter Hardy, "Modern Muslim Historical Writing on Medieval Muslim India," in *Historians of India, Pakistan, and Ceylon*, ed. C.H. Philips (London: 1961), p. 297.
53. Ishwari Prasad, *The Mughal Empire* (Allahabad: 1974), p. 435.
54. S.R. Sharma, *The Crescent in India: A Study in Medieval History* (Bombay: 1954), pp. 506-10. For Prasad's evaluation of Roe, see Prasad, *History of Jahangir*, p. 399.
55. Pramod Sangar, *Growth of the English Trade Under the Mughals* (New Delhi: 1993), p. 260.
56. Sangar, *Growth of the English Trade*, p. 24. The quote comes from William Foster's introduction of *English Factories, 1618-21* (Oxford: 1906), p. XI.
57. Anil Kumar, *Asaf Khan and His Times* (Patna: 1986), p. 45.
58. Bamber Gascoigne, *The Great Moguls* (London: 1971) p. 144.
59. Findly, *Nur Jahan*, p. 56.
60. Findly, *Nur Jahan*, p. 65.
61. Findly, *Nur Jahan*, p. 72-74.
62. Abdur Rashid, "Jahangir," in *The History and Culture of the Indian People*, Vol. 7, ed. R.C. Majumdar (Bombay: 1974), p. 195.
63. Prasad, *History of Jahangir*, p. 459.
64. Mill, *The History of British India*, Vol. 1, p. 610.
65. Lane-Poole, *Medieval India*, p. 320.
66. Smith, *The Oxford History of India*, p. 369.
67. S.R. Sharma, *The Crescent in India*, pp. 504-507.
68. Haig and Burns, *The Cambridge History fo India*, p. 163.
69. S.M. Ikram, *Muslim Rule in India and Pakistan (711-1858 A.C.)* (Lahore: 1961), p. 315.
70. Richards, *The New Cambridge History of India*, p. 102.
71. Kumar, *Asaf Khan and His Times*, pp. 46-47.
72. Prasad, *History of Jahangir*, p. 160.
73. Prasad, *History of Jahangir*, p. 165.
74. Prasad, *History of Jahangir*, p. 170.
75. Prasad, *History of Jahangir*, p. 171.
76. Gascoigne, *The Great Moghuls*, p. 138.
77. Findly, *Nur Jahan*, p. 57.
78. Findly, *Nur Jahan*, p. 58.
79. Findly, *Nur Jhan*, p. 62-63.
80. Findly, *Nur Jahan*, p. 7.
81. Findly, *Nur Jahan*, p. 7.

CONCLUSION: SIR THOMAS ROE AS ORIENTALIST

While researching in Aligarh and other Indian cities, I remember distinctly how many of my friends would describe how superior and refined Indian culture stood when compared to its various counterparts in the West. After harshly condemning 'the Britishers' and what they had done to India, these friends would then, invariably, turn around and conspiratorially ask if there was some way I could help with their written and spoken English. In many ways, I see such paradoxes as indicative of a larger tension for twentieth-century Indian society. With the overwhelming legacy of the British Raj, and with global communication and dialogue reaching unparalleled heights, Indians are more than ever aware of the degree to which they exhibit some of the trappings of western societies while at the same time finding themselves undeniably unique. Part of this tension can also be explained by India's relatively rapid propulsion into the world of 'nation-states' after two centuries of colonial subservience. What Carol Breckenridge and Peter van der Veer describe as the "postcolonial predicament" is essentially the problem of how Indians and scholars of India will interpret South Asian civilization now that they are free to cast away the Orientalist tradition established by the British in the eighteenth and nineteenth centuries. As Breckenridge and van der Veer both caution, "for scholars who think with and about the (ex)colonial world, this awareness [of 'Orientalism'] is strongest when applied to colonial scholarship and weakest when it comes to a critique of the present and to the formulation of critical alternatives and methods for approaching the study of other world regions."[1]

For many scholars of South Asia, the paradigmatic arguments of Edward Said have a logical application to eighteenth and nineteenth-century India; the creation and patronage of Oriental studies by the English East India Company was designed to facilitate the administration and, ultimately, control of the Indo-Pak subcontinent. Said, however, has been criticized for extrapolating his arguments beyond their reasonable boundaries, suggesting there existed a discourse of 'Oriental other' long before the expansion of Europe in the sixteenth century. More contentious is his claim that the entire phenomenon of scholarly Orientalism was linked at a fundamental level to the European political program of subjugating non-European cultures. In the case of colonial India, the Saidian framework has some applicability but, as Rosane Rocher warns, we must examine closely "the connections of political and intellectual concerns at given points in history and in different mileus" and, in doing so, we can "identify the multiple processes that come into play."[2]

Said's framework has deeply influenced those scholars concerned with the "postcolonial predicament" and historians have begun to reinterpret how we should look at early European accounts of India and the Islamic world. For Said and others, seventeenth and eighteenth century travel accounts should be seen as deliberate, early attempts to create juxtaposition between Europe and the 'Other.' This juxtaposition, in turn, facilitated the later Orientalist caricatures of non-European societies as culturally stunted and politically harmless. In the case of the seventeenth century and the Mughal empire, there have been renewed efforts to examine how such early European sources were designed to create and expand a politically and economically appealing image. This image, of course, would show the rapid decline of the Mughal empire in complete contrast to the growing ascendancy of the English East India Company.³

Kate Teltschner can be considered one of these efforts with her recent publication of *India Inscribed: European and British Writing on India 1600-1800*. More to the point regarding this present discussion, she provides a healthy description and interpretation of Roe's writings and what they came to mean in subsequent historiography. She contends that Roe and other texts of the early-modern era "are preoccupied with a wide-ranging set of questions about authority in India" and that this, in turn, is indicative of an early attempt by the West to reinforce a "sense of European superiority"⁴ and plant the seeds of future submission. However, to my mind, it seems unlikely that the only institution to have a stake in such matters at such an early date, the East India Company, was organized or focused enough to conceive of such ambitions. Interest in India and the East Indies was far removed from the Crown; the only people involved with Mughal India at this time were a handful of mercantile agents whose sole concerns were to guarantee returns on their modest investments. At this stage of the early seventeenth century, the EIC was certainly not interested in confining its mandate to India; in fact, in the same year that Sir Thomas Roe arrived at the Mughal court, the Company had sent its first trading mission to Iran and had just organized its first embassy to Japan. Moreover, there is evidence to suggest that high placed EIC officials had reservations regarding India's potential economic yield. In 1615, Nicholas Downton counselled Sir Thomas Smythe to reduce trade in Sûrat, while Francis Fettiplaces insisted in Dececember 1617 that the Board of Directors "recall the factories both at Brampore (Burhānpir), Amadavas (Ahmadâbâd), and Agra all down to Surat, and not to send thither but only on occasion."⁵ In addition, Company officials were leery of the high overhead costs introduced by numerous, fortified trading stations, a trend which continued well into the eighteenth century.⁶

With respect to Roe's behaviour, Teltscher is right to comment how "Roe implies the dignity and integrity both of his own sovereign and himself."[7] Her discussion of theatrical analogies makes no reference to popular Jacobean perceptions of the monarch as actor; for Teltscher, such comparisons were part of his larger program of "denigrating" the Mughal court in the hopes of implying a "positive Western counterpart."[8] I would not agree that Roe was so committed to comparing the two societies in the hopes of reinforcing the virtuous qualities of his own culture. Telscher ignores how, after one meeting with the Jahângîr, Roe was "fvll of admiration of such a virtue in a heathen prince" and commented that "wee, hauing the true vyne, bring forth crabbs, and a bastard stock grapes: that either our Christian princes had this deuotion or that this zeale were gvided by a true light of the gospell."[9] Roe, no doubt, had his difficulties with the Mughal court but, as a true Tacitean scholar, he was aware that vice and voraciousness were truly universal phenomena: "soe that comparing the vices of some cittyes in Europe, which I once iudged treasvries and sea of synne, I find them santuaryes and temples in respect of these [Mughal cities]."[10]

When we contemplate how Mughal court events and courtier divisions read like a Jacobean tragedy, or how Roe paints Jahangir's absolutism with a veneer of Tacitean commentary, we have to wonder whether *The Embassy* had more in common with Jacobean England than it did with mediaeval Islamic rule in the Indo-Pak subcontinent. In essence, this study of *The Embassy of Sir Thomas Roe* has been a study of context and its fluidity from one period to another. Its production in the early seventeenth century was congruous with a singular stream of language and world consciousness, and Roe's characterization of the Mughal empire from 1615 to 1618 parallels many Jacobean literary devices and mechanisms of expression. One of the critical features of Renaissance Humanism was the imbrication of factional and fictional representation where historical topics and themes were interwoven with literary milieus, while historians repeatedly catered to literary motifs and styles in their discussions of the past. It is difficult, knowing this, to qualify *The Embassy of Sir Thomas Roe* as a factual enterprise, with inherent qualities of objectivity and realism. If anything, this text, from a seventeenth-century perspective, floats in an environment where fiction and fact were often difficult to discern. Despite recent efforts to point out such qualities in historical sources such as Roe's peripatetic styles of writing histories, with intriguing moral conundrums and dramatic personal conflicts, continue to be produced.[11] In the case of Roe's text and its subtle inclusion of Jacobean pre-generic plot structures, a comfortable connection resulted between the impelling qualities of a juicy narrative and *The Embassy's* status as a contemporary account. Bound by a modern conceptual system where Roe's text should be naturally construed as objective, scholars are still influenced, consciously or subconsciously, by the subjunctive, narrative element of this written work. The alleged irreconcilability between fact and fiction is conveniently overlooked by historians while using *The Embassy of Sir Thomas Roe* as a source for understanding Mughal India. Consequently, we look to Roe's observations to objectively conclude certain interpretations, yet we are still motivated by Roe's dramatic undertones to present the years of 1615 to 1618 as a narrative, complete with characterization, plot movement, and conflict. Until we recognize this about *The Embassy of Sir Thomas Roe* and other early modern European travelling accounts, we will always conceive of Mughal history with the same dramatic framework.

NOTES

1. Carol A. Breckenridge and Peter van der Veer, "Orientalism and the Postcolonial Predicament," in *Orientalism and the Postcolonial Predicament: Perspectives on South Asia*, eds. C.A. Breckenridge and P. van der Veer (Philadelphia: 1993), p. 2.
2. Rosane Rocher, "British Orientalism in the Eighteenth Century: The Dialectics of Knowledge and Government," in *Orientalism and the Postcolonial Predicament: Perspectives on South Asia*, eds. C.A. Breckenridge and P. van der Veer (Philadelphia: 1993), p. 215.
3. Nancy G. Cassels, "Introduction," in *Orientalism, Evangelicalism and the Military Cantonment in Early Nineteenth Century India: A Historical Overview*, ed. N.G. Cassels (Lewiston: 1991), p. 1.
4. Kate Teltscher, *India Inscribed: European and British Writing on India 1600-1800* (Delhi: 1995), p. 2, p. 22.
5. Letters Received by the East India Company Vol. 3, p. 28, Vol. 6, p. 251.
6. Chaudhuri, "Foreign Trade:1. European Trade with India," p. 395.
7. Teltscher, *India Inscribed*, p. 7.
8. Teltscher, *India Inscribed*, p. 22.
9. Roe, *The Embassy of Sir Thomas Roe*, p. 328.
10. Roe, *The Embassy of Sir Thomas Roe*, p. 271.
11. Norman L. Jones, "History Without Teleology: Framing the Historical Narrative," in *Perspective as a Problem in the Art, History, and Literature of Early Modern England*, eds. M. Lussier and S.K. Heninger (Lewiston: 1992), p. 137.

BIBLIOGRAPHY

Printed Primary Sources

Abdullah Yusuf Ali (ed.). *The Holy Quran: Text, Translation and Commentary.* Washington. 1946.
'Abd al-Qâdir ibn Mulûk Shâh Badâ'ûnî. *Muntakhab al-tavârîkh.* Trans. and ed. G. Ranking. 3 Vols. Calcutta. 1898-1925.
Abû al-Fazl 'Allâmî. *Â'în-i Akbarî.* Trans. and ed. H. Blochmann. 3 Vols. Calcutta. 1927.
_____. *Akbar nâma.* Trans. and ed. H. Beveridge. 3 Vols. New Delhi. 1993.
Ashton, Robert (ed.). *James I By His Contemporaries.* London. 1969.
Bacon, Sir Francis. *Novum Organum or true suggestions for the interpretation of nature.* London. 1844.
Bernier, François. *Travels in the Mughal Empire.* Trans. A. Constable and ed. V.A. Smith. London. 1916.
Carew, Lord George. *Letters From George Lord Carew to Sir Thomas Roe, Ambassador to the Court of the Great Mogul, 1615-1617.* Ed. John Maclean. London. 1860.
Correia-Alfonso, John. *Jesuit Letters and Indian History, 1542-1773.* Bombay. 1969.
Cowell, John. *The Interpreter.* Cambridge. 1607.
Danvers, F.C. and Foster, William (eds.). *Letters Received by the East India Company From its Servants in the East.* 6 Vols. London. 1902.
De Callières, François. *On the Manner of Negotiating with Princes.* Ed. Stephen Kertesz. Notre Dame. 1963.
De Wicquefort, Abraham. *L'Ambassadeur et ses fonctions.* The Hague. 1682.

Fekete, L. (ed.). *Einführung in die persische Paläographie.* Budapest: 1977.
Ghiyâs al-Dîn ibn Humâm al-Dîn Muhammad Khvândamîr. *Habîb al-siyar.* Bombay. 1857.
Great Britain. *Commons Debates, 1621.* Vol. 7. New Haven. 1971.
Jahângîr. *Tûzuk-i Jahângîrî.* Trans. and ed. A. Rodgers and H. Beveridge. 2 Vols. London. 1909.
Jonson, Ben. *The Complete Plays of Ben Jonson.* Ed. F. Schelling. 2 Vols. London. 1910.
———. *The Selected Plays of Ben Jonson.* Ed. J. Procter. 2 Vols. Cambridge: 1989.
Khvâjah 'Imad al-Dîn Mahmûd Gâvân Sadr-i Jahân. *Manâzir al-inshâ'.* Istanbul, 1800.
Khvâjah Kâmgâr Khân. *Ma'âsir-i Jahângîrî.* In *History of India As to Told By Its Own Historians.* Trans. and ed. H.M. Elliot and J. Dowson. Vol. VI. London. 1875.
———, *Ma'asir-i Jahângîrî.* Ed. A. Alvi. Bombay. 1978.
Lach, Donald F. *India in the Eyes of Europe: The Sixteenth Century.* Chicago. 1965.
Marlowe, Christopher. *Tamburlaine.* Ed. J.W. Harper. London. 1971.
McIlwain, Charles H. (ed.) *The Political Works of James I: Reprinted from the Edition of 1616.* Cambridge. 1918.
Mîrzâ Ibrâhîm Zubairî. *Basâtîn al-salâtîn.* Bombay. 1968.
Monserrate. *Commentary of Father Monserrate, S.J. on his journey to the Court of Akbar.* Trans. and ed. J.S. Hoyland. London. 1922.
Muhammad Bâqir Najm-i Sânî. *Advice on the Art of Governance: An Indo-Islamic Mirror for Princes: Mau'izah-i Jahângîrî.* Trans. and ed. S.S. Alvi. Albany. 1989.
Muhammad Hâshim Khâfî Khân. *Muntakhab al-lubâb.* Ed. W. Haig. 2 Vol. Calcutta. 1909-1925.
Muhammad ibn Hindûshâh Nakhjuvânî. *Dastûr al-kâtib fî'l ta'yyin marâtib.* Ed. 'Abd al-Karîm 'Alî Ûghlî 'Alîzâdih. 3 Vols. Moscow. 1964.

Mu'tamad. Khân. *Iqbâl nâmâ Jahângîrî*. In *The History of India As Told By Its Own Historians*. Trans. and ed. H.M. Eliot and J. Dowson. Vol. 6. London. 1875, pp. 400-438.

———. *Iqbâl nâmâ Jahângîrî*. Ed. Maulana Maulavi Muhammad Rafi' Sahib Fazil Divband. Allahabad. 1931.

Nizâm al-Mulk. *Traité de Gouvernement (Siyaset-Name)*. Trans. and ed. C. Schefer. Paris. 1984.

Roe, Thomas. *The Embassy of Sir Thomas Roe to the Court of the Great Mogul, 1615-1619, As Narrated In His Journal and Correspondence*. Ed. William Foster. 2 Vols. London. 1899.

Roemer, H.R. *Staatsschreiben der Timüridenzeit: des Sharaf Nâmâ des 'Abdullâh Marwârîd im kritischer Auswertung*. Weisbaden. 1952.

Sainsbury, E.B. (ed.) *A Calendar of Court Minutes of the East India Company*. 2 Vols. London. 1909.

Shakespeare, William. *The Complete Works of Shakespeare*. Ed. W.J. Craig. London. 1900.

Sujan Rai Khatrî. *Khulâsat al-tavârîkh*. Ed. Muhammad Zafar Husain. Delhi. 1918.

Tacitus, Cornelius. *The Annals and the Histories*. Trans. A. J. Church and W.J. Brodribb. Vol. 1. Chicago. 1952.

Treswell, Robert. *A Relation of...the Journey of the...Earl of Nottingham...London. 1605*. Reprinted in *Harleian Miscellany*. London. 1745, pp. 405-28.

Winwood, Sir Ralph. *Memorials of Affairs of State in the Reigns of Queen Elizabeth and King James I*. Ed. E. Sawyer. 2 Vols. London. 1725.

Zâhir al-Dîn Muhammad Bâbur. *Bâbur nâma*. Trans and ed. A.S. Beveridge. 2 Vols. New Delhi. 1970 (reprint).

Ziyâ al-Dîn Baranî. *Fatawa-i Jahândârî*. Trans. and ed. M. Habib in *The Political Theory of the Delhi Sultanate*. Allahabad. 1960.

———. *Târîkh-i Fîrûz Shâhî*. In *The History of India, As Told By Its Own Historians*. Eds. H.M. Elliot and J. Dowson. Vol. 3. London. 1875, pp. 97-268.

Secondary Sources

Adams, Simon. "Spain or the Netherlands? The Dilemmas of Early Stuart Foreign Policy." In *Before the English Civil War*. Ed. H. Tomlinson. London: 1983, pp. 79-101.
Ahmad, Aziz. "The Role of Ulema in Indo-Muslim Writing." In *Studia Islamica*. Vol. 31 (1970), pp. 1-13.
Akrigg, G.P.V. *Jacobean Pageant or the Court of King James I*. Cambridge. 1962.
_____, "Akbar and Islam (1581-1605)." In *Islamic Society and Culture: Essays in Honour of Professor Aziz Ahmad*. Eds. M. Israel and N.K. Wagle. Delhi. 1983, pp. 123-134.
Ali, M. Athar. *The Apparatus of Empire: Awards of Ranks, Offices, and Titles to the Mughal Nobility (1574-1658)*. Delhi. 1985.
_____. *The Mughal Nobility Under Aurengzeb*. Bombay. 1965.
Alvi, M.A. *Jahangir - The Naturalist*. New Delhi. 1968.
Alvi, Sajida S. "Mazhar-i Shâhjahânî and the Mughal Province of Sind: A Discourse on Political Ethics." In *Islam and Indian Religions*. Eds. A.L. Dallapiccola and S.Z. Lallemant. Vol. 1 (Stuttgart. 1993), pp. 239-58.
_____. "Religion and State During the Reign of Mughal Emperor Jahângîr (1605-27): Non-juristical Perspectives." In *Studia Islamica*. Vol. 69 (1989), pp. 95-119.
Aubin, Jean. "Les relations diplomatiques entre les Aqqoyunlu et les Bahmanides." In *Iran and Islam*. (Edinburgh. 1971), pp. 11-16.
Beach, Milo C. *The Grand Mogul: Imperial Painting in India 1600-1660*. Williamstown. 1978.
Beckingham, C.F. "The Quest for Prester John." In *Between Islam and Christendom: Travelers, Fact and Legend in the Middle Ages and the Renaissance*. Ed. C.F. Beckingham. London. 1983, pp. 291-310.

Beveridge, Henry. "Preface." In *Tûzuk-i Jahângîrî*. Trans. and Eds. A. Rogers and H. Beveridge, Vol. 1. London. 1909, pp. vii-xv.
Bhatia, M. and Behari, K. "The Mughal Court Etiquette and Matters of Protocol." In *Journal of Indian History*. Vol. 56 (1978), pp. 111-18.
Blake, Stephen. "The Patrimonial-Bureaucratic Empire of the Mughals." In *Journal of Asian Studies*. Vol. 39 (1979). No. 1, pp. 77-94.
Bolgar, R.R. *The Classical Heritage and Its Beneficiaries*. Cambridge. 1954.
Braunmuller, A.R. "Robert Carr, Earl of Somerset, As Collector and Patron." In *The Mental World of the Jacobean Court*. Ed. L.L. Peck. Cambridge. 1991, pp. 230-50.
Breckenridge, Carol A. and von der Veer, Peter. "Orientalism and the Postcolonial Predicament." In *Orientalism and the Postcolonial Predicament: The South Asian Perspective*. Eds. Carol A. Breckenridge and Peter von der Veer. Philadelphia. 1993, pp. 1-19.
Brown, Michael. *Itinerant Ambassador: The Life of Sir Thomas Roe*. Lexington. 1970.
Buckler, F.W. "The Oriental Despot." In *Legitimacy and Symbols*. Ed. M.N. Pearson. Ann Arbor. 1985, pp. 176-87.
Cassels, Nancy G. "Introduction." In *Orientalism, Evangelicalism and the Military Cantonment in Early Nineteenth Century India: A Historical Overview*. Ed. N.G. Cassels. Lewiston. 1991, pp. 1-17.
Chakrabarty, Phanindranath. *Anglo-Mughal Commercial Relations*. Calcutta. 1983.
Chaudhuri, K.N. "Foreign Trade: 1. European Trade with India." In *The Cambridge Economic History of India*. Eds. T. Raychaudhuri and I. Habib. 2 Vols. Cambridge, 1982, pp. 382-407.
Christianson, Paul. "Royal and Parliamentary Voices on the Ancient Constitution, c. 1604-1621." In *The Mental*

World of the Jacobean Court. Ed. L.L. Peck. Cambridge. 1991, pp. 71-95.

Cohn, Bernard. "The Command of Language and the Language of Command." In *Subaltern Studies IV: Writings on South Asian History.* Ed. R. Guha. Delhi. 1985, pp. 276-329.

Colebrooke, T.E. *Life of the Honourable Mountstuart Elphinstone.* 2 Vols. London. 1884.

Collingwood, R.G. *The Idea of History.* Oxford. 1946.

Collinson, Patrick. "The Jacobean Religious Settlement: The Hampton Court Conference." In *Before the English Civil War.* Ed. H. Tomlinson. London. 1983.

Cox, John. *Shakespeare and the Dramaturgy of Power.* Princeton. 1989.

Cuddy, Neil. "The Revival of the Entourage: the Bedchamber of James I, 1603-1625." In *The English Court: From the Wars of the Roses to the Civil War.* Ed. D. Starkey. New York. 1987, pp. 173-226.

Dale, Stephen F. *Indian Merchants and Eurasian Trade, 1600-1750.* Cambridge. 1994.

———. "Steppe Humanism: The Autobiographical Writings of Zahir al-Din Muhammad Babur, 1483-1530." In *International Journal of Middle East Studies.* Vol. 22 (1990), pp. 37-58.

Dickson, Martin "Uzbek Dynastic Theory in the Sixteenth Century." In *Trudy XXV-ogo Mezhdunarodnogo Kongressa Vostokovedov.* Vol. 3. Moscow. 1960. pp. 208-16.

Disney, A.R. *Twilight of the Pepper Empire.* Cambridge. 1978.

Edwards, E. *The Life of Sir Walter Raleigh.* London. 1868.

Elliot, Henry. "Preface." In *The History of India As Told By Its Own Historians.* Eds. H.M. Elliot and J.D. Dowson. Vol. 1. London. 1867, pp. xv-xxix.

Elphinstone, Mountstuart. *History of India.* 2 Vols. New Delhi. 1988.

Farooqi, Naimur R. *Mughal-Ottoman Relations: A Study of Political and Diplomatic Relations Between Mughal India and the Ottoman Empire, 1556-1748.* Ann Arbor. 1986.

Findly, E.B. *Nur Jahan: Empress of Mughal India.* Oxford. 1993.

Finkelpearl, Philip J. *John Marston of the Middle Temple: An Elizabethan Dramatist in His Social Setting.* Cambridge. 1969.

Foster, William. "The East India Company, 1600-1740." In *The Cambridge History of India: British India 1497-1858.* Ed. H.H. Dodwell. Vol. 5. Delhi. 1958, pp. 76-115.

_____. "Introduction." In *The Embassy of Thomas Roe to the Court of the Great Mogol 1615-1619, As Narrated In His Journal and Correspondence.* Ed. W. Foster. Vol. 1. London. 1899, pp. i-lxviii.

_____. "Preface." In *The Embassy of Sir Thomas Roe to the Court of the Great Mogul, 1615-1619).*

Friedman, John B. "Cultural Conflicts in Medieval World Maps." In *Implicit Understandings: Observing, Reporting, and Reflecting on the Encounters Between Europeans and Other Peoples in the Early Modern Era.* Ed. S. Schwartz. Cambridge. 1994, pp. 64-95.

Furber, Holden. *Rival Empires of Trade in the Orient, 1600-1800.* Minneapolis. 1976.

_____. "The Theme of Imperialism and Colonialism in Modern Historical Writing on India." In *Historians of India, Pakistan, and Ceylon.* Ed. C.H. Philips. London. 1961, pp. 332-43.

Furet, Francois. *In the Workshop of History.* Chicago. 1984.

Gascoigne, Bamber. *The Great Moguls.* London, 1971.

Goldberg, Jonathan. *James I and the Politics of Literature.* Baltimore. 1983.

_____. "James I and the Theater of Conscience." In *English Literary History.* Vol. 46 (1979), pp. 379-98.

Gosse, Edmund. *The Life and Letters of John Donne.* 2 Vols. London. 1899.

Green, A. Wigfall. *The Inns of Court and Early English Drama*. New Haven. 1931.

Greenblatt, Stephen. "Invisible Bullets: Renaissance Authority and Its Subversion." In *Glyph*. Vol. 8 (1981), pp. 40-61.

Grewal, J.S. "Characteristics of Early British Writing on Medieval India." In *Historians of Medieval India*. Ed. M. Hasan. New Delhi. 1968, pp. 225-33.

_____. *Muslim Rule in India: The Assessments of British Historians*. Delhi. 1970.

Habib, Irfan. *An Atlas of the Mughal Empire*. Delhi. 1982.

_____. "The Family of Nur Jahan During Jahangir's Reign: A Political Study." In *Mediaeval India - A Miscellany*. Vol. 1 (1969), pp. 74-95.

Haig, Lt. Col., Sir Wolseley and Burns, Sir Richard. *The Cambridge History of India*. Vol. 4. Delhi. 1937.

Hanley, Cecile C. *Jacobean Drama and Politics*. Ph.D. Dissertation. Ann Arbor. 1972.

Hansen, Waldemar. *The Peacock Throne*. New York. 1972.

Hardy, Peter. "The Authority of Muslim Kings in Mediaeval South Asia." In *Islam and Society in South Asia*. Ed. M. Gaborieau. Paris. 1986, pp. 37-55.

_____. "Modern Muslim Historical Writing on Medieval Muslim India." In *Historians of India, Pakistan, and Ceylon*. Ed. C.H. Philips. London. 1961, pp. 294-309.

_____. "Unity and Variety in Indo-Islamic and Perso-Islamic Civilization: Some Ethical and Political Ideas of Ziyâ' al-Dîn Baranî of Delhi, of al-Ghazâlî, and of Nasîr al-Dîn Tusî Compared.' In *Iran*. Vol. 16 (1978), pp. 127-35.

Hasan, Nurul. "The Theory of the Nur Jahan 'Junta' - An Examination." In *Proceedings of the Indian History Congress, Trivandrum Session*. Vol. 21 (1958), pp. 324-35.

Hay, Denys. *Annalists and Historians: Western Historiography from the VIIIth to XVIII Century*. London. 1977.

Heninger, S.K. "Framing the Narrative." In *Perspective as a Problem in the Art, History, and Literature of Early*

Modern England. Ed. M. Lussier and S.K. Heninger. Lewiston. 1992, pp. 3-25.

Herford, Charles H. and Simpson, Percy. *Ben Jonson*. 11 Vols. Oxford. 1954.

Holderness, Graham. "Endgames." In *Shakespeare Out of Court Dramatization of Court Society*. Ed. G. Holderness. New York. 1990, pp. 236-44.

──────. "Introduction: Theatre and Court." In *Shakespeare: Out of Court; Dramatization of Court Society*. Ed. G. Holderness. New York. 1990, pp. 129-35.

Hunter, W.W. *History of British India*. New York. 1966.

Ibn Hasan. *The Central Structure of the Mughal Empire*. New Delhi. 1970.

Ikram, S. M. *Muslim Rule in India and Pakistan (711-1858 A.C.)*. Lahore. 1961.

Islam, Riazul. *A Calendar of Documents on Indo-Persian Relations*. 2 Vols. Tehran. 1979.

──────. *Indo-Persian Relations: A Study of the Political and Diplomatic Relations Between the Mughal Empire and Iran*. Tehran. 1970.

Jones, Norman, L. "History Without Teleology: Framing the Historical Narrative." In *Perspective as a Problem in the Art, History, and Literature of Early Modern England*. Eds. M. Lussier and S.K. Heninger. Lewiston. 1992, pp. 131-141.

Judson, Margaret A. *The Crisis of Constitution, An Essay in Constitutional and Political Thought 1603-1645*. New Brunswick. 1949.

Kay, W. David. *Ben Jonson: A Literary Life*. London. 1995.

Keens-Soper, H.M.A. and Schweizer, Karl W. "Diplomatic Theory in the Ancien Régime." In *The Art of Diplomacy*. Eds. H.M.A. Keens-Soper and Karl W. Schweizer. New York. 1983, pp. 19-52.

Khan, Iqtidar Alam. "The Nobility Under Akbar and the Development of His Religious Policy, 1560-1580." In *Journal of the Royal Asiatic Society*. 1968, pp. 29-36.

Khan, Kunwar Refaqat Ali. *The Kachwahas Under Akbar and Jahangir*. New Delhi. 1976.

Kumar, Anil. *Asaf Khan and His Times*. Patna. 1986.

Lambton, A.K.S. "Justice in the Medieval Persian Theory of Kingship." In *Studia Islamica*. Vol. 17 (1962), pp. 91-119.

———. "Quis costodiet custodes? Some Reflections on the Persian Theory of Government." In *Studia Islamica*. Vol. 5 (1955), pp. 125-48; Vol. 6 (1956), pp. 125-46.

———. *Theory and Practice in Medieval Persian Government*. London. 1980.

Lane-Poole, Stanley. *Mediaeval India Under Mohammedan Rule*. New York. 1906.

———. "Thomas Roe." In *Dictionary of National Biography*. Vol. 49. Ed. S. Lee. London. 1897, pp. 89-93.

Lawson, Philip. *The East India Company: A History*. London. 1993.

Lévi-Strauss, Claude. *The Savage Mind*. Chicago. 1966.

Limon, Jerzy. "The Masque of Stuart Culture." In *The Mental World of the Jacobean Court*. Ed. L.L. Peck. Cambridge. 1999, pp. 209-29.

Loades, D.M. *Politics and the Nation*. London. 1973.

Lyall, Alfred. *The Rise and Expansion of the British Dominion in India*. New York. 1968.

Majeed, Javed. *Ungoverned Imaginings: James Mill's* The History of British India *and Orientalism*. Oxford. 1992.

Mattingly, Garrett. *Renaissance Diplomacy*. New York. 1955.

Metcalf, Thomas. *The New Cambridge History of India (Vol. III•4): Ideologies of the Raj*. Cambridge. 1994.

Miles, Rosalind. *Ben Jonson: His Life and Work*. London. 1986.

Mill, James. *The History of British India*. 3 Vols. New Delhi. 1972.

Mitchell, Colin Paul. "Safavid Imperial *Tarassul* and the Persian *Inshâ'* Tradition." In *Studia Iranica*. (1997), pp. 173-209.

Mohiuddin, Momin. *The Chancellery and Persian Epistolography Under the Mughals*. Calcutta. 1971.

Moir, Thomas L. *The Addled Parliament of 1614*. Oxford. 1958.

Momigliano, Arnaldo. "The First Political Commentary of Tacitus." In *Essays in Ancient and Modern Historiography*. Ed. A. Momigliano. Oxford. 1977, pp. 205-29.

―――. "Tradition and the Classical Historian." In *Essays in Ancient and Modern Historiography*. Ed. A. Momigliano. Oxford. 1977, pp. 161-178.

Mujtabâ', Fath-Allâh. "Correspondence: ii. In Islamic Persia." In *Encyclopaedia Iranica*. Ed. Ehsan Yarshater. p. 290.

Naqvi, H.K. *History of Mughal Government and Administration*. Delhi. 1990.

Neale, J.E. *Elizabeth I and Her Parliaments, 1584-1601*. 2 Vols. London. 1965.

Nietzsche, Friedrich. *The Use and Abuse of History*. Trans. Adrian Collins. Indianapolis. 1957.

Nizami, Khaliq Ahmad. *Akbar and Religion*. Delhi. 1989.

―――. "Aspects of Muslim Political Thought in India During the Fourteenth Century." In *Islamic Culture*. Vol. 52 (1978), pp. 213-40.

Notestein, Wallace. *The House of Commons, 1604-1610*. New Haven. 1971.

Oman, Carola. *Elizabeth of Bohemia*. London. 1938.

Peck, Linda L. *Court Patronage and Corruption in Early Stuart England*. Boston. 1990.

―――. "The Mental World of the Jacobean Court: An Introduction." In *The Mental World of the Jacobean Court*. Ed. L.L. Peck. Cambridge. 1991, pp. 1-17.

Pedersen, J. "Nadhr." In *Encyclopaedia of Islam*. Vol. VII, pp. 846-47.

Philips, C.H. "James Mill, Mountstuart Elphinstone, and the History of India." In *Historians of India, Pakistan, and Ceylon.* Ed. C.H. Philips. London. 1961, pp. 217-29.
Prasad, Beni. *The History of Jahangir.* Allahabad. 1940.
Prasad, Ishwari. *The Mughal Empire.* Allahabad. 1974.
Queller, Donald E. *The Office of Ambassador in the Middle Ages.* Princeton. 1967.
Qureshi, I.H. *Administration of the Mughal Empire.* Karachi. 1966.
Rahim, A. "An Aspect of Diplomacy of the Mughal Age." In *Journal of the Pakistan Historical Society.* Vol. 9 (1961), pp. 289-95.
Rahim, Abdur. *Mughal Relations With Persia and Central Asia.* Aligarh. 1936.
Rashid, Abdur. "Jahângîr." In *The History and Culture of the Indian People.* Ed. R.C. Majumdar. Vol. 7. Bombay. 1974, pp. 175-96.
Rees, J.D. *The Muslim Epoch.* New Delhi. 1978.
Richards, John F. *Document Forms for Official Orders of Appointment in the Mughal Empire.* Cambridge. 1986.
_____. "The Formulation of Imperial Authority Under Akbar and Jahangir." In *Kingship and Authority in South Asia.* Ed. J.F. Richards. Madison, 1978, pp. 252-85.
_____. "Mughal State Finance and the Pre-Modern World Economy." In *Comparative Studies in Society and History.* Vol. 23 (1981), pp. 285-308.
_____. *The New Cambridge History of India (Vol. V • 1): The Mughal Empire.* Cambridge. 1993.
_____. "Norms of Comportment Among Imperial Mughal Officers." In *Moral Conduct and Authority: The Place of Adab in South Asian Islam.* Ed. B.D. Metcalf. Berkeley. 1984, pp. 255-89.
Ricoeur, Paul. "The Metaphorical Process as Cognition, Imagination, and Feeling." In *Critical Theory Since 1965.* Eds. H. Adams and L. Searle. Tallahasee. 1986, pp. 424-34.

Rizvi, S. Rizwan Ali. *Nizam al-Mulk Tusi: His Contribution to Statecraft, Political Theory and the Art of Government.* Lahore. 1978.
Rocher, Rosane. "British Orientalism in the Eighteenth Century: The Dialectics of Knowledge and Government." In *Orientalism and the Postcolonial Predicament: The South Asian Perspective.* Eds. Carol A. Breckenridge and Peter von der Veer. Philadelphia. 1993, pp. 215-49.
Russell, Conrad. "Parliamentary History in Perspective, 1604-29." In *History.* Vol. 61 (1976), pp. 1-27.
Said, Edward W. *Orientalism.* New York. 1978.
Salmon, J.H.M. "Seneca and Tacitus in Jacobean England." In *The Mental World of the Jacobean Court.* Ed. L.L. Peck. Cambridge. 1991, pp. 169-98.
Sangar, Pramod. *Growth of the English Trade Under the Mughals.* New Delhi. 1993.
Sarkar, J.N. "A Little Known Chapter in Indo-Iranian Diplomacy in the Mid-Seventeenth Century." In *Indo-Iranica.* Vol. 25 (1972), pp. 51-56.
_____. *Mughal Polity.* Delhi. 1984.
Sharma, S.R. *The Crescent in India: A Study in Medieval History.* Bombay. 1954.
Sharpe, Kevin and Zwicker, Steven N. "Politics of Discourse: Introduction." In *Politics of Discourse: the Literature and History of Seventeenth Century England.* Eds. Kevin Sharpe and Steven N. Zwicker. Berkeley. 1987, pp. 1-20.
Sherwani, H.K. "The Bahmanids." In *History of Medieval Deccan.* Eds. H.K. Sherwani and P.M. Joshi. Vol. I. Hyderabad. 1973, pp. 183-93.
Singh, Nihar Nandan. *British Historiography on British Rule in India.* New Delhi. 1986.
Smith, Alan G.R. "Crown, Parliament and Finance: the Great Contract of 1610." In *The English Commonwealth, 1547-1640.* Eds. P. Clark, A.G.R. Smith, and N. Tyacke. Leicester. 1979, pp. 111-27.

Smith, Vincent A. *Akbar the Great Mogul, 1542-1605.* Oxford. 1892.

_____. *The Oxford History of India.* Oxford. 1923.

Smuts, Malcolm. "Court-Centred Politics and the Uses of Roman Historians, c. 1590-1630." In *Culture and Politics in Early Stuart England.* Eds. K. Sharpe and P. Lake. London. 1994, pp. 21-43.

_____. *Court Culture and the Origins of a Royalist Tradition in Early Stuart England.* Philadelphia. 1987.

_____. "Cultural Diversity and Cultural Change at the Court of James I." In *The Mental World of the Jacobean Court.* Ed. L.L. Peck. Cambridge. 1991, pp. 91-112.

_____. "Introduction." In *The Stuart Court and Europe: Essays in Politics and Political Culture.* Ed. R. Malcolm Smuts. Cambridge. 1996, pp. 3-19.

Sommerville, J.P. "James I and the Divine Right of Kings: English Politics and Continental Theory." In *The Mental World of the Jacobean Court.* Ed. L. L. Peck. Cambridge. 1991, pp. 55-70.

Spivak, G.C. "Subaltern Studies: Deconstructing Historiography." In *Subaltern Studies IV: Writings on South Asian History.* Ed. R. Guha. Delhi: 1985, pp. 330-63.

Steensgaard, Niels. *The Asian Trade Revolution of the Seventeenth Century: The East India Companies and the Decline of Caravan Trade.* Chicago. 1973.

Stokes, E.T. "The Administrators and Historical Writing on India." In *Historians of India, Pakistan, and Ceylon.* Ed. C.H. Philips. London. 1961, pp. 385-403.

_____. *The English Utilitarions and India.* Oxford. 1959.

Stone, Lawrence. *The Crisis of the Aristocracy 1558-1641.* Oxford. 1965.

Strachan, Michael. *Sir Thomas Roe, 1581-1644: A Life.* London. 1989.

Subtelny, Maria E. "Mîr `Alî Shîr Navâ'î." In *Encyclopedia of Islam.* Vol. 7, pp. 90-93.

Tanner, J.R. *English Constitutional Conflicts of the Seventeenth Century.* Westport. 1983.
Teltscher, Kate. *India Inscribed: European and British Writing on India 1600-1800.* Delhi. 1995.
Tennenhouse, Leonard. *Power on Display: the Politics of Shakespeare's Genres.* New York. 1986.
Tirmizi, S.A.I. *Ajmer Through Inscriptions.* New Delhi. 1968.
_____. *Mughal Documents (1526-1627).* New Delhi. 1989.
Tricomi, Albert H. *Anticourt Drama in England, 1603-1642.* Charlottesville. 1989.
Tuck, Richard. "The 'Ancient Law of Freedom': John Selden and the Civil War." In *Reactions to the English Civil War.* Ed. J.S. Morill. London. 1982, pp. 137-161.
White, Hayden. "The Fictions of Factual Representation." In *Tropics of Discourse: Essays in Cultural Criticism.* Ed. H. White. Baltimore. 1978, pp. 121-34.
_____. "The Historical Text as Literary Artifact." In *Tropics of Discourse: Essays in Cultural Criticism.* Ed. H. White. Baltimore. 1978, pp. 81-99.
_____. "Interpretation in History." In *Tropics of Discourse: Essays in Cultural Criticism.* Ed. H. White. Baltimore. 1978, pp. 51-80.
Woolf, D.R. *The Idea of History in Early Stuart England.* Toronto. 1990.
Ziegler, Norman P. "Some Notes on Rajput Loyalties During the Mughal Period." In *Kingship and Authority in South Asia.* Ed. J.F. Richards. Madison. 1978.

INDEX

A

'Abbâs I, shâh of Iran, 16, 17, 41, 150, 158, 160, 165, 166
'Abbâs II, shâh of Iran, 171
Abbot, Archbishop George, 34, 98, 99, 100, 110, 128
'Abd Allâh Khân, 5, 17, 18 108, 119, 149
'Abd al-Nabî Fakhr al-Zamânî Qazvînî, 15
Abû al-Fazl ibn Mubârak, 12, 13, 114, 115, 116, 117, 121, 122, 160, 165, 194, 195
Abû al-Hasan, 14
Abû al-Hasan Âsaf Khân, xv, 17, 20, 24, 72, 73, 75, 76, 81, 83, 84, 107, 108, 112, 113, 146, 151, 152, 167, 189, 216, 221, 223, 224, 229
'Addled' Parliament, see Parliament of 1614
Adham Khân, 5
'Âdilshâhs, 158
Afghân Lodîs, 2
Âgrâ, 3, 4, 13, 22, 73, 109, 112, 194, 232
Ahmadâbâd, 22, 23, 25, 41, 144, 196, 232
Ahmadnagar, 6, 17, 18, 39, 73
Â'în-i Akbarî, 10, 42, 44, 114, 115, 116, 118, 121, 124, 129, 130, 131, 165, 203, 236
Ajmîr, 5, 22, 23, 24, 25, 69, 70, 76, 105, 109, 122, 126, 144, 147, 148, 149, 187, 191, 196, 223, 228

Akbar, see Jalâl al-Dîn Muhammad Akbar
'A'lâ al-Dîn Khaljî, 1, 38
Allâhabâd, 13
Alvarez de Cabral, 6, 214
Amber, 6, 10
Amîr Khusrau, 155,
Amsterdam, xvi, 27, 138
Anthony and Cleopatra, 78, 88
Anti-Catholicism, 100
Âqâ Rizâ, 14
Archian, 2
Arjun, fifth Sikh Guru, 16
Armenian, 15, 16, 151
Âsaf Khân, see Abû al-Hasan Âsaf Khân
Âsaf Khân Ja'far Beg, 14
'Askarî (brother of Humâyûn), 4
Astrakhân, 21

B

Bâbur, see Zahîr al-Dîn Muhammad Bâbur
Bacon, Sir Francis, 28, 31, 49, 62, 86, 177, 236
Bahâdur Shâh, xix, 3
Bahmanids, 39, 154, 155, 170, 248
Bairâm Khân, 4, 5, 9, 40
Balkh, 21
Bandar 'Abbâs, 21
Bâqir Khân Najm-i Sânî, 15
Basilikon Doron, 57, 60, 64, 86, 95
Bengâl, 1, 2, 3, 4, 5, 6, 18, 20, 41, 207

INDEX

Best, Thomas, 23, 45, 147
Beveridge, Henry, xix, xx, 43, 237, 240
Bihâr, 1, 5, 13, 40, 73
Bîjâpûr, 39, 157, 171
Birar, 17, 39
Bishân Dâs, 14, 163
Brooke, Christopher, 50, 180, 183
Bukhârâ, 155
Bundî, 4
Bûrhânpûr, 17, 18, 24, 25, 69, 104, 144, 232
Bustrode, Lady Cecilia, 54

C

Calvinist, 56, 57, 101, 112, 174
Carew, Lord Thomas, 32, 35, 71, 105
Carr, Lord Robert, 99, 100, 101, 105, 128, 240
Catholic Church, 7, 48, 49
Catholics, 28, 101
Cecil, Lord Robert, 97, 100, 101, 178, 182
Chamberlain, John, 96, 179
Charles, Prince of Wales, 187
Chandirî, 3
Chausâ, 3
Chitor, 6
Church of England, 56, 57, 173
Colet, John, 49,
Collingwood, R.G., 46, 241
Cornwallis, Charles, 185, 207
Coromandel, xvi
Cowell, John, 176, 201, 236
Cuffe, Henry, 184
Cymbeline, 79, 88

D

Damân, 22, 111
Daulat Khân, 2, 3, 39
de Callières, François, 141, 143, 150, 168, 169, 236
Deccan, 2, 6, 39, 43, 73, 75, 76, 82, 158, 248
de Gama, Vasco, xvi
de Voga, Father Christopher, 8
de Wicquefort, Abraham, 150, 168, 236
Delhî, 2, 4, 5, 40, 109, 117, 130, 154, 170, 227, 228, 235, 236, 238, 239, 241, 243, 246, 248, 250
Digges, Sir Dudley, 99, 180
Dilâvar Khân, 15
dîn-i illâhî, 12
Diu, 6, 7
dîvân-i 'âmm, 104, 109, 164
dîvân-i khâss, 109, 164
Divine Right of Kings, 57, 175, 186, 201, 202, 249
Donne, John, 28, 50, 51, 53, 55, 56, 66, 85, 92, 242
Dow, Alexander, 208, 209
Downton, Nicholas, 23, 45, 232

E

Earl of Carlisle, 97
Earl of Essex, 100, 184
Earl of Exeter, 94
Earl of Lincoln, 94
Earl of Pembroke, 94, 97, 100
Earl of Southhampton, 94
Edwards, Arthur, xvii, 169
Elizabeth I, Queen of England, 28, 50, 56, 86, 87, 92, 94, 104, 111, 135, 173, 174, 238
Elizabeth (daughter of James I), 53, 93, 99, 100, 101, 104, 138
Elliot, Henry, 38, 43, 44, 211, 217, 227, 241
English East India Company, (xvi, xvii, 21, 26, 29, 34, 45, 47, 98, 133, 215, 227, 228, 231, 232, 235, 236, 245, *passim*

INDEX

Estado da India, 6, 8, 22, 108, 111, 112, 215, 216

F

Fargânah, 2
Fâtihpûr Sikrî, 7, 109
Findly, E.B., 88, 223, 225, 226, 229
Fîrûz Tughluq, 1
Fitch, Ralph, xvii
Foster, William, 32, 45, 46, 47, 167, 172, 214, 217, 218, 219, 227, 228, 229, 238, 242
Frederick, Elector Palatine, 100, 101, 138, 139
'French faction', 63, 97, 98
Fulbrooke, Nicholas, 99
Fuller, Nicholas, 180

G

Gainsford, Thomas, 190
al-Ghazâlî, 11, 115, 243
Ghijdavân, 3
ghulâmân, 10
ghusâl khânah, 73, 109, 164
Goa, 7, 111, 129
Goghra, 3
Golkundâ, 22, 39, 157, 171
Great Contract of 1610, 63, 201, 248
Greneway, Richard, 184, 185
Gujarât, 1, 2, 3, 6, 7, 39, 41, 74, 76, 108, 112, 167, 197

H

Hackwill, William, 35
Haidighat, 6
Hakluyt, Richard, 34, 35
Hampton Court Conference, 57, 86
Hâtim Beg, 171

Hawkins, William, 45, 147, 163, 169, 196
Henry, Prince, 96, 97, 100, 1110, 185
Herât, 9, 16, 155
Hindus, 10
Holland, xvi, 20, 27, 56, 101, 134, 158, 206
Holland, Hugh, 50
Hoskyns, John, 63, 180, 181, 183
Howard, Charles, Earl of Nottingham, 97, 135, 136, 137, 138, 139, 168
Howard, Thomas, 97
Howards, 63, 174
Humanism, 31, 42, 48, 177, 233
Husain Beg, 16
Hushang, 197

I

Ibrâhîm Husain Mîrzâ, 7
Ibrâhîm Lodî, 3
Inns of the Court, 50, 51, 53, 60, 86, 184, 191, 243
Isfahân, 21, 84, 158, 162
Islâm Khân, 18
Islâm Shâh Sûr, 4, 40
Isma'îl I, *shâh* of Iran, 2
Istânbûl, 10, 36, 55, 68, 171, 237
I'timâd al-daulat, see Mîrzâ Ghiyâs̱ al-Dîn Muhammad

J

jâgîrdâr, 8, 41, 197, 198, 199
Jahângîr, see Nûr al-Dîn Muhammad Jahângîr Pâdshâh Ghâzî
Jaisalmîr, 4
Jalâl al-Dîn Muhammad Akbar, xv, xix, 1, 4, 5, 6, 7, 8, 9, 10, 11, 12, 13, 14, 15, 16, 18, 20, 39, 41, 42, 43, 68, 108, 114,

115, 116, 117, 118, 119, 120, 121, 122, 125, 129 130, 131, 155, 160, 171, 195, 196, 199, 237, 239, 245, 246, 299
Jamâl al-Dîn Husain Injû, 15
James I, King of England, 22, 28, 29, 32, ,34, 36, 52, 53, 58, 59, 61, 62, 64, 65, 71, 86, 87, 93, 94, 96, 99, 100, 101, 102, 104, 107, 109, 110, 112, 127, 128, 133, 134, 139, 142, 144, ,147, 149, 152 167, 168, 173, 174, 176, 178, 182, 186, 193, 200, 201, 202, 237, 238, 249
Jaunpûr, 5, 13, 41
Jenkinson, Anthony, xvii, 29
Jesuits, xv, 7, 22, 28, 29, 42, 90, 101, 111, 112, 149
Jodhpûr, 4
Jones, William, 209, 210
Jonson, Ben, 28, 50, 51, 52, 53, 55, 56, 65, 66, 70, 74, 75, 80, 85, 87, 88, 186, 237, 244, 245

K

Kâbul, 3, 4, 6, 16, 17, 19, 20, 40, 41, 44, 84, 155
Kachwâha Râjah, 6, 10
Kâlinjar, 4, 6
Kâlpî, 13
Kâmrân (brother of Humâyûn), 3, 4, 40
Kashmîr, 6, 41, 163
Kaye, John William, 210
Keeling, Captain William, 23, 104
khânazâd, 118, 119, 122, 130, 131
Khân 'Âlam, 160, 162, 163, 197
Khân A'zam, 81
khândân, 8, 149
Khândesh, 2, 17
khân-i jahân, 18
khân-i khânân, 5, 17, 24, 40, 69
Khânwâh, 3

Khurâsân, 2, 9, 40, 43
Khurâsânîs, 16, 20, 77
Khurram, xv, 19, 24, 25, 72,73, 74, 75, 76, 77, 78, 81, 82, 83, 84, 108, 112, 113, 124, 149, 167, 188, 189, 191, 197, 221, 222, 223, 224
Khusrau, 13, 15, 16, 17, 44, 73, 74, 75, 76, 77, 78, 83, 84, 112, 119, 188, 224
Khvâjah Kâmgâr Husainî, 82, 131, 221, 224
Khvâjah 'Imad al-Dîn Mahmûd Gâvân Sadr-i Jahân, 155, 160, 170, 171, 237
Khvâjah Nizâm, 73
Khvâjah Vais, 17

L

Lahore, 4, 5, 8, 15, 16, 21, 171
La Clavière, Maulde, 140
Lâl Beg, 13
Lancaster, James, xvii
Leiton, Father Edward, 8
Lipius, Justus, 184
London, xvi, 25, 27, 29, 35, 36, 43, 44, 51, 53, 79, 85, 87, 92, 93, 98, 127, 142, 181, 201, 203, 220, 228, 229, 236, 237, 238, 239, 240, 242, 245, 246, 249,
Lord Chamberlain's Company, 51, 65
Lord Pembroke, 36
Loyola, Saint Ignatius,
Lyall, Alfred, 212, 228, 245

M

Macbeth, 78, 88
Mahâbat Khân, 13, 17, 81, 119, 224
Mahâl Angâh (foster-mother of Akbar), 5

INDEX

Malabar, xvi
Malik 'Ambar, 18, 73, 83
Malwâ, 2, 5, 39
Mândalgarh, 14
Mandû, 25, 109, 124
mansab, 81, 82, 118, 119, 160, 163, 165, 198, 224
mansabdâr, 105, 118, 122, 198, 199
Marathas, 206, 207
Marlowe, Christopher, 69, 70, 76, 77, 88, 104, 237
Marston, John, 50, 51, 65, 70, 85, 242
Marv, 2
Masque plays, 59, 60, 182
Mazhar Decree of 1571, 115
mehmândâr, 163, 164
Mermaid Tavern Club, 50, 51
Mewâr, 4, 13, 17, 18, 19, 73
Middleton, Herny, 26, 45
Mihrpûr, 17
Mill, James, 210, 211, 212, 222, 227, 229, 245, 247
Mîr 'Alî Shîr, 155, 170, 249
Mîr Jamâl al-Dîn Husain, 73
mirrors for princes, 15, 44
Mîrzâ 'Abd al-Rahîm, 17, 69, 119
Mîrzâ 'Azîz Koka, 13, 41, 44
Mîrzâ Ghiyâs al-Dîn Muhammad, 20, 73, 81, 83, 112, 160, 189, 221, 222, 223, 224
Mîrzâ Muhammad Hakîm (brother of Akbar), 4, 5, 41
Monserrate, Father Anthony, 7, 42, 237
More, Sir Thomas, 49
Muhammad 'Âdil, 4
Muhammad ibn Tughluq, 1
Muhammad Rizâ Beg, 147, 150, 151, 153
Muhammad Sultân Mîrzâ, 5, 40
Multân, 3, 5, 41

Muqarrab Khân, 22, 73, 111, 112, 144, 145, 147, 148
munshî, 15, 120, 121, 155, 160, 161

N

Nasîr al-Dîn Muhammad Humâyûn, 3, 4, 5, 8, 9, 39, 40, 68, 159, 165
Nasîr al-Dîn Tûsî, 11, 43, 115, 171, 243
nazr, 124, 125, 126, 165, 166, 167
Neile, Bishop, 181, 183
Neville, Sir Christopher, 181
Nietzsche, Friedrich, 31, 46, 246
Nizâm al-Mulk, 11, 156, 157, 171, 196, 238
Nizâmshâhs, 6, 17
Nûr al-Dîn Muhammad 'Abd Allâh, 15
Nûr al-Dîn Muhammad Jahângîr Pâdshâh Ghâzî, *passim*, xv, xvii, xix, xx, 1, 13, 14, 15, 16, 17, 18, 19, 20, 22, 24, 25, 26, 29, 41, 43, 44, 66, 68, 69, 71, 73, 74, 79, 80, 81, 82, 83, 88, 89, 90, 105, 108, 109, 112, 114, 119, 120, 121, 122, 123, 124, 125, 126, 128, 129, 130, 131, 133, 149, 151, 153, 160, 162, 163, 165, 166, 167, 169, 171, 172, 187, 190, 192, 194, 196, 197, 199, 204, 216, 217, 219, 220, 221, 222, 224, 225, 229, 237, 243, 247, "passim"

O

Ottomans, xv, 9, 10, 11, 12, 36, 42, 67, 104, 150, 154, 157, 158, 164, 242

INDEX

Oxford, 28, 46, 50, 85, 88, 128, 129, 180, 184, 201, 202, 227, 228, 229, 242, 244, 246, 249

P

Parliament of 1604, 175,177
Parliament of 1610, 63, 175, 176, 179, 192
Parliament of 1614, 103, 139, 174, 175, 180, 181, 182, 192, 201, 202, 246
Panîpât, 3, 4
Panjâb, 3, 10, 15, 16, 196
Parvaiz, 14, 17, 24,69, 70,73, 82, 104
Persia, xvi, 5, 8, 16, 153, 170, 172, 215
Phillip III, King of Spain, 100, 110, 135, 137, 158
Pîr Khân Lodî, 17, 18
Polo, Marco, xivi
Portugal, xvi, 20
Portuguese,7, 8, 21, 22, 24, 25, 41, 42, 45, 67, 90, 98, 108, 111, 112, 129, 152, 154, 158, 167, 215
Prasad, Beni, 88, 128, 219, 222, 223, 224, 226, 229, 247
Prester John, 67, 68, 87, 239
Protestantism, 134
Protestants, 28, 56, 85, 96, 99, 100, 101, 102, 134, 136
Purchas, Samuel, 29, 32, 34, 35, 36, 45

Q

Qanauj, 3
Qandahâr, 4, 6, 16, 17, 21, 39, 40, 41, 166
Qutb al-Dîn Khân, 13, 38
Qutbshâhs, 22, 158

R

Râjah Amar Singh, 19
Râjah Bhagwân Dâs, 10
Râjah Bihârî Mal, 10
Râjah Mân Singh, 6, 10, 13, 17, 41, 44, 119
Râjah Todar Mal, 10
Râjasthân, 3, 6
Râjpûtânâ, 1, 6, 215
Râjpûts, 6, 10, 18, 19, 43, 123
Raleigh, Sir Walter, 93, 96, 214, 228, 241
Rânâ Partâb Singh, 6, 14, 19
Ranpûr, 17
Ranthanbhûr, 6
Râthor, 1
Roman classicism,
Royal Asiatic Society of Bengal, 209
Royal Council for Virginia, 133

S

Sâbit Khân, 83
Safavids, xv, 9, 10, 12, 41, 42, 43, 120, 154, 157, 158, 159, 164
Sa'îd Khân Chaghtâ'î, 196
Said, Edward, 206, 227, 231, 248
Savile, Henry, 184, 185, 189
Salîm I (Ottoman sultan), 12
Samarqand, 2, 39, 84, 155
Sandys, Sir Edwin, 93, 99, 177, 180
savâr, 19, 82, 105, 107, 163
Sayyid Khân Bârha, 13
Sejanus, 52, 53, 54, 65, 74, 75, 80, 88, 186
Seneca, 94, 185, 190, 202, 203, 248
Senecan tragedy, 65
Shâh Beg Khân, 16, 39
Shâh Jahân (see also Khurram), xv, 81, 82, 158, 221

INDEX

Shibânî Muhammad Khân, 2, 5, 39
Shakespeare, William, 28, 51, 65, 70, 86, 87, 88, 238, 241, 244
Shams al-Dîn Muhammad Atga Khân, 5
sharî'ah (Islamic law), 1, 11, 114, 194, 197, 199
Sharîf Khân, 17
Sharîf ibn Mu'tamad Khân, 81, 82
Sher Shâh Sûrî, 40, 130
shî'ism, 2, 40
Shîrâz, 21, 150, 155
Shujâ'at Khân, 18
Sindh, 3, 6, 41
Smythe, Sir Thomas, 33, 78, 93, 133, 216, 232
Spain, xvi, 27, 48, 63, 85, 93, 97, 100, 128, 134, 135, 136, 137, 174, 215, 239
'Spanish faction', 63, 97
Steele, Richard, xvii, 45
sûbadâr, 73, 167
sufism, 11
Sultân Husain Bâiqarâ, 39, 155
Sultân Iskandar, 2
Sultânpûr, 15
Sûrat, xvii, 7, 21, 22, 23, 24, 25, 41, 45, 73, 76, 111, 129, 144, 148, 167, 191, 214, 232
Swally Road, 21

T

Tabrîz, 2, 12
Tacitus, Cornelius, 184, 185, 186, 188, 189, 190, 202, 203, 238
Tâlib Âmulî, 15
Tamurlaine, 76, 77, 88, 104, 237
Teltschner, Kate, 232, 233, 235, 250
Timon of Athens, 79, 88

Tîmûr, 2, 5, 40, 68, 69, 77, 103, 155
Titus Andronicus, 78
Transoxania, 2
The Trew Law of Monarchies, 57
Tûzuk-i Jahângîrî, xix, 15, 43, 44, 82, 88, 89, 119, 129, 130, 131, 150, 169, 171, 172, 197, 204, 237, 240

U

'ulamâ, 3, 11, 43, 115, 129, 155, 239
umarâ, 11
'Usmān Khân, 18
Ustâd Mansûr, 14
Uzbeks, 5, 41, 43, 158, 159, 164, 241

V

vakîl, 5, 10, 12, 20, 83, 198
vazîr, 20, 116, 155, 160
Vereenigde Oost-Indische Compagnie, xvi, 21
Vijayanagar, xvi, 39
Villiers, George, Duke of Lennox and Buckingham, 63, 64, 105, 178, 182
Volpone, 52, 53, 54

W

Westminster, 56, 103, 108, 126, 174, 175
White, Haydn, 46, 47, 70, 228, 250
Winwood, Sir Ralph, 99, 180, 183, 193, 238
Wotton, Sir Henry, 180, 183
Wright, Father Thomas, 101, 139

INDEX

Y

Yatîm Bahâdur, 13
Yazd, 20
Yûsuf Mîrak, 120

Z

Zahîr al-Dîn Muhammad Bâbur, 2, 3, 5, 8, 39, 40, 42, 68, 116, 155, 158, 165, 171, 172, 212, 238, 241
Zain al-Beg, 163
Zambîl Beg, 165, 166
zât, 19, 105, 107, 163
Zû al-Faqâr Khân, 25, 73, 76